A GROUND FOR COMMON SEARCH

Edited by

Reginald G. Golledge, Helen Couclelis, and Peter Gould

The Santa Barbara Geographical Press
267 Forest Drive
Goleta, CA 93117

ISBN 88-60900

The contributors

Helen Couclelis

Department of Geography
University of California
Santa Barbara, California, USA

Reginald Golledge

Department of Geography
University of California
Santa Barbara, California, USA

Peter Gould

Department of Geography
The Pennsylvania State University
University Park, Pennsylvania, USA

Gunnar Olsson

Nordplan
Nordiska Institutet för
Samhällsplanering
Skeppsholmen
Stockholm, Sweden

John Pickles

Department of Geology and Geography
West Virginia University
Morgantown, West Virginia, USA

Allan Pred

Department of Geography
University of California
Berkeley, California, USA

Dagmar Reichert

Department of Geography
University of Vienna
Vienna, Austria

Pierre Walther

Department of Geography
University Zürich-Irchel
Zürich, Switzerland

Barney Warf

Department of Geography
University of Connecticut
Storrs, Connecticut, USA

Michael Watts

Department of Geography
University of California
Berkeley, California, USA

Contents

i

Editors' preface

It is customary for those who decide to add another volume to the world's overloaded bookshelves to offer a justification, if not an apology, for their presumption. Our claim to printed space stems from the belief that the concerns that led to this publication continue to be shared by a large number of human geographers and others with an interest in the study of human affairs. Though few can afford the luxury to pause, sit back, reflect, and write on these 'philosophical' issues, many, we think, will find raised in the following pages some major questions of their own.

At issue are the labels "scientific" and "humanistic" geography, the intellectual divide they are supposed to describe, the state of the art of these "two cultures" within our discipline, and the question of whether or not a synthesis of science and humanism in geography looks possible, desirable, or forthcoming. Not everyone will agree that this last question is worth asking: for some, the notion of a *humanistic science* (or a scientific humanism) is a contradiction in terms. We believe that such a synthesis is not only meaningful but also necessary. *A Ground for Common Search* is a result of that belief.

The questions raised in this volume are clearly not new, and this collection of essays is only the latest in a long series of writings about philosophy in geography addressing similar issues. The themes of the present essays have all, in some way or other, been discussed before: the interface between individual, society, and space; the question of spatio-temporal constraints to human decision and action; the relation between experiential and objective realities; the problem of language as the medium scientists and scholars are talking in, and its significance in shaping the realities they are talking about; the nature of theory, when its objects are human subjects. It's all been asked before.

But though our questions might sound like the old ones, by being asked today they point toward different answers. Geography in the late nineteen-eighties is not what it was in the sixties or seventies, nor is our understanding of either science or humanism the same as yesterday's. A few years ago, our concern for a synthesis of science and humanism in geography might have reflected no more than a benign wish for intra-disciplinary reconciliation. Today, with developments in the wider intellectual community threatening to abolish traditional boundaries between scientific, technical, and critical forms of thought, we are more concerned about human geography's ability to keep up with the times. Many of the essays in this volume grapple with that challenge, though we clearly still have a long way to go.

The beginnings of this book go back to 1985, when we set in motion the process that eventually brought together for a few days some very young and some well established human geographers with an active interest in the philosophy of geographic thought. Initial ambitious plans for a medium-size international conference were thwarted by the realities of insufficient funding. Instead, we opted for a two-stage approach that allowed us to combine the breadth we had hoped for with the conditions necessary for the more in-depth deliberation and reflection conducive to the expression of original thinking. The first stage consisted of three special sessions on the theme "Science and Humanism in Geography" that we organized as part of the AAG annual meetings in May of 1986; the second stage, a small three-day symposium, took place in Santa Barbara a month later.

Some of the participants in the Santa Barbara meeting were among the contributors to two earlier landmark volumes in the same tradition of inquiry as the present one. The first, Gale and Olsson's *Philosophy in Geography*, published in 1979, reflected the intense preoccupation of its age with positivism, whether in a critical or in a supportive vein. The second, Gould and Olsson's *A Search for Common Ground*, which appeared in 1983, clearly showed that the humanistic alternatives to positivist thought had grown into mature and important perspectives in human geography. Yet, behind the now established diversity, there were some deep common concerns -- a common search, if not a common ground, as the title of that book would have it. *A Ground for Common Search* picks up the thread where its predecessor left it, and carries forth that same tradition of inquiry, renewed by the thinking of a few unusually talented younger people.

Participants at the Santa Barbara symposium included Nick Entrikin, Roger Friedland, Peter Gould, Harvey Molotch, John Pickles, Waldo Tobler, and the organizers, Reg Golledge and Helen Couclelis, from the U.S.A; Derek Gregory, from the U.K.; Gunnar Olsson, from Sweden; Eric Moore and Yorgo Papageorgiou, from Canada; Dagmar Reichert, from Austria; Nori Sugiura, from Japan; and Pierre Walther, from Switzerland. Most of the essays in this book were first presented at the Santa Barbara symposium. Barney Warf presented his in one of the special sessions at the AAG conference. Allan Pred and Michael Watts contributed to this collection, though neither of them was able to attend any of the meetings.

All the participants, whether or not their name appears in the list of contents of this volume, contributed to the success of this whole endeavor. Our thanks to each and all of them for making this such a memorable and worthwhile experience, both intellectually and in human terms. Karen Harp deserves more than thanks. She was the soul and mind in the machine that converted our good intentions into a tangible product. Without her there might have been no book. The same is true of the Academic Senate of the University of California at Santa Barbara, which made the symposium materially possible through a grant. We are happy to be able to show that the seeds sown with the funds they entrusted us with have borne fruit.

Reg Golledge
Helen Couclelis
Peter Gould

Prologue: A ground for common search

This book continues an endeavor that will never finish, and in this sense it stands in the philosophical tradition that has informed the Western world for over two and a half millennia. It is important to point to this tradition of reflection, a tradition that encourages a quiet setting aside from time to time to create moments when one may ask the meaning of formal and sustained inquiry. The last phrase is chosen deliberately: not 'scientific inquiry' in its many forms, not 'humanistic inquiry' in its many forms, as though these were juxtaposed in some natural antagonism, but the 'formal and sustained inquiry' that is the hallmark of all efforts to illuminate rather than entertain. Not that the latter are mutually exclusive either, for the performing arts can lay claim to both. No matter what words we choose at the ends of our dialectical continua, they weaken the fabric of thought once we allow them to become exclusive categories. Poetry may respond for or against a scientific and technological world, but the deepest insights of science have a truly poetic quality.

It is to a continual renewal of the reflective tradition that this book points, and in so pointing it reminds us of two things. First, that the philosophical tradition stands as the originator of most of what we see in the university today, and what we see in the university informs the larger society. Is this too grandiose a claim? One con-tradicting the detached image of the ivory tower? Is it a claim with a touch of absurdity, when all too frequently the university stands obedient to the state? Then reflect: students become the society, and few reach positions of power and prominence today without passing through this institution. Does the fragmentation of the modern university reflect the society? Or does the society, made up of men and women shaped by an intellectually partitioned 'gatekeeper', reflect the university?

Reflecting upon the intellectual tradition that lies at our origin reminds us that the partitioning and fragmentation we see all around us is relatively recent. It is only since the seventeenth century that we name the individual physical sciences, and only since the eighteenth that the biological braid becomes detached from the philosophical core. The human sciences are children of the nineteenth century, including geography in its human variety. Like many disciplines of 'formal and sustained inquiry', geography relaxed its hold on the reflective tradition that constantly renewed the questions of meaning. But inquiry that lets go completely soon finds itself in trouble, and the trouble may be most severe at those moments of pragmatic arrogance and explanatory success when the need for reflection is seen no more.

Which reminds us of the second aspect of renewing the tradition. All fields of formal and sustained inquiry are human endeavors, and to say so is more than a simple tautology. The human presence is at the core of all of them, but nowhere more crucially than in those self-reflective inquiries that look inward to the human condition itself. Here the questions are never laid to rest, but are themselves questioned and answered again and again as each generation renews or reacts to the previous quest. The reason is obvious: the structures and conditions of the human world are constantly unfolding into something that was not before. In a new and constantly becoming world the old questions of theory and practice, the individual and society, the unique and the general, and all the

other juxtapositions and comforting dichotomies, take on new meaning. And
new meaning demands in turn new explication, interpretation and elucidation.

Titles of books may also be juxtaposed, intentionally, reflectively, and not just
for effect. In 1980, from the shores of Lake Como at Bellagio, came *A Search
for Common Ground*, reflective essays on some of the many conditions of
geographic inquiry. In 1986, from the shores of the Pacific at Santa Barbara,
the reflective discussions were renewed on the old conditions, and on those that
had emerged in the interval. *A Ground for Common Search* is the result. It
acknowledges that the ever-renewed search itself might be grounded in the
caring and intentional stance that characterizes the best efforts by geographers
to further the task of illumination, to create geographical perspectives that
provide unexpected understanding rather than the "so what" that forms the last
words of this book.

Understanding can come in many ways, and from many unexpected
directions. Understanding is always personal, and meaning depends upon what
a person brings to a text as much as the text itself. An essay in its entirety may
bring understanding to one and not another. A single phrase may trigger a
reflection that alters the course of a professional life and yet leaves another
untouched. All we can ask for is an initial stance of openness as a precondition
essential for meaningful interpretation, but not guaranteeing it. The text and
the interpreter are always locked in a joint endeavor. As interpreters
themselves change, so it may be difficult to recapture an initial enthusiasm
engendered by first and fresh acquaintance. As interpreters themselves change,
old texts may take on new and fresh meanings.

Santa Barbara is the site for one of the few annual lecture series in
geography, and the first essay by Peter Gould deliberately retains the freer
format and style of its presentation as the 1986 Golledge Lecture. The marxist
perspective has emerged as an important and informing one in human
geographic inquiry, and strong claims for its exclusive authority have been put
forward. For the most part these have been challenged only lightly. What
Gould attempts is to place that perspective back in the non-exclusive arena of
discourse where questioning is possible, and to provide a critique that raises
questions about the claims made. The marxist claims are essentially theoretical,
and in a following essay Gould attempts to examine the meaning of 'theory'
itself in the human, as opposed to the physical, sciences. It is these that provide
an authoritative meaning to 'theory' today, but are the mechanistic
underpinnings appropriate when they are transferred into the human world?

Challenging the marxist claims is not to dismiss them in their entirety. The
power of that particular perspective to illuminate a 'geographic situation' is
highlighted in the essay of Michael Watts, an essay focusing upon the concrete
conditions of a particular time, place and people. Here we see the way in which
an economic system at a global scale has the capacity to reach down to the
filaments of everyday life and drastically alter social and individual
relationships, even as those same cultural conditions thwart the intentions of
those who would impress a traditional economic system with an alien one.
What is central is the way human meanings change, and the way these altered
meanings are played out in both space and society.

Watt's case study exemplifies a thesis that is close to that of structuration
theory, for Barney Warf a conceptual framework and 'sensitizing device' that
recognizes the role of human consciousness, while acknowledging at the same
time the limitations of specific human 'worlds'. These 'worlds' are always
regionally based, and require a regionally reconstituted social science to

explicate them. Such a renewed regional geography would ground the notion of local uniqueness in the recognition that no region stands by itself, but can only be understood as a part of an interconnected system that sets certain conditions within which a region may develop. At the same time the specific or unique features are contingent upon the human choices made within the larger structures defining the possibilities available. Thus regions without theories, and theories without regions, are avoided.

Traditionally, the regional approach has tended to evoke the humanistic concern within the discipline, while systematic-theoretical stances have been associated with scientific concern. Both may be indicative of the lions and the unicorns of Reg Golledge, who points to the great difficulties that members of both species have had in communicating with each other. Seen from different perspectives, a 'reality' becomes multiple realities requiring multiple languages for their enunciation. How does a geographic Tower of Babel start to understand the task of translation required? Careful attention to the question of aggregation may help, so that a more astute awareness of what is clustered together into categories may lead to greater communication. Objects, persons, events and processes in lion and unicorn worlds become communally shared when there is a more precise understanding of the sets both species are talking about. Uncertainty shatters single realities into multiple ones, which shift and turn in unstable states until unified by communicable language and common thought and action.

Theoretical concern produces a set of distinct problematics, but its application in the realm of everyday practical life raises equally difficult questions. How does one use such insight to shape and intervene in everyday life and yet avoid the charge of engaging in modern social engineering? How do we foster an emancipatory science, or at least a science, a knowing, that does not thwart democratic participation? For any geographer, whether teacher, researcher, consultant or citizen, these are questions of worrisome concern, questions teased apart by John Pickles as he invites us to reflect upon the way geographic thinking is embedded in a modern opposition between the scientific and humanistic. Not that these terms are to be brushed over lightly. Unless we understand what is truly human about action, we shall never have a science of action in the sense of a knowing about science and humanity, as opposed to the scientism and humanism that are so frequently substituted in discourse.

Questions of application and practical life translate to a pragmatic geography for Pierre Walther, who uses the question of land abandonment in the small Sambuco region of his native Switzerland as a thread throughout his essay. Pragmatism refuses to acknowledge the closed and absolute which tend to turn in on themselves. Meaningful discourse is shaped by specific purpose, and the Sambuco thread is used to support a purposive discussion of a variety of geographic perspectives. In the end, appropriately and pragmatically, they inform a methodological stance that allows him to approach quite concrete and complex situations, and put into speech and writing something about "the wicked problems" which do not fit neatly into the disconnected boxes that knowledge, and therefore understanding, have become.

For Dagmar Reichert form and content are inextricably entwined. The unwary reader may think the editors have been remiss in their duties, but read carefully and allow yourself to experience a rather special version of the hermeneutic circle of spiralling understanding and self-reference. In the course of the journey many themes are touched upon, but at the end ask yourself whether you are exactly the same person as the one who started, and what

would a second self-referential circulatory jaunt do? The journey is not simply
an intellectual exercise but a bodily one as well. You can feel yourself at the
beginning again, but the beginning is not quite the same as before. Not simply
because you think you know now what is coming, but because the exercise itself
has changed you.

The sense of bodily journey in a verbal discourse is no accident. As Gunnar
Olsson points out, philosophers as different as Augustine and Wittgenstein
acknowledged that language is more, much more, than flat and disembodied
speech, or simple marks on a page - symbols. Meaning is also contained in a
complex and subtle set of bodily acts, and sometimes true meaning is
surreptitiously and unintentionally given 'away'. Think of the analogy between
breaking linguistic conventions and breaking bodily taboos. Here Olsson
continues his own journey towards the meaning of identity and existence,
certainty and ambiguity. At the end is the question of what sort of word is
'word'. For some, including John, it is in the beginning.

But sometimes words are lost, and when formed again reveal a lost world of
reference. As thinking beings, we are our language, and language cannot be
separated from the spatial and temporal conditions, the 'worlds' in which people
live out their lives. All memories, all rules, norms and practical knowledge are
conveyed by word to each other and to future generations. Language, with its
words and rules, is itself passed along more or less intact, yet always with subtle
changes. Language is always becoming, reflecting an always becoming and
unfolding human world. Not simply a changing physical and material world, but
an always-changing world of meaning. Grounded in his empirical experience
and research on nineteenth century Stockholm, Allan Pred's essay lays out the
broad conceptual underpinning that allows him to bring back a lost world by
recapturing the meaning of lost words.

Finally, Helen Couclelis focuses our attention on the difficulty of keeping
conceptual categories apart and properly pinned down so that they 'know their
place'. The problem with categories is that their meaning seems to be forever
shifting, as it needs to be in order to keep up with the changing experience of
humans interacting with an ever-changing world. Unexpected behavior by
objects as well as astute and novel uses of language to describe familiar
situations (machines that think or toys that come alive) often elicit in us
dissonant cognitive schemas: that is, they force us into modes of interaction not
compatible with our prior experience of the categories to which these objects or
situations are known to belong. The result at first is cognitive, even emotional,
tension; eventually, the redefinition of a category, and a new truth about what
these things 'really' are.

The bodily/cultural experience of dealing with a world in flux that is at the
same time physical and social is then, according to this view, what determines
meaning in language and ultimately, truth. Cognitive science, the source of this
insight, thus brings together the intuitions of both Olsson, who points at the
grounding of meaning in the bodily, and Pred, for whom language is embodied
in everyday practice and social relations. Here we also find again Pierre
Walther's confidence in the pragmatist view of truth as relevance-in-concrete-
experience, and Dagmar Reichert's practical demonstration of the inseparability
of subject and object - for aren't the two always bound by expectation and
experiencing? What a remarkable consensus! Is this then the new Truth? A
shifting truth at best, undermined by its own definition: but one that is possibly
the most appropriate given our current state of experience in the world.

In an endeavor that seeks to renew a tradition of reflection that we call philosophical, it is hardly surprising that the old questions of language, truth and meaning appear as connecting threads, weaving and holding so many apparently disparate essays together in a single volume. Perhaps it is these that form the ground for a common search, even though the paths do not run parallel. None of the essays seeks to be definitive, or makes such a claim. They are thoughts on the way, along many ways, attempts to address, thoughtfully and reflectively, some aspects of inquiry in the human realm as it changes through time and over geographic space with all its particularity of place.

It is endeavor . . .

. . . to be continued.

Peter Gould   Santa Barbara
Reg Golledge   December, 1987
Helen Couclelis

The only perspective: a critique of marxist claims to exclusiveness in geographical inquiry *

Peter Gould

Granted the privilege, and all the attendant responsibilities, of delivering the Golledge Lecture, one suddenly becomes aware of what a series like this may come to mean in the future, as one annual lecture follows another to form a sequence of statements in our field that inevitably take on an historic cast as soon as they are delivered. Inevitably, any topic worthy of choice immediately begins to expand beyond the time available for its full and proper explication and it will simply not be possible to unfold all the questions in detail. For this reason some of the arguments must appear superficial, and the charge of superficiality may be especially tempting when a topic touches upon deeply held convictions. But no matter what your convictions, I ask you to let your thinking remain open for the moment, to release it from set vocabularies whose words so often betray closure, and to join with me in a concern to examine, rethink, and clarify a series of questions that form part of the ethos of marxist claims to the 'only perspective'.

There will be some, of course, who will accuse me of simple 'Marx bashing',[1] but I hope I can persuade you that my concern lies at a much deeper level. The issue is not simply the claims to a single, truthful perspective by those who have adopted a marxian viewpoint in geography today, because this is only one of several, rather similar claims that could be examined - even though it is a particularly strident and forceful one at the moment. Rather, my concern is to raise, in the context of a quite specific and concrete example, the question of all claims to Fundamentalism. That those holding to a marxist viewpoint make such claims should not surprise us; indeed, our job is not to be surprised, but to understand. Fundamentalist claims to the truth are nothing new, and a nineteenth century perspective, arising out of a Hegelian Idealism grounded in an Absolute,[2] could hardly claim anything less. And when I say 'nothing new', realize that the following was written over 100 years ago, even as the great marxian doctrine was being hammered into shape.[3]

"When a doctrinaire attitude, ensconced in what has become a rigid and dogmatically closed world view, considers itself to have arrived at the summit of wisdom and now employs all its sagacity in elaborating all the subtlest ramifications of the finished conceptual system that it holds to be true ... then the reaction against such hypertheorizing follows in natural sequence, and

---

* This essay was originally given as the second annual *Golledge Lecture*, University of California, Santa Barbara, California, June 5, 1986. With the exception of a few oratory excisions, stylistic revisions, and explanatory annotations, the essay deliberately retains the freer form appropriate to verbal presentation.

[1] The phrase used by a few sociologists at the lecture who appeared to have missed the deeper point of examining *all* Fundamentalisms. This was my fault for not being clear enough.

[2] Many contemporary Hegelians, whether professional philosophers or not, appear greatly embarrassed by Hegel's insistence on an Absolute, and usually avoid discussing it if they possibly can. The word 'Hegelian' itself is indicative of those willing to adopt an absolute viewpoint, or a rigid *a priori* perspective, rather than being prepared to keep thinking open to new, and always unfolding possibilities.

[3] Liebmann (1884, pages 4-5), quoted in Blumenberg (1983, page 235).

subsequent generations cautiously assessing the evidence, will have to invest half their efforts in the critical clearing out of overflowing Augean stalls."

So we are dealing with an old, recurring, and thoroughly human problem, one more manifestation of the longing to find a place of security from which to view the world.

It is no longer necessary to emphasize the distinction between the philosophical use of the word *critique*, as a laying out and examining of the conditions of possibility for claims made, as well as the implications they contain, and *criticism* as an intended damaging thrust. But it is a distinction important to point to as one of three preliminary remarks. The second is that the adjective and noun 'marxist' covers such a broad spectrum of claims and beliefs, that one begins to doubt whether we can use it meaningfully anymore. To emphasize the ambiguity such breadth of meaning provides, I started to use the totally unwieldy phrase Those Holding Onto Marxist Perspectives ..., and since they might well be considered the intellectual sons and daughters of Marx, the acronym Thomp(son) rapidly came into view. But I think any honest marxist would be immediately, and quite properly, insulted, so 'marxist' it will have to be, with the context providing the exact vibrational frequency in the broad spectrum.

The third, preliminary remark is to acknowledge that the titular phrase "the only perspective" is David Harvey's,[4] and then to state immediately that I have adopted it only as a symbol of many strong claims to exclusiveness often implicitly, if not explicitly, made within a marxist analysis. But in adopting this strong and excluding claim as the focus of this lecture, I want to make it quite clear that I am not adopting an aggressively critical stance to Harvey's thought and writing. On the contrary, much of what he has written genuinely illuminates a part of the human condition in its spatial and temporal context, and no one who is familiar with his last four books - *Social Justice and the City, The Limits to Capital, The Urbanization of Capital*, and *Consciousness and the Urban Experience* - can be unaware that there is a highly intelligent and imaginative geographer at work, deeply informed and driven by humane concern. No one can criticize the larger context of such thinking and retain a shred of humanity themselves.

But it is in these books and contemporary articles that the exclusive claim is made and constantly reaffirmed. This is not the slip of a temporarily over-enthusiastic pen, but a claim to Truth made over a number of years. It is a claim saturated with implications, implications that must be laid out, and thoughtfully assessed to the extent that time allows. Thus my aim is to sketch out three broad, and what we might call 'questionable', areas for reflection, giving these the rough and ready labels of Conditions of Possibility, Economic Grounds, and Philosophical Considerations.

Conditions of possibility

Few marxists, even if they attempt to stand outside of history, as so many appear to do, would detach a theory of human history from its historical context. Neither can we. What, then, was the 'world' into which Marx was thrown, a nineteenth century 'world' that formed the conditions of possibility for his own thinking? It was a world overwhelmed by Newtonian Law, standing at the forward edge of nearly two hundred years of confirmed and amazed conviction. The laws of nature, inevitable, unalterable, eternal, had finally been pinned

---

[4] Harvey (1984, page 1; 1985a, page x; 1985b, page xi).

vn: in Marx's lifetime, physicists announced that there were only a few pping up operations left to do. Thus, it was argued, if such laws existed for physical world, then why not for the human? In Marx, and of course in ers, such thinking now becomes possible. One of the others was August mte, whose writing on a 'science of society', and a three-phase development history, immediately precedes Marx, and so allows Marx's thinking to roach a now reified society in a manner considered only appropriate for the sical world before.

But the most immediate 'presence' of the mid-l9th century world is Hegel, l I would suggest that the way he most deeply conditions Marx's own thinking ot so much through the dialectical quest (undoubtedly important, on which much emphasis has been placed, and an idea to which we shall return), but what I can only call the Idealist 'drive to system' (Heidegger, 1985). It is gel's colossal project, paralleled by Fichte's bridge building from Kant, and elling's forty years of silent struggle, that allows thinking, in a morally raged and committed man, to attempt the construction of a single, holistic tem, a social theory that would account not only for the conditions of his day, for the course of societies at all times. This holistic view, the refusal to inter the social, political, economic, temporal, and perhaps even the spatial,[5] s truly important consequences for marxist thought in geography today, hough there is not time to explore these ramifications here. No thinking rson of the mid-nineteenth century German world (and Marx, above all, was hinking person), could fail to be touched by the giant in Berlin, even though rx's views towards philosophers were often equivocal. An early and thusiastic Marx felt that philosophy was "the spiritual weapon of the letariat," but later, as his own work became increasingly scrutinized, he elled such worries about truth as mere "philosophical crochets". Which is ply to note that in a body of work, spanning several genres of writing over ty years, a man is certainly allowed to change his views. But we should nember that these views had an early philosophical grounding, and I nmend his student notebooks, prepared for his dissertation on Epicurus, as ssible sources for our understanding (Marx, 1975). Perhaps those early quiets about Epicurean individual releasement is one source of the ntradrive to a concern for collective emancipation.

But the conditions of possibility represented concretely by Marx's world were ing laid not just decades, but centuries, and even millenia, before. Marx is ly a 'child of his time' - and, I might add, of his place, the Western World - as all, and always, are. A Descartes has already pushed the human being to terstage, even as astronomers were displacing an earth through heliocentric rganization, and the God so displaced will be declared dead by Nietzsche in rx's own lifetime. Less than fifty years after Descartes, Pierre Bayle will clare that competent government will only be found in a state of atheists - a te, presumable Marx would say, in which the people have overcome the igious opiate. But theological matters are not so easily detached, and ntinue to inform and shape a 'world' by the constant resurgence of their estions and their responses. It is tempting, in a rather shallow way, to pursue rallels between the developments of christian and marxist thinking, including e difficulties that arise when a system containing an eschatological event of ochal closure - the Second Coming and the Revolution - has to deal with ntinually disappointed anticipations. Systems claiming to have found the

---

is Harvey's constantly reaffirmed insistence that the spatial dimension enriches and extends the marxist perspective marks his writing.

ground of truth, so that philosophy can now safely fade away, take on a terrible burden of holistic accountability. Add to these a strong teleological component, and faith becomes virtually obligatory. In Marx's 'world', the fortuitous arrival of a theory of evolution allows a newly emerged, and appealing scientific authority to reinforce a teleological element of the social theory that is now impossible to justify on older, religious grounds of faith. But the last thing I want to imply is that the marxist perspective is in any way the result of a secularization process. Nevertheless, these sorts of parallel developments and problems underpin my own concern to point to the mythologizing of the marxist position into one bordering religious faith - and I use both 'mythologizing' and the notion of 'religious faith' respectfully.

Economic grounds
For the marxist, the grounds of truth in the human realm lie in the economic - a region of concern we can properly label 'first among equals' in the larger, integrative theory that Marx tried to insist upon, although many of his followers, as Louis Dupré (1983) has noted, have demoted culture to simply a byproduct of production, rather than part of a mutually informing and shaping relationship. Yet even with a 'first among equals' designation, the economic realm, by itself, cannot be ignored in our reflective concern, although the arguments rapidly become so technical that one is sorely tempted to bypass them altogether. Yet, they insistently demand our attention, for these are the grounds in which Marx actually roots his social theory, and so gives priority to them. In doing so, he openly defends Ricardo, and speaks a language of pure social Darwinism that sociobiologists today can only approve. "The higher development of individuality," says Marx (1963, pages 117-118), "is thus only achieved by a historical process during which individuals are sacrificed, for the interests of the species in the human kingdom, as in the animal and plant kingdoms ..." Today we hear that translated as 'you cannot make an omelet without breaking eggs', an argument in which all ends justify the means. We cannot follow these things in any depth here, but let me point to a few questions I feel are worth our careful, reflective thought.

As a general rule, I prefer not to appeal to authority, and try to stand responsibility for my own ideas, but for many of the technical arguments I can only point here to the extremely careful scrutiny of such economists as Okisho, von Weizsacker, Roemer, Samuelson, Steedman, and the more sympathetic Morishima. Two points, out of many, are worth briefly following here (Elster, 1985). First, the labor theory of value - that the sole source of profit lies in the expropriation and exploitation of labor - is so shot through with misunderstanding and contradiction that it cannot stand as a ground, let alone an explanation, of anything. A quite mystical, and unmeasurable, 'social unit of labor' is incapable of explaining the formation of prices, and therefore rates of profit, and in Elster's words (1985, page 136), "It is hard to see what is proved by showing values do not depend on prices, when there is nothing that depends on values." And yet attempt after attempt is made to shore up these foundations, to explain away the contradictions, and to account for the inability to make such an idea operationally defined and empirically verifiable. So called 'transformation problems' are examined, to translate actual prices, varying across space, time and culture, into mystical values which allow rates of exploitation to be somehow computed from prices on which the 'true' values do not, according to the ground of the theory, depend.

I confess to a personal bafflement as to why the hold of marxists upon the body of these ideas is so tenacious, but I would like to put forward the suggestion that it is because a deeply moral issue is closely intertwined. Marx, in moral outrage at the conditions he observed, grounded his social theory in the economic domain. It is as though marxists today feel that if the economic theory is shown to be logically inconsistent and mystically grounded, then somehow the moral force of the marxist position will be destroyed. This is a totally specious, non-sequiturial argument, for the ontological ground of human morality is quite different from, and has nothing to do with, the regional ontology underlying the construction of economic theory. But I challenge you, gently, to find a more appropriate explanation for all the theoretical 'bandaiding' we see in the literature today.

The second point to consider is the theory of over-accumulation and crisis, cyclical dislocations in the capitalist system that lead ultimately to the eschatological event of revolution. This closes off an older stage of human development, and starts a new era of collective emancipation in which the means of production are placed in the hands of the people, constituted as a state that will ultimately wither away as each gives according to his or her abilities, and takes according to his or her needs. And here again, rather than relying on 'expert witnesses', I would like to offer a possibility of my own for your consideration. It seems to me increasingly clear that the so-called phenomena of 'over-accumulation' and 'crisis of consumption' are cyclical phenomena whose roots do not at all lie exclusively in the capitalist mode of production and ownership. Nor are they simply the result of natural events (for example, droughts), playing out their perturbations through an otherwise equilibriated system. The same cyclical behavior is displayed by the Soviet economy, where the ownership is quite different and conforms to marxist recommendations. Both Bettleheim, and Charance in *Le Systeme Economique Sovietique*, show how the autonomy of economic levels in the Soviet Union results in over-accumulation and economic crisis. The planned economy must produce 12 million products in a plan containing 48,000 'aggregated' slots. No one can understand, order, and control such complexity. Shortages result precisely from over-accumulation in certain sectors attempting to anticipate future shortages to meet exogenously set production targets. The result is structural crisis and a stagnant economy - a growth rate of 8.6 percent in 1966 falling to 2.0 percent today. We are seeing now some tentative, still experimental attempts to correct these problems.

What I would like to suggest is that in economic systems today, all of them state-managed in varying degrees, that over-accumulation and 'crises' of cyclical behavior are not grounded in any particular modes or ownerships of production, but are simply characteristic of *all* very large and intricately connected systems whose parameters, say production coefficients, are not, and cannot be, stable. *All* complex systems display such behavior, and no one, capitalist on the Federal Reserve, or soviet on the Planning Praesidium, knows how to steer with precision. As a simple example, I think it is worth pointing to the model building of the U.S. economy by Jay Forrester over the past four or five years. Starting, in a sense, in 'innocence', building the model from the ground up as an engineer, without too many prior intellectual preconceptions and hang-ups from current, often quite contradictory, economic theories, his model produces with remarkable fidelity some broad cyclical characteristics of the past 100 years of the U.S. economy. Let it be pointedly noted that such cyclical behavior was not consciously built into the model (Forrester, personal conversation). It appeared as a result of the non-linear feedback relations, which produced not only the business cycles whose amplitudes are meant to widen in Marxist theory, to produce the final crisis of capitalism, but also 'strange' 60 year cycles that Forrester admitted he had no idea how to interpret initially. They are perhaps simulating the Kondriatieff waves related to innovation phases.

Now I am well aware of the criticism leveled at much of this modeling tradition - much of it rather unfair, given the extraordinary, almost 'invitational' openness of those who employ it - and any reader of this essay will be much too sophisticated to believe that an economy is just a system of non-linear differential equations working out their destined trajectories. But even with such gross oversimplification of actual complexity, two things are worth reflecting upon. First, the model displays extraordinary resilience, a robustness, a capacity to absorb enormous jolts, whether 'exogenous', as in the case of the impact of the Second World War and the arms race with Soviet Union, or 'endogenous' as in the case of the Great Depression in the West. Although I would note that in such global contexts I have grave doubts that we can use these words 'exogenous' and 'endogenous' with any precision, or even meaning. We live in one world, and a simple structural analysis of international trade flows shows immediately what a highly connected world it is.

But the major point of this section is simply this: an economic theory, ill founded and illogical, is still held to be the ground of marxist theory. National rates of profit, in which the entire structural complexity of a modern economy is mapped to a single index, are still assiduously computed as signs and portents to foretell the 'Final Coming', apparently unaware that high profit may well reflect an historical moment of initial innovation that can *only* come down over time as new entries saturate a previously empty market. What we see here is the same problem that arises in any theoretical structure that is essentially closed because it has captured, at last, the truth. Psychoanalysis faces a similar problem, and Blumenberg (1983) in a long, historical analysis of *curiositas*, shows how theory has the capacity to satisfy curiosity, and he then asks "What motive takes the place of curiosity when it has been satisfied?" After believing, and having made sure, that one is grounded in truth - the only perspective - then only the documentation or exposure of truth is possible, since curiosity *for* Truth has dissolved. The consequences for scholarship are deadly, as people take on research topics whose conclusions have been written before the 'research' has even been undertaken.

Philosophical considerations

I would now like to turn to two broader issues, labelling these, with a certain generosity, 'philosophical considerations'. They involve claims to a certain form of thinking - the dialectical - and to the definition of the marxist perspective and its argumentation as 'scientific'. Along the way, we shall have to touch again upon moral issues, for these, I believe, form the greatest strength of the marxist perspective - and, in some sense, its greatest weakness.

Marxist thought constantly claims that its mode of thinking is *dialectical*. Like many other words whose origins lie in philosophy, the meaning of 'dialectical' becomes less precise as it moves into arenas of social theory, but it seems fair to characterize it, in fairly concrete terms, as a broad awareness that within capitalist society there are internal contradictions that gradually negate the structures of that society to produce its ultimate collapse. There is the additional awareness and claim that dialectical thinking is not mechanistic, and some point specifically to the notion that the negation of a negation does not produce the original conditions. Putting it another way, negating the negation of A does not bring A back, as in those logics available to the nineteenth century; negating the negation of feudalism, does not bring back a feudal society. Rather, society dialectically negates itself, and unfolds into something new that was not before. Fair enough - providing we do not have something close to a simple tautology here - but difficulties arise which are worth considering. One problem is that just as Marx was unable to resist being drawn into the algebraicized arguments of Ricardo, so many marxists today feel they must couch their economic arguments in the common calculi available to them. These are all computable, and, therefore, mechanical. But, virtually by definition, dialectical thinking is non-mechanical, and therefore non-algebraicizable since algebraicization requires strict conformance to the binary operations that are unambiguously defined to work upon carefully specified elements of sets. Any algebraic operation, or sequence of operations, is computable, with the derived consequences always contained in, and constrained by, the mechanical operations allowed. This confrontation of general dialectical claims, and algebraicized theoretical arguments, can lead to grave difficulties. In any algebraic argument, the internal contradictions claimed by marxist theory for a capitalist economic system, ought to be, in principal, statable, and should indicate how the amplitudes of the oscillations reach such undampenable values that the system cannot survive. I am not aware that this has been done. But unalgebraicizable dialectical thinking is more patient, and as a posture of research appears to look always backwards to account, naturally with hindsight, for the contradictions that produced the unique and particular historical unfolding. Putting aside any short term predictions because of the mechanical, computable basis it requires, dialectical thinking nevertheless boldly predicts the final event of system collapse. For a marxist, there must be a tension here that is difficult to resolve. Either a functional, algebraic argument must be discarded, or dialectical claims must go. One cannot be contained within the other.

On the other hand, there may be good grounds for defending non-mechanical dialectical thought as the only form with the capacity of looking backwards to account for changes - cyclical or catastrophic. At least it is prepared to take as given the particular historical event, rather than trying to predict it. It is a form of thinking that tries, in a sense, to argue backwards, through time, to unfold the 'conditions of possibility' that allowed such an event to appear.

But it is also the dialectical approach, with its deep sense of negation and the production of the 'opposite', that leads thinking to a highly dichotomous view of the world. It is this that produces the view of society divided into two essential parts, a partition that provides one of the main underpinnings of marxist theory in the form of 'class struggle' - a view of society unfolding as a result of a constant confrontation of Us and Them. Again, a difficult tension is apparent, particularly in geography today as constant appeals are made by marxists to a Realist position. Dialectical thinking, in its dichotomous drive, was annealed in the furnace of early nineteenth century Idealist thought, thought that shaped Marx in his typically Idealist drive to system. Let us leave aside the obvious question of transcending both extremes, extremes that can only exist in historical opposition to each other, and take a realistic look at this wholly idealistic conception of class and the constant struggle it is supposed to produce.

Partitioning society into two parts through fuzzy, and now much disparaged, Idealist thinking constitutes the imposition of an idea that no hard headed Realist can possibly allow. If we are to look, clear eyed, at reality, we see societies in which people are distributed in various ways along many axes of differentiation which may claim our attention. In a Latin American country today - a Mexico, a Brazil - the distributions may be extreme, and they may tempt us, perhaps quite appropriately, to impose a simplifying two-part partition. But in many other cases - a Denmark, a Japan, a New Zealand - the dimensions are shorter, and the distributions much more even. We should not forget that these partitions and categories arise out of mid-nineteenth century European conditions, and constitute ideas formulated by a man who was intimately familiar with the censuses and statistics (literally the state numbers) of his day. Where categories arise out of careful observation of the things themselves, the simplifications may well be used to throw into sharp relief some basic structural properties of the society. Which is perhaps why, in skillful and imaginative hands, they illuminate a mid-nineteenth century Paris in all its dynamics of urban renewal and change (Harvey, 1985a, 1985b). Nevertheless, we still have a case here of a theory requiring that we impose a dichotomous idea on a reality that in many other cases refuses to fit. Yet if that partitional idea goes, a main support of the theory goes with it. The only answer is to make the reality conform to the idea.

This points, once again, to the idea that thinking must constantly be kept open, and the way in which, in Dupré's words (1983, page 11), a "critique undertaken from a radically historical perspective must, at least in principal, extend to its own judgments ... to acknowledge the conditioning of all thought is not to become infallible oneself, but rather to submit all modes of consciousness, including the critique, to the test of fallibility." It is the same admonition that Allen Scott (1982) gave us six years ago, when he called geographers to that sense of 'critical vigilance and analytic self-consciousness' that never allowed thinking the comfort of closure.

I noted above that I thought that moral questions formed both the greatest strength and greatest weakness of the marxist perspective. I would certainly defend my claim about the former, but the latter may appear contradictory or paradoxical, and I think some explication is in order. It involves what we might call a 'hidden agenda', a set of issues that have, I believe, to be addressed forthrightly, and in public, by those who are touched deeply by the moral concern.

Marxism, in practice (and we are all exhorted by marxists to think in terms of *praxis*), too frequently means *sovietization*. By this rather loose term I mean the enforcement of views whose wholesale acceptability might be placed in doubt if a plebiscite (regulated, say, by the United Nations) were held. In the same way that the excesses of the West (including such champions of freedom and democracy as Bokassa and Mobutu, with $2 billion and $5 billion in Zürich respectively, and Marcos with $10 billion ... who knows where?) are a source of outrage to all decent people still unpersuaded by the totality of marxist claims, so the excesses of marxism *in practice* can only form an equally acute embarrassment to those who feel kindred to this perspective. But these issues of marxism *in practice* are seldom, if ever, addressed forthrightly, and whatever cursory attention is directed, it is too often only to explain away such excesses as purely temporary phenomena ... after all, you cannot make an omelette without breaking eggs. But people are not eggs, and after Budapest 1956, Prague 1968, Gdansk and Warsaw in the 1980s, Afghanistan still today ... well, those who insist we should reflect upon *praxis* should, perhaps, reflect on these things. Read Milan Kundera (1983, 1985), not for his tiresome eroticism, but read him to understand the meaning of the Prague Spring (after which 140 historians lost their positions - they were, after all, the national memory bank - and 150,000 Czechs left their homeland). These connected, essentially moral issues, cannot be ignored by geographers, and all others, who feel exactly that sense of outrage that informed Marx himself.

Finally, we have to take seriously the marxist concern and claim, often made and repeated, that marxist theory, concerning the deep structural rules that dialectically unfold the historical narrative, is *scientific*. Let us take Thom's statement at face value that "the aim of science is to reduce the arbitrariness of description" (Berlinski, 1986, page 74), and add the suggestion that such science requires us to posit theoretical rules that indicate how the particular follows from the general. In the physical realm such statements appear quite acceptable, but in the realm of human meaning - literally meaning-full human behavior - disquieting questions arise. John Searle, in both linguistic research and human face recognition, has raised some grave doubts about the assumption that computational rules either exist, or are required, as explanations, and notes that once the nature of the assumptions are understood "their implausibility is manifest ... [and] that we do not actually have sufficient empirical evidence for supposing that these assumptions are true" (Searle, 1984, page 55). I would like to suggest that at the macrolevel of human societies unfolding in historical time, the assumption of the existence of generative rules is equally suspect.

Consider the requirements for computing, and therefore predicting, the future, either deterministically or probablistically, where the latter has a secure basis - something unavailable to macrosystems, even if we count the banal arithmetic of proportions of prior events. Whether the computational task is cast pretentiously in the conceptual arena of bifurcation theory (Prigogine and Stengers, 1984; Gould, 1987), seen in the more general problematic light of 'maximal complexity' (Kolmogorov, 1968); Chaitin, 1974), or loaded into the latest seductive bandwagon of chaos theory (Crutchfield, et al , 1986), the mechanism of both mathematics and marxism is there.

But this raises, in turn, the question of whether *theory*, with the modern mechanical meaning we place upon that word, is even writable in human affairs for which time is constitutive. Perhaps Edmund Husserl was right in tracing "the agony of his times to a failure in the original formulation ... of the theoretical attitude" (Blumenberg, 1983, page xiii). But this must be the subject of another lecture at another time.[6]

References

Berlinski D, 1986 *Black Mischief: The Mechanics of Modern Science* (William Morrow, New York)

Blumenberg H, 1983 *The Legitimacy of the Modern Age* (MIT Press, Cambridge, Mass)

Chaitin G, 1974 "Information-theoretic computational complexity" *IEEE Transactions on Information Theory* **IT-14** 662-664

Crutchfield J, Farmer J, Packard N, Shaw R, 1986 "Chaos" *Scientific American* **255** 46-57

Dupré L, 1983 *Marx's Social Critique of Culture* (Yale University Press, New Haven)

Elster J, 1985 *Making Sense of Marx* (Cambridge University Press, Cambridge)

Gould P, 1987 "A critique of dissipative systems in the human realm" *European Journal of Operational Research* **30** 211-221

Harvey D, 1984 "On the history and present condition of geography: an historical materialist manifesto" *Professional Geographer* **36** 1-11

Harvey D, 1985a *The Urbanization of Capital* (Johns Hopkins University Press, Baltimore)

Harvey D, 1985b *Consciousness and the Urban Experience* (Johns Hopkins University Press, Baltimore)

Heidegger M, 1985 *Schelling's Treatise on the Essence of Human Freedom* (Ohio University Press, Athens, Ohio)

Kolmogorov A, 1968 "Logical basis for information theory and probability theory" *IEEE Transactions on Information Theory* **IT-20** 10-15

---

[6] See the following essay in this volume, "What does chaos mean for theory in the human sciences?".

Kundera M, 1983 *The Joke* (Penguin Books, Harmondsworth)
Kundera M, 1985 *The Unbearable Lightness of Being* (Harper and Row, New
    York)
Liebmann 0, 1884 *Die Klimax der Theorien* (Strasbourg)
Marx K, 1975 *Frühe Schriften* (Wissenschaftliche Buchgesellschaft, Darmstadt)
Marx K, 1963 *Theories of Surplus Value* (Progress Publishers, Moscow)
Prigogine I, Stengers I, 1984 *Order Out of Chaos* (Bantam Books, New York)
Scott A, 1982 "The meaning and social origins of discourse on the spatial
    foundations of society," in *A Search for Common Ground* Eds P Gould and
    G Olsson (Pion, London), pp 141-156
Searle J, 1984 *Minds, Brains and Science* (Harvard University Press, Cambridge,
    Mass)

What does chaos mean for theory in the human sciences?*

Peter Gould

In reflecting upon inquiry in the human realm, we face two choices. We may think within the horizon of the tradition given to us, within the conventions that are generally accepted, trying to come to a deeper appreciation of that tradition for the mode and manner of our inquiries. Those concerned to explicate a large body of thought and writing generally labelled the 'philosophy of science' stand within such a horizon. Alternatively, we may attempt to think beyond the horizon, to enlarge it, and in so doing perhaps undermine and endanger the conventions within the accepted horizon (Gould, 1985a).

At first glance, any claim to push the horizon outwards, to enlarge the space or clearing within which we may reflect upon the nature of our inquiries, must appear pretentious. And not simply pretentious, but futile as well. Any attempt to move thought to a region where others are few or absent means breaking away from a sharing community where thoughts may be presented for acceptance. Communication breaks down.[1] But to deny such a possibility is to deny any enlargement of the horizon, so that human thought takes on a static and constrained quality that obviates the constant openness of possibilities that is constitutive of being human. Nevertheless, such claims must be examined critically and with care, and in the full realization that we always stand within an informing tradition containing the interpretive seeds from which any enlargement springs. Claims to originality are always suspect.

I wish to put forward a thesis to provoke thinking in such a way that others will find it rewarding to make a reasoned move into the clearing it provides. From this act of intellectual colonization a new community may be formed, and a 'new world' may be discovered from which we may look back with appreciation and sympathy to the 'old world' that gave it birth. Such an endeavor requires rather dangerous exploration, but this is what geographers are for.

I am going to argue that the word 'theory' is essentially (and I choose my words with care - I mean truly, *in its essence*), meaning-less as it is used and applied in the realm of human inquiry today. This apparently outrageous statement is not made mischievously or insincerely, but is offered as a genuine and thoughtful thesis which I will try to convince you is defensible because of its intrinsic merit. Of course, 'defensible' implies that it may be attacked, and I certainly hope you will try. If it is not defensible it should be discarded, and thinking may then be directed to other, more fruitful possibilities.

I suspect that those objecting to the thesis most strenuously will be either of marxist persuasion, or those working in the tradition of mathematical modeling. Or conceivably both, despite the equivocal attitudes both perspectives bear towards one another on occasion. Initially, these may seem strange bedfellows, but their alliance of possible opposition is actually quite conjugal because both

---

* Certain passages and ideas in this essay are contained, in a much compressed and précised form, in a sequence of three, invited editorials (Gould, 1986a, 1986b, 1987a), and an extensive review for the Spanish-speaking world (Gould, 1987b).

[1] The language of community and sharing is etymologically deliberate, underpinned by *communicare*, to share, itself arising from *munere*, to send a present.

believe deeply in, and actually require, the notion of *mechanism* in human affairs. We shall examine these misconceived requirements as we go along, but it seems likely that I shall be branded either anti-marxist or anti-mathematical. Both communities contain adherents who are quite certain of the claims they make, so allowing them to partition the world into Us and Them. It seems doubtful that I shall be able to convince anyone that I am respectful of some insights from these perspectives, because such a declaration may well appear contradictory. Although why contradiction should prove disturbing in a marxist or mathematical context is difficult to understand, because it is employed constantly in mathematical proofs by mathematicians, and it forms a Hegelian wellspring of creative thought for any properly-grounded marxist. In fact, it is contradictory in appearance only. Properly stripped of their mechanistic implications, both the marxist and mathematical perspectives may be used descriptively to illuminate limited domains of the human realm.

So the first question is: what do we *mean* by 'theory' today? And notice that in italicizing the word 'mean', I am immediately invoking and emphasizing a hermeneutic stance or perspective of interpretation. If we are inconsistent in the meanings we place upon our language, we are inconsistent in our thinking, because we think in language, and our language is, in a very fundamental sense, ourselves as thinking beings. If we cannot agree upon meaning, then we cannot think together, and if we cannot think seriously together, any sense of intellectual community breaks down.

Although the initial reaction may be one of antagonistic disparagement, and the consequences ultimately uncomfortable, I ask you to reflect that the fundamental meaning we place upon the word 'theory' today comes to us, with enormous and fully justified authority, from the physical sciences, the sciences of physical things. Newton's *theory* of celestial mechanics stood for nearly 300 years (we celebrated the 300th anniversary of the *Principia* in 1987), and we still use it to guide our spacecraft to the nethermost reaches of Pluto. At the low velocities involved, no relativity corrections are required, for they are smaller than our ability to make those corrections. Not a bad *theory*, certainly a useful theory, held as the truth, without a shadow of doubt, for 200 years; but, and quite literally, wrong as a description. It is swallowed, at the turn of this century, by Einstein's Special and General theories (Stegmuller, 1976), which constitute better statements, more truthful theories, because they encompass wider ranges of phenomena, and have successfully passed every test we can devise for them, from the stars to subatomic particles.

At the subatomic scale, at which even the topological structure of space comes into question, quantum mechanics, in all its many elaborations, again confirms the authority of the meaning of theory, for this extraordinary realm of physics not only informs its sister discipline of chemistry, but makes unthinkable predictions in the world of things which are confirmed again and again by observation. In theoretical physics today, one thinks the absurd and finds that it is true. I put it to you that we have, today, no choice but to accept the meaning of the word 'theory' as it comes to us from the physical realm, even though we may wish to harken to a more primal, etymological meaning later. This older meaning, not incidentally, is still in total accord with the best that we continue to receive from the physical sciences today, as the bright torch of the human presence is thrust into the dark fissures of *phusis* - that non-human world of Aristotle's 'nature' that slowly enters into the realm of human inquiry (Heidegger, 1979).

So in conformance with such meaning, let us agree that a 'theory' is a well-tested set of statements about the way things *will* be under carefully specified conditions. Such a definition is in strict accordance with the *Oxford English*

Dictionary's "A scheme or system of ideas or statements held as an explanation or account of a group of facts or phenomena; a hypothesis that has been confirmed or established by observation or experiment, and is propounded or accepted as accountable for the known facts; a statement of what are held to be the General Laws, principles, or causes of something known or observed." But the matter is more subtle, and those who will object, immediately and strongly, to such an apparently constrained meaning may repair to the same authority and there find evidence for their claim that 'theory can mean all sorts of things', so seemingly justifying their extensions of meaning to a framework for communication, a ground for discourse, a guide to inquiry and action, and so on. But this is precisely my point: many meanings have been loaded onto the word 'theory', and it is this ambiguity, this distressingly 'anything goes' attitude to language, that so often makes the word meaning-less. Much of the time we literally do not know what we are talking about as meanings slide back and forth on skids of discourse often well-greased by thoughtless pretension.

A full explication of such a claim would require another essay, but it is worth pointing to the sort of evidence available in order to draw an important distinction today between *theory* and *speculation* in the English language. The confusion is an old one, and probably rests upon the medieval translation of Aristotle's *theoria* into *contemplatio*. The conventional, and perfectly sound, etymological ground points to *thea* as 'outward appearance' and *horao* as 'to view closely or attentively' (Heidegger, 1977). There are many other important implications in this transition from the Greek to the Latin for thinking that can only take place in language, not the least the total reversal of meaning that arises when the full implications of *templum* become 'templating', the construction of *a priori* frameworks into which things will fit even before their outward appearances have been viewed attentively. But we only need to note here that by 1611 the Italian Florio's *theoria* of 1598 has entered the English language as "theorie, contemplation, deepe studie; a sight, or beholding, speculation" through Randle Cotgrave's *A Dictionarie of the French and English Tongues*. The implication is that 'theory' and 'speculation' (itself etymologically grounded on *specula*, a watch tower, and *speculari*, to observe) are synonymous, their meanings are interchangeable. The synonymity is initially maintained in discourse that we would label 'scientific' today, as William Harvey, in his *Anatomical Exercises Concerning the Motion of the Heart and Blood* of 1653, noted "All their theory and contemplation (which they count Science) represents nothing but waking mens dreams and sick mens phrensies," a justified and disparaging comment on the state of anatomical studies by a man whose own work was marked by attentive looking, not 'mere speculation'.

But then an important teasing apart and separation of meaning occurs, and we have strong evidence that it was 'in the air' as the poet Dryden anticipates the scientist Newton when he writes, in 1674, "Your theories are here to practice brought/As in mechanic operations wrought." It seems legitimate to construe these lines as saying that 'theory' is beginning to take on a sense of something tested (to practice brought), and the testing is similar to the experiments conducted in the mid-17th century with simple mechanical systems of cogs and levers. Thirteen years later the *Principia* appears, and shapes everything that comes after it. Book after book appears in the 18th century on celestial mechanics shaped by the enormous authority of the *Principia*, while tables of navigation are published based on the constantly tested predictions computed from Newton's laws. By 1798, even a man trying to understand the human world, Thomas Malthus in *An Essay on the Principle of Population*, insists "A theory that will not admit of application [i.e., that cannot be tested] cannot possibly be just [i.e., true]." The testing of statements deriving from theoretical concern has become an explicit part of the meaning of 'theory', and already, in 1829, James Mill, in his *Analysis of Phenomena of the Human Mind* will decry the coming slippage with "The word theory has been perverted to denote an operation ... which ... consists in supposing [i.e., speculating] and setting down matters supposed as matters observed. Theory in fact has become confounded with Hypothesis." Once again, theory contains within it the idea of something tested, its mark and meaning are grounded on "matters observed." In 1864, Francis Bowen, in his *A Treatise on Logic*, will note "A Theory, sometimes incorrectly used as a synonym for Hypothesis." And the *Oxford English Dictionary* will acknowledge, almost reluctantly, such deterioration of meaning, carefully defined in the scientific realm, by providing a sixth, and final definition as "In loose and general sense: A hypothesis proposed as an explanation; hence, a mere hypothesis, speculation, conjecture."

Thus, my desire to retrieve and stiffen the meaning of 'theory', making the tested and testable an explicit part of the meaning, is not whimsical or idiosyncratic. It is grounded upon that separation from 'speculation' that arises with, and out of, the authoritative stance that a body of well-tested, and not merely speculative, knowledge provides. That body of knowledge we call today Science, and I maintain my claim that the authoritative meaning of 'theory' today must come from that rich, though limited, realm of inquiry. I take it as a reasonable statement that those who take 'theory' out of its scientific domain take with it its authoritative meaning of a well-tested body of statements, not to be confused with conjecture and speculation, themselves honorable and necessary tasks that always precede theory, and may, with time and testing, become it.

It is pertinent to ask why 'theory' is taken out of this realm, and constantly given other meanings ranging from the old synonym 'speculation', to the more recent definitions such as 'framework for communication', etc. First, theory as a well and constantly tested body of knowledge may certainly be used as a secure framework within which communication and discourse can take place by those who share a high degree of confidence in it precisely because constantly tested knowledge provides a secure base. Moreover, theory as a well and constantly tested body of knowledge may certainly be used as a secure guide to inquiry and action. We built, not unnaturally, from those areas we believe are our secure ground out to those areas where speculation and ignorance reign. But secure, theoretical ground is hard won, and not to be cheapened by those who wish to borrow the term to give an authoritative gloss to their own speculative statements, nor to be confused with speculations that are untested, and frequently untestable.

Secondly, borrowing the word 'theory' from the physical sciences constitutes yet another instance of that thoughtless sideways transfer into the language of the human world whose meaning is inconsistent with the new realm of inquiry. We have here a purely linguistic example of the same inappropriate borrowing represented by mapping the human world onto mathematical structures whose developments proceeded hand in hand with the need to describe faithfully the mechanical world of physical things. In the same way that a mechanical, essentially functional, mathematics can only allow the human world to appear mechanical, so the words of inappropriately borrowed language can only allow meaning whose authority has been annealled in a furnace of thinking directed to the physical world. To take the authoritative meaning of 'theory' arising in the world of things into the world of human beings is to imply, by thoughtless analogy, that similar sets of well-tested statements and laws may be found.

Finally, the desire to use the word 'theory', instead of the appropriate 'speculation', itself arises precisely because the authority of the former, and the untested nature of the latter, are implicitly recognized. We frequently speak of social *theory* when we refer to an untested, and frequently untestable, set of statements, instead of social *speculation*, because we appear to need the authoritative assurance of the scientific meaning that gains its authority from testable and confirmed predictions. We cover the shallowness of our discussions and statements in the complex human realm with the dignity of the meaning we assume is available in the physical realm. We stretch meaning from one world to cover another, and by so stretching we disclose the etymological ground of *pretension*.

Given the strong desire to move language and modes of inquiry from one realm to another, it comes as no surprise that both theoretical and speculative statements in the physical sciences are invariably couched in mathematics, and rather simple algebras at that, in which well-defined binary operations work on well-defined elements of sets, to deduce, in strict logical order, the consequences contained in the initial definitions.[2] This implies that mathematically stated theory contains within it the possibility of prediction, at least in some manner and to some degree, ranging from the highly precise to the much more qualified. We shall examine such qualifications in both micro and macro systems later, but the meaning, both implicit and explicit, of 'theory' requires the sense of testing that can only come from anticipated states or events, i.e., those predicted in advance of actual observations made. If the predicted events or states are observed, no matter how absurd or unlikely they were thought to be given the current state of knowledge, then the theory whose mathematical statements predicted them gains credence and authority. Simply as a stage aside, and not something that can be explored in depth here, the meaning of *ta mathemata* has been philosophically retrieved as "that which man knows in advance in his observation of whatever is ..." (Heidegger, 1977). Its root, of course, is *mathesis*, 'the teaching' or 'what can be learned from lessons', but notice that we can only teach that which we know in advance (Heidegger, 1967). Thus, both the ancient Greek, and our modern meaning, imply that mathematical statements point to things that are capable of being anticipated, i.e., predicted.[3]

Notice also that the mathematical statements made out of theoretical concern are invariably *functional*, in the strict mathematical sense of a one-to-one or many-to-one mapping.[4] Thus, they are essentially (again, in their

---

[2] "Invariably", in its quite literal sense, must be slightly qualified here, since the relatively new field of Artificial Intelligence is currently making quite extraordinary and sweeping claims to its own powers, grounded upon the purely mechanical mathematics of computational theory which provide for n-ary operations. To the degree that anything in the physical or human worlds has been genuinely illuminated by such approaches - a point that is still moot despite the stridency of the claims made - then the statement here must be qualified. In fact, even the claim to the illuminating power of n-ary operations is contradicted by an even stronger claim in AI, that all mathematically statable theories are simply special cases of Turing machines. These, however, rely upon simple binary operations, to which all n-ary operations are reducible.

[3] This retrieved meaning causes distress to those unwilling to listen carefully to the process of retrieve employed by a man who read Greek every day of his life, and who always discussed the plausibility of such retrieved meaning with the philogist Lohman, who had a written command of 140 languages. The full argument is contained in pages 69-76 of Heidegger's *What is a Thing?*, pages which even the most skeptically outraged should approach in a spirit of thoughtful openness.

[4] Again, 'invariably' must be somewhat qualified in light of two areas of mathematics which have recently assumed some prominence in limited domains of Science (catastrophes and bifurcations), and in view of the all-inclusive claims to computational wisdom made by some working in AI. Some functional statements may be characterized by regions within which a transition may be specified as one-to-many, and statements made in AI may be set down as many-to-many

essence) *mechanical*, for they embody the concept of mechanism (Gould, 1985b). It is hardly surprising that we find ourselves today in a world of mechanism, for it is certainly our Cartesian inheritance, even though it need not constitute the limit to our horizon of thinking. Nor is it surprising that the mathematical forms we generally employ were developed in, and came out of, celestial *mechanics*, statistical *mechanics*, continuum *mechanics*, and quantum *mechanics*. So when we map the human world onto the mathematics arising in the world of mechanics, the human world can only look mechanical. The structures we employ to express ourselves, literally to 'push out' our thoughts onto these symbolic structures, do not allow this human world of ours to look anything else except mechanical.

But now what meaning, what sound and consistent meaning, do we give the word 'theory' in the human sciences? And before we consider this, perhaps we should ask: what do we mean by the phrase 'human sciences'? Is it perhaps an oxymoron, a phrase that contains a contradiction within itself? If it turns out that a science is characterized by theoretical structures as I have carefully tried to define them here, and 'theory' turns out to be meaningless within the human realm of inquiry, what happens to the meaning of the word *science* as it is used to characterize the human world? Perhaps the meaning of this word will also have to shift, or perhaps we shall have to qualify its meaning to a term more appropriate to the human world.

So the second, basic question I would like to ask is: *where* are the mathematical statements, whose predictions are well-tested, again and again, against empirical evidence, that are characteristic of theory in a physical science? I challenge you to find them. Economics? Here we have a discipline that dresses its computations in the most elaborate notations, when most of its interpolating arithmetic could be put down on the back of an envelope by an eight-year-old child. It makes the strongest claims to computational science, it still speaks of laws, and yet is unable to predict anything of intellectual worth. How much contrary empirical evidence do we require before graduate training in this discipline becomes a genuine education to help people illuminate the economic condition, rather than the *rite de passage* in which the niceties of 19th century functional mathematics are passed on to the next generation? In sociology, political science, and, I suggest, in human geography, the claims are often, and quite properly, more modest, for the mechanistic functions appear to be as incapable of making predictions in these areas of human life as they are in the economic. I ask you again: *where* are the predictions to be tested? And where, therefore, is the meaning of *theory* maintained (MacIntyre, 1984)? It is true, of course, that there is much more to science than prediction, not the least genuinely illuminating description arising from acts of considerable imagination. But there is not much more to theory when its true meaning is allowed to be kept intact. It is the predictions that allow a speculation to be tested, and so become part of a consistent, and intellectually authoritative, theory.

We must reflect that prediction is the mark of a *theoretical* science, and consider the possibility that a theoretical science, in which theory is so marked and tested, may well be constrained and confined to the physical world of things. But so powerful, so intellectually powerful, are the physical sciences within their own, and highly limited, realm of things that their authority tends to act like a Judas goat to the sheep of the human sciences. In our attempts to

---

mappings. Such mappings (and strictly not functions) may arise in empirical work; for example, responses of crops to environmental conditions modified by agricultural practices (Chapman, 1982). But for the last 500 years functional statements, *sensu strictu* have overwhelmingly dominated Science.

theorize, in our attempts to emulate the form of theorizing, we betray our own lack of intellectual self-confidence, a self-disparagement that may well arise from cutting ourselves loose from the tradition of philosophical thinking from which all the sciences hived off from the 17th century onwards. After all, 300 years ago even physics was 'natural philosophy', and sociology's original meaning, when it was first used in the English language in 1843, was 'social ethics'.

The result is that we have witnessed a thoughtless, almost Gadarene, rush over the past thirty years to find, and jump on, every passing mathematical bandwagon, with little, if any, thought for the appropriateness of such totally mechanical descriptions for the human world. Let us consider some of these briefly. Catastrophe theory, an extraordinary and brilliant feat of mathematics by Rene Thom (Thom, 1975), became the darling of the non-physical sciences about ten years ago, because it pointed to the possibility of describing, in a few canonical mathematical forms, sharp breaks or discontinuities, discontinuities that were often observed in the human world. For example, a sudden decision to fast if you are anorexially gorging, or the precise application of a new tax law, treaty or cease fire at midnight on the 31st of March. The result was that everyone started seeing folds and cusps and butterflies, but all this was at the level of *Scientific American* analogy (Zeeman, 1976), where dogs put their ears back and cringed, or leapt forward to attack as they tipped over the edge of the fold in their three-dimensional behavior space. But where is catastrophe theory today? Where have all the catastrophes gone ... long time passing? Gone to graveyards, every one; perhaps to join game theory in the heaven where all good mathematical models go after they have had a brief, fleeting life in the human sciences. There are those who remember the excitement of game theory in the 1960s, but when did someone last see a reference to it in the 1980s that genuinely illuminated some aspect of the human world? In 1983, I spent five days with Rene Thom in a small biological research station north of the arctic circle, and held a number of discussions with him outside of the formal presentations that were made (Casti and Karlqvist, 1986). He said he knew of no calibrated examples of catastrophe theory in the human sciences, no examples whatsoever of concretely examining the appropriateness of a particular catastrophe as a description, no empirical examples of actually fitting and calibrating such a description to a real set of data. Of course, this did not bother him in the least as a mathematician, but even in the physical world of things there are few examples where these structures describe discontinuous phenomena with fidelity. I know, for example, from colleagues in meteorology and topology, that the actual fitting of atmospheric turbulence to the butterfly catastrophe is no easy matter.

Then we had bifurcation theory, the great opportunity to bring order out of chaos led by Ilya Prigogine (Prigogine and Stengers, 1984). I certainly do not quarrel with him as a physical chemist, and I trust the judgment of his peers who awarded him a Nobel Prize ... for *chemistry*, where he described remarkable flip-flop chemical reactions in terms of the bifurcations of non-linear equations as parameter values were altered; for example, the splitting of a function's trajectory as heat was applied. But with recognized authority in the physical domain of things, there is a temptation to assume authority in the human domain of people. Many-valued functions (as they used to be called), were first investigated in the middle of the 19th century by Riemann, and they were greatly extended by some of the great Italian algebraic geometers, such as Levi-Civitas. They require as a condition of their possibility the set of the reals, and even if a bifurcation point should occur in the set of integers (the only set whose elements can actually be observed),[5] continuation of the trajectory requires the additional specification of random input, often the accumulated rounding error in computed applications. Regrettably, enlarging the mathematical possibilities to still highly constrained one-to-many mappings does not result in a solution to all of mankind's ills. When chemists, armed with 19th century mathematics, enter the human realm and declare Napoleon and John Locke to be bifurcation points in European history, I exhibit a distressing tendency to doubt for the sake of the truth (Gould, 1987c). Once again, we have a mechanical description upon which we map the human world.

Today, drawn by our ever-increasing involvement with computers, we have a growing concern with random and chaotic behavior, and sometimes the fractal representations that represent chaotic forms (Mandelbrot, 1977). Now popular as they are today, I shall not deal with fractals here, for the simple reason that I do not know what to do with them, except to print them for the aesthetic pleasure they give people in the popular magazines, or to hang them as posters on the wall - like the old maps of land use that were once so diligently compiled on geographical field courses, or the satellite pictures that are produced at such vast expense and technical expertise today. Fractals constitute a perfectly valid domain of mathematical inquiry, with some power to illuminate older areas of concern; for example, numerical approximation methods devised by Newton (Peterson, 1987). But mathematicians are expressing grave doubts that these intellectually seductive visual forms actually illuminate anything in the worlds of things or human beings. Indeed, if we wish to be correct and consistent within the very mathematical domain out of which the claims are made, then the simple fact that fractals require the continuum of the set of the reals is inconsistent with any quantum description limited by the finiteness of Planck's constant. You cannot stop a fractal process at some, quite arbitrary level, and then declare a fractal dimension, for you have broken an axiom constituting a condition of possibility for the fractal domain. These may appear pedantic objections, but claims of application made from the mathematical realm should be consistent with the axioms and requirements of that perspective. However, these fractal requirements do not have to be exhaustively addressed here if we are concerned with chaotic behavior and the philosophical questions it raises for the methodology of human geographical inquiry. They will, however, enter the discussion again for the doubts they cast upon the appropriateness of chaotic models.

The relatively recent concepts of chaos have intellectual precedents that are important for thinking through their implications in both the physical and human realms. These cannot be explicated in any detail here, but they are important to consider briefly as a context for the more recent concern for chaos, and the claims that are made out of this body of thought. The concept of randomness itself has a long and important history that has engaged both scientists and philosophers (Brown, 1957), and the term itself begins to accrete its meaning from the 13th century onwards.[6]

---

[5] In our observations we can only count, and we can only count integer numbers (Atkin, 1974), since we do not observe elements of the rationals, and we are always obliged to truncate the transcendentals to values that may be recorded as integers by simple scaling.

[6] The sense of impetuousness contained in *random*, a sense that will later inform the question of predictability, arises etymologically in the Old French *randon*, meaning a headlong rush or gallop. It appears in English in 1305, but by 1561 the sense of haphazardness is already there, and quite rapidly insinuates itself into the meaning. Thus does the everyday language of hunting and hawking inform the Brownian motion of Einstein.

To help us think about chaos, and its implications for 'theory' in the sciences, let us return to some earlier concerns for the formal properties and consequences of randomness and complexity (Kolmogorov, 1968; Chaitin, 1974). Although less than two decades old, the doubts and disquiet that these raise inform more recent developments, even as they may be indicative of a considerable enlargement of possibilities. However, we must examine the claims to enlarged possibility with great care. Paradoxically, the clearing available for thinking may be enhanced by a simple awareness that binding and unreleasable constraints may exist in certain areas of human inquiry into macrosystems. Perhaps such an awareness is analogous to the earlier constraints of uncertainty claimed for micro (i.e., quantum) systems, although the ground here is quite different.

Our contextual discussion starts in the now classical fashion by directing thought to the description of sequences of events, sequences that we shall assume can be mapped to, and coded as, a binary string, say S:

$$S = 1\ 0\ 1\ 1\ 0\ 1\ 0\ 0\ 1\ 1\ 0\ 1\ ...$$

Notice that such a sparse representation does not appear to be essential to the argument that follows, for it simply says that any piece or sequence of information, can, *in principle*, be coded in this way. Even Mahler symphonies are coded now in digital form on laser-read disks, and we shall see that this is not an unimportant example to consider later.

The question arises: is it possible to find a shorter string, say D, that could act as the input or instructions to a computer to generate S:

$$D = ?\ \rightarrow \rightarrow\ \boxed{\quad ?\quad}\ \rightarrow \rightarrow\ S = 1\ 0\ 1\ 1\ 0\ 1\ 0\ 0\ 1\ 1\ 0\ 1\ ...$$

By definition, finding such a shorter string D means that there is some pattern in S, so that S is not random:

$$D = 1\ 1\ 0\ 1\ ... \rightarrow\ \boxed{\begin{array}{l}\text{If 1, write 1 0 1}\\ \text{If 0, write 0 0 1}\end{array}}\ \rightarrow S = 1\ 0\ 1\ 1\ 0\ 1\ 0\ 0\ 1\ 1\ 0\ 1\ ...$$

However, not finding a shorter string D does not mean that S is necessarily random, and, in fact, demonstrating that S is random is unsolvable - what a mathematician would call recursively unsolvable. Both Kolmogorov and Chaitin have provided some fundamental proofs of theorems that support this statement.

Now in classical Newtonian physics, still the ground of so many sciences dealing with the physical world of things (geology, meteorology, etc.), the D strings are presumably the binary digits that record the ticking away of clock time, or record spatial coordinates, input terms to the functional statements computing the outputs. Just think of $s = u.t + 1/2.a.t^2$ ... record the acceleration LT^{-2} and the time T, turn the cogwheels on the right hand side of the equation, and out comes the mechanically derived distance s. In classical physics, other terms (for example, mass), remain constant, while in relativistic statements they vary with the input string in well-specified ways. Such specifications imply a high degree of predictability of the S strings, and we often term the computational instructions 'laws'. We find them inductively, or we confirm those deduced from highly imaginative and fruitful definitions, by choosing to consider a very limited number of things, constructing scales, counting integer numbers, and then relating the scales by making some bold assumptions about the set of the real numbers. That, essentially, is all (Atkin, 1965). It is often difficult work; we spend billions each year doing it; and we call such activity Science.

The 'sciences' that deal with human beings also examine S strings of events, and try to find shorter D strings that will compute them. Relative to the physical sciences, we only spend pennies each year to understand ourselves in this way, and, as I have already indicated, predictability is, generally speaking, a joke. Ironically, we usually ignore future demographic structure, generally considered to be the most predictable human variable, as any life insurance company will confirm, except those that took the premiums of Jewish clients in Europe between the years 1939-1945. Only when a national classroom-teacher, or social security, crisis 'suddenly' appears as a great surprise (Atkin, 1981), do we realize with regret the potentialities we once had for meeting the future. Notice, however, that even here the S string of tomorrow, the 'prediction' of demographic structure in the future, is shorter than the D string of today that computes it, namely the present demographic structure. No demographic theory, no shorter theoretically compressed D string, is involved. All that is required is simple extrapolating arithmetic, the sort conducted on the back of an envelope by our eight-year-old child.

It is both interesting and important to ask why prediction, computed on 'theoretical' grounds, fails so frequently in the human sciences and, as we shall see, in an increasing number of the physical sciences concerned with macrosystems, such as plate tectonics and atmospheric circulation. Quite apart from the human capacity to reflect upon itself individually, or collectively as a society, and so invalidate any computational statement and its input string, it is, perhaps, because many sequences of events, in both the human and physical worlds, are *maximally complex*. This means that the string S is not compressible to a shorter string D. It simply *is what it is*, namely itself, and as a maximally complex string it is not computable except by another maximally complex string. For example, I generated this particular S string 'at random' using the last digit of first references in the Index of Ron Johnston's (1986) *On Human Geography*:

$$0\ 1\ 1\ 0\ 0\ 0\ 1\ 0\ 0\ 0\ 1\ 1\ 1\ 1\ 0\ 0\ 0\ 0\ 1\ 1\ 0\ ...$$

But the only way I can 'compute it' is by constructing a D string, together with a rule that says 'map all the ones to zeros and all the zeros to ones', or simply 'reverse everything':

D		**S**
1 0 0 1 1 1 0 1 1 1 0 0 0 0 1 1 1 1 0 0 1 ... →	"Reverse Everything" →	0 1 1 0 0 0 1 0 0 0 1 1 1 1 0 0 0 0 1 1 0 ...

Another rule might be 'keep everything as it is', for which I would have to use the S string as its own D string. But in either of these totally banal cases, I would have to use a D string of the same length as S. In other words, I cannot find any 'compressible order' in the original S string. Unfortunately, for those seeking the D strings in the human sciences, it can be shown that for a string of events of reasonable length, say n, any shorter D strings that might generate it are going to be minutely shorter, which means empirically they are going to be quite uninterestingly shorter, and even these will be overwhelmed by the huge number of maximally complex strings.

At this point, I believe there only remains one other thing to consider, and that is the choice itself that is made to restrict observation to a very limited number of events involving human beings (Figure 1). Such an initial choice

CHOICE: S ———————> S' AGGREGATION: S' —> S"

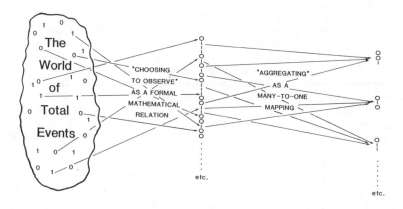

Figure 1: Our observations as a binary string S', formally stated as a relation CHOICE, an act of human freedom not available to a machine. These may be subsequently aggregated to S" by the many-to-one mapping AGGREGATION, another free act of human inquiry not available to the machine existing in a space incommensurable with, and subservient to, the human presence.

constitutes, in the fullest mathematical sense, a relation, an act of specification taking elements of S→S', while any aggregation forms a many-to-one mapping of S'→S". Such relations and mappings are initially powerful, even violent, compressions, that are arbitrary and artificial in the well-defined sense that they are purely human constructs undertaken contingently and historically. It is these that produce the observed S" strings. So if we now find corresponding, let us call them D" strings, and some appropriate computational statements to generate the corresponding S" strings, what is it that we are computing and predicting? We cannot go back to S' or S, because inverses do not exist for many-to-one mappings and relations. Do we then model with our D" strings and computational statements the nonrandomness we have imposed by our choices. Do we end up modeling the compressional rule of observational choice producing the highly simplified structures? Are we modeling, in mechanistic mathematics, the order-forming mappings of our own choices, the relation CHOICE and the mapping AGGREGATION? Are we mathematizing our own historically contingent, and thus will-o'-the-wisp, perceptions in a maximally complex world? In brief, are we chasing our own tails, and disappearing up our own Klein bottles?

Seeing order and predictability by writing D strings and computational instructions, whether in an algebra, or stated in verbally specified systems, is an activity usually denoted today as 'theoretical'. Yet perhaps, in David Berlinski's words, " ... vast sections of our intellectual experience might be so very rich in information that they stay forever outside the scope of theory and remain simply what they are - unique, ineffable, unaffiliated, insubsumable, irreducible" (Berlinski, 1986, page 80).

It is important to note that this problem is not confined to the human world. At the quantum mechanical level, "the source of randomness ... is an inherent limit on the precision with which certain variables can be measured," (Scientific American, 1987), and there is a well-tested *theoretical* basis for such genuinely scientific statements about probability that are grounded in Planck's constant. But to indulge in probabilistic statements as genuine expectations about 'macroscopic systems (such as the global atmosphere), is to put forward pseudo-probabilities without genuine scientific merit. The statement that there is a 40 percent chance of rain tomorrow can be a legitimate, if banal, declaration about simple tallies of prior events, but it cannot be grounded upon genuine scientific and predictive computation that stands any chance of being tested in finite human time. Such pseudo-probabilities, like the likelihood estimates about nuclear accidents, have nothing to do with science, and they may be subject to grossly unethical manipulation. In the atmosphere, even minute perturbations can amplify quickly, and with the finest data grid, and the largest and fastest computers we can imagine, errors are transmitted hierarchically to limit weather predictions *absolutely* to about two weeks (Lorenz, 1969). In other words, and in the future, the S weather strings two weeks away may conceivably be computed from D weather strings that are of the same length. No *theory* is involved, just extrapolating arithmetic. As things are today, even with the dynamic, essentially Newtonian equations in place, the weather reasserts its maximal complexity after three or four days. Even 400,000 compared comparisons of weather map sequences produced no repetitions, no good analogues. In other words, in terms of relatively short term prediction, what happened before cannot tell us what will happen again.

In marked contrast, and in what appears initially as a paradox, the gross long term 'trajectories' of historical climatology now appear postdictable to a quite extraordinary degree (Imbrie, 1985) giving rise to some confidence that predictions may be made.[7] But the matter is more subtle, and the apparent paradox is rooted in what we might almost term a 'Laplacian ground', in the sense of what is deemed knowable and unknowable. It is not accidental that the fidelity of the gross climatological trajectory arises because the forcing functions are those grounded in planetary motion described by the classical functional statements of celestial mechanics. Computations of precession, eccentricity and tilt, all based on Newtonian mechanics, constitute the numerical inputs that the binary operations of arithmetic then map to the single valued system state that is matched by oxygen isotope ratios. But the leap from planetary motion to

---

[7] It is here that the finitude of a human life comes starkly to the fore, since predictions of ice ages can never be confirmed by those who make them - nor, for that matter, by the hundred or more generations that follow the predictor and their foretelling of events. The gods must be smiling at mortals who cannot foretell in times meaningful to them while they do appear able to predict in times so vast that they are pragmatically meaningless. However, these mortal endeavors should neither be dismissed nor diminished. First, they bear witness to the human spirit to understand the physical world of things, and they constitute magnificent instances of that intentionality towards the world that is constitutive of being human. Secondly, they point to ethical stances and responsibilities towards future generations that cannot be ignored any more out of ignorance (Apel, 1986). The 'climatological trajectory', described by a single variable state in the phase space, is currently at an extreme value that does not appear to have been exceeded during the past 400,000 years. There appears to be no sign at the present time of the typically sharp reversal to an ice age, brought about by mechanisms of negative feedback that are little understood (Lovelock, 1979). Thus, the question arises as to whether the intensity of the human presence (overpopulation, destruction of the tropical forests, atmospheric pollution, desertification, the loosening of distance constraints on the transmission of disease, e.g, AIDS, etc.) constitutes a change in the system itself, or an additional 'forcing function' driving the system into states not previously encountered.

isotope ratios leaves out all the extraordinarily complex couplings between land, ice and water surfaces by atmospheric circulation, all driven by changes in the radiation balance. It is these that are recorded in the ice cores of the Greenland icecap, the tree rings of bristlecone pines, the cores from lake beds (Petit-Maire, 1984), and even varve sequences in the geological record spanning hundreds of millions of years. It is in these sequences recording the coupling mechanisms that order appears to break down, in much the same way that apparent cycles and periodicities of populations unaccountably break down in the world of bank voles and other living things (Gripps, et al., 1986). In this biological realm, specialists like Nils Stensteth, probably the world's authority on lemmings, calls for "another mathematics" (Stensteth, 1986), while others acknowledge that traditional forms may be inadequate, since any application requires that we describe quite specifically and concretely what is. For example, the spread of rabies in a cellular space of fox territories requires the arithmetic of finite element analysis based on a description that illuminates a particular time and place (Källén, Arcuri, Murray, 1985). This constitutes legitimate, careful, important, useful and illuminating description, but no theory is involved in the proper sense that might be applied to the conduction of heat through a copper plate.

But it is precisely here, in the midst of such 'event sequences' that traditionally would have been described as random, maximally complex, and so unpredictable, that new voices are heard enunciating claims that some chaotic and unpredictable sequences are not random after all. There is a distinction to be made between 'purely' random and chaotic sequences. What such a distinction brings to us, what chaotic sequences *are* in the deeply human sense of what meaning may be given to them to illuminate the physical, biological and human worlds, is something that we shall have to examine with the utmost care. As the claims made for the mathematics of games, catastrophies and bifurcations to illuminate the world around us fade into the past, we can only approach the equally strident claims of this new area of concern with caution, and even some legitimate skepticism.

Frustrating though it may be to someone who approaches the distinction between randomness and chaos for the first time, it is not possible to provide anything like an elementary introduction here (Crutchfield, et al., 1986). But like many areas obfuscated by operational computation, the basic ideas, and the claims made from them, are quite simple. What I shall call 'chaotic thinking' - thinking about chaos distinct from randomness as it has been traditionally thought - arises with the discovery that sequences of 'events', represented by numbers, may be generated by deterministic processes. The sequences are indistinguishable from those traditionally thought to be random, where 'indistinguishable' means they cannot be discriminated by the usual tests employing runs and moments of distributions. The deterministic process is often represented by a machine, with a pendulum regularly pulsed by an electromagnet serving as a classical, and archetypically simple, mechanism. If we measure some characteristic state of this simple mechanical system, say the width of the swing and the velocity, a chaotic sequence, without any apparent order or pattern, will be generated. Similarly, we can write three very simple differential equations in x, y and z, and get a small personal computer to plot out the integrated trajectory on the screen. The system makes a series of closely aligned loops in one part of the 'state space', and then suddenly flips to another sequence of loops. The number of loops in each part of the 'pretzel' form a series that appears to be random, although the generating process is completely deterministic. There are, in fact, an infinite number of such totally deterministic models that will produce such chaos, and such a plethora of possibilities will raise some uncomfortable conceptual issues later.

But even at this point there is an important caution and qualifying condition to be stated. All computable models are grounded on the set of integers, while the purely mathematical ground requires the set of the reals. The reason is obvious: if chaotic sequences are constrained to the integers, the continuum is broken, integer values will repeat in a state space constrained to a hyperlattice, so that eventually the same conditions will occur that occurred previously. Thus, the sequence will eventually repeat - much more frequently than the equivalent 'Poincaré recurrence' on the reals - and the trajectory will follow a path already taken, and so cycle. Finite outputs from observable machines are not expansions of the transcendentals. We are not concerned operationally with a big Π in the sky. As I have already pointed out, *all* our observations employ the integer numbers, and perhaps this simple fact alone undermines chaotic models as faithful descriptions of the observable human world. The same question arises in the observable physical world, where the long-accepted integer constraint at the quantum level now appears in a different guise at the macrolevel.

These qualifying conditions are not pedantic: the mathematics of chaos are properly grounded in axiomatic statement, and are well tested in the sense that no contradiction has yet appeared that would cast doubt on the adequacy of these axioms. But we must reflect carefully upon the claims made when they are moved out of the mathematical realm to stand as statements purporting to illuminate the human, biological and physical worlds.

The heart of the claims made by chaotic thinking lies in the familiar representation of a dynamic system's trajectory as a sequence of 'time points' in a state space whose orthogonal dimensions are the variables used to characterize the state of the system. For example, positions and velocity suffice to fix the state of a simple, unpulsed pendulum, and the system trajectory of simple harmonic motion is either the radius circle in an ideal, frictionless world, or the spiral to the fixed point at the center. Both are termed 'closed solutions', and both allowing precise Laplacian predictions if the boundary conditions are known by substituting values of t in the appropriate classical equations. The trajectory of a magnetic, and regularly pulsed, pendulum cannot be stated in such a simple way, although the trajectory may be sequentially computed by always finite methods. While these methods themselves give rise to uncertainty, uncertainty that magnifies exponentially and quickly obviates prediction, trajectories may tend to remain in certain regions of the state space. And it is here that we have to deal with a major claim, based on a misnomer (the first of two), and examine the meaning of that which is named.

Trajectory behavior in a state space is called chaotic if it is confined to a region of the space,[8] even if no closed solution exists. The regions have been misnamed 'strange attractors', and the misnomer is grave for it leads thinking astray. Both the etymological roots, and the common meaning, imply that there is some *thing*, some entity in the state space that is drawing the system's trajectory to it, exerting some force rather like the intense gravitational force of

---

[8] A mathematician would insist, quite properly, that the phrase 'a subset of the states' should be substituted for 'a *region* of the space', the latter implying mathematically that it is open. I have retained 'region' here in its more colloquial, even geographical, sense, realizing that the distinction will not be meaningful to most, non-mathematical readers. Confining the trajectory to a limited region of the state space is important not only for the misnomer to come, but because it distinguishes chaotic from random behavior under carefully stated dimensional conditions.

a black hole sucking everything into itself. In brief, the existence of an entity is posited that has, and can have, no existence. There is no *thing* there, no attractor existing that can attract in any sense meaningful in the English, or any other, language. 'To attract' is an active transitive verb, by definition taking an object. Unfortunately, in predicative Indo-European languages, a subject, some thing, is also required, simply because a predicative statement must affirm or deny a subject to be meaningful.

This is not linguistic pedantry: we think in language, and if the language we use implies the existence of things which do not exist, then our thinking is led totally astray. Having posited existence to no thing, we try to give meaning to that which does not exist. By using language carelessly, we end in trying to interpret a no thing that, by tautological definition, can have no interpretation. This becomes crucial as we move out of the *purely mathematical* realm and try to interpret, i.e., give meaning to, possible things that may actually exist and act as constraints on the trajectory, so allowing us to name, and thus categorize, system behavior as chaotic instead of random. It is the difference between positing real things in the human or physical worlds (for example, limits to human abilities or mechanical friction), things that constitute genuine bounds to behavior exhibited in a confined region of state space, as opposed to positing nonexistent things and ascribing predicative powers of attraction to them. The language of science should lead thinking to the possibility of the real, to the truth, not to figments of the imagination more appropriate to astrology.

But it is here that other difficulties arise, and with them the second misnomer. A region of a state space confining a trajectory is currently considered to be of interest if it displays some *form*, a concept with deep aesthetic roots, notoriously difficult to specify, and lying, perhaps like beauty, in the eye of the beholder. The misnomer arises precisely because all previous meanings of 'chaos', on either etymological or traditional religious grounds (Genesis 1:2), imply *without form*. Yet those who name this realm of thinking are forced to ground their claims on the detection of form denied by the word itself, an unbelievably perverse and casual use of language that actually reverses meaning. But the gravest difficulties do not lie here, but in the technical and hermeneutic tasks that lie outside of the pure mathematical realm. It is these difficulties that must give pause to even the most enthusiastic proponents of 'this year's model'.

The mathematical statements, from which the hopes of application spring, lie in a theorem of Taken that states the precise conditions under which a model (in the sense of delimiting a region of the state space) may be discovered or created out of the sequence of states observed.[9] If the conditions, and, it should be emphasized, if these *purely mathematical* conditions hold, then it would appear that an enormously exciting and promising methodology opens up. The implication would seem to be that we can 'work backwards' from any numerically stated sequence of states to the 'model', where 'model' here means a region (subset) of the state space.

Mathematically the road has been smoothed to a broad highway by Taken's theorem; operationally we are on a rough track full of potholes. The first technical difficulty lies in the discovery of the form of the region or 'model'. It

---

[9] Briefly, given a sequence of numerically expressed states, say x_1, x_2, x_3 ... then there is a model if:

a) M is a finite dimensioned smooth manifold

b) $T: M \rightarrow M$

c) $\Psi: M \rightarrow R$ the reals and these conditions are generic.

is quite possible that it may not be visualized, which is why I used the phrase 'detection of form' rather than 'perception of form'. In fact, the concept of form has been operationalized to the detection of dimensionality in the model less than that of the phase space. The second technical difficulty lies in the fact that the dimensions computed may be fractals, with all the conceptual difficulties this raises for moving back and forth between the integers of observation and the reals of the mathematics. Thirdly, the mathematical conditions require that the states in the sequence are known precisely, without error. Any error of observation will raise the dimensionality of the model, although conceivably it may be possible to compute the 'weight' or relative importance of the dimensions required. Notice at this point we are not far from the conceptual realm of traditional factor analysis which asks how many 'significant' dimensions are required to span a 'state space'. Finally, in these purely technical matters, the computation of the dimensionality of the confining region may be a very poor guide to the question of form. One only has to think of a stove pipe bent in such a way that it requires the three dimensions of its state space to contain it. There is no reduction in the dimensionality of the stove pipe 'region', yet it constitutes a highly significant form that could lead thinking to consider what constraints are operating in the observable world to produce such a configuration. To state it flatly, simple dimensionality, computed in and of itself, does *not* disclose form, and in higher dimensional spaces our inability to visualize form obviates any possibility that we can think towards the constraints that confine the observed states to a formed region, for which structure is claimed, rather than the formless region of unstructured, i.e., random events.

But in raising the question of thinking away from misnomered 'attractors' and towards real constraints on real processes giving rise to real events, we have crossed the threshold into the hermeneutic realm of interpretation. The argument is no longer mathematical and technical: the mathematician does not care what meaning is placed upon the constructs of dimensionality, either integer or fractal, or anything else mathematical. The mathematics is consistent and gives pleasing results within the precisely stated axiomatic conditions. The real difficulty lies in the meaning, the power to illuminate, of a model region with a computed fractal dimensionality of 4.31 in a state space of 5.0 dimensions. For all the computing, what has been achieved? Is the confining region a hyperpancake? A hypertorus? A topological form shaped by a hyperMoore? Above all, what does it *mean*? What meaning, in terms of quite specific and concrete interpretation, can be placed upon such computed entities? Is it just an accident that a fractal representation is possible, and that no one has yet given meaning to fractals?

Consider the Mahler Symphony as a sequence of precisely specified integer vibrations, and suppose, at least in principal, that the region or model in the state space could be reconstructed. What would we have? Just a huge number telling us that the dimensionality of the model region to which Mahler's Symphony was confined was less than the even greater dimensionality of the orchestral state space because Mahler did not use every instrument in every note over its full range. Moreover, Three Blind Mice, played on a penny whistle, would have a model region of even lower dimensionality. This might have been suspected before the computations were undertaken. However, since computation is involved, both the Mahler Symphony and Three Blind Mice could, in principle, have been composed by a Turing machine.

The above paragraph is, of course, deliberately mischievous, but it points to a number of important matters. First, the distinction between random and chaotic behavior appears to hold little promise for writing meaningful descriptions of anything but the simplest and most bathetic mechanical systems, and even less promise for writing meaningful theory. In terms of our ability to illuminate the world, it appears that neither long and 'uninterestingly shorter' D strings, nor 'uninterestingly compressed' dimensions, lead anywhere, for the simple reason that no meaning or interpretation can be placed on either. Even in the physical world it is admitted that "[al]though a given system may be known to be chaotic, the fact alone does not reveal very much" (Crutchfield, et al., 1986, page 56). And in the human world, 'theory' as compressible mechanism, or as compressed dimensionality, begins to veer towards the absurd. What sound and consistent meaning can be placed upon the word 'theory' when no statements can be made that constitute testable propositions?

Secondly, we have another mathematical realm that points to the fact that prediction, even in certain mechanical systems, may be intrinsically impossible. This is a lesson to be learnt, and obviously one that has to be learnt again and again. It is the lesson pointed to by Kolmogorov and Chaitin, and, on a somewhat different, but closely allied, ground by Linhart (1973), with his epidemics of uncertainty and ignorance times. Again, if this is true of the mechanical world of physical things, how much more cogent is it for the world of human beings?

Thirdly, we should have reasoned evidence enough to direct thinking once again to the attentive looking on 'the things themselves', thus releasing so many intelligent people from what are little more than computer games towards genuinely illuminating description that allows us to see something we did not see before. After all, if it is acknowledged that an infinite number of models can simulate the dimensionality of a region to which no meaning can be given, then we might hope that those so enamored will turn to ways towards knowledge (methodologies) that lead to greater understanding.

Nowhere are the implications of this lesson to be reflected upon more deeply than in the human realm, where the unexamined discourse of 19th century mechanical thinking claims to state a theory in verbal, rather than mathematical, form. Whether prediction of an eschatological event of revolution is made, or whether prediction is deliberately eschewed (Johnston, 1986), it appears that those standing somewhere in the broad marxist spectrum will face grave difficulties when they try to claim the meaning of theory as a set of well-tested and confirmed statements. Indeed, those concerned to write 'social theory' cannot be comforted by a body of speculation that so often appears not simply untested, but untestable. Nor can they gain support from recent chaotic thinking that emphasizes, once again, the inability to predict. The mechanical basis is still there. Perhaps, where 'theory' is concerned, it always will be. And perhaps that is why theory, as a well-tested body of knowledge, may be confined to the physical world after all. If theory, in this established and authoritative sense, is in partial disarray in the world of things, then what meaning can it have in the world of sentient and self-reflective human beings? Speculation is quite proper to this world, but there must be grave doubts that it can become theory when those whom the 'theory' is about may break it at will.

I have little doubt that there will be some who will object, perhaps violently, to the words and thoughts of this essay. I can only assure them that these remarks are made in the spirit of positive critique, rather than negative criticism. If we are professors, not by academic title, but by a calling, then presumably we are professors of truth. We may not always speak truly, but our hope is that we may be able to do so, and the notion of truth is surely our ultimate touchstone. As I noted elsewhere (Gould, 1987a, page 2):

"Truth appears to be unpopular today, and talking about it makes the sophisticated squirm with embarrassment, or indulge in knowing winks directed at the naïveté of the poor fool who does not realize that 'all truth is relative'. But if a concern for Truth is not our touchstone, what are we as researchers, as professors (of what?), or as human beings?"

Even examined discourse, if not constantly exercised and reflected upon, too quickly becomes part of the great mass of unexamined discourse that congeals and hardens into ideology. All members of the academic community stand in an old and honorable tradition of constantly questioning, of doubting for the sake of the truth. But let me end on two more positive notes, one in the realm of real and practical affairs, the other in the realm of guiding ideas. Notice, even here, that I use and contrast the *real* and the *ideal*, for the current fashion of juxtaposing realism with idealism is yet another false dichotomy that must be transcended. We must dig beneath the buzz of the current buzz words, and a sense of our intellectual heritage is invaluable to help us see clearly.

First, how do we engage in the thoroughly human and humanely informed task of trying to create a more decent world? If the events coming to us out of the future unfold in random or chaotic, but equally unpredictable, ways, how do we get from *here* to *there*? The answer may come as a disappointment: it means monitoring where we are now, and trying to judge the directions in which we are heading. This is precisely the sort of thing that Stafford Beer tried to do in Chile, in those few dramatic years before Salvadore Allende was murdered by the geographer (and general) Pinochet (Beer, 1981). His monitoring system recognized explicitly the hierarchical nature of a complex economy, and refused to acknowledge the artificial dichotomy between total centralization and total decentralization. We are also much more sensitive today to the fact that intervention, even for the most impeccable, thoughtful, and humane purposes, may well create effects that are counterintuitive to what we intend. Let me suggest, not exactly *contra* Forrester (1973), but regarding the problem from the point of view of chaotic behavior, that these effects do not arise because human society is structured in a mechanistic way by nonlinear equations, but because we simply cannot tell the future. Even the insurance companies did not foresee the Holocaust. As human beings, we are truth-sayers, not soothsayers. What we can do is try to understand what is coming to us in what Beer called 'real time', and then hope to meet the variety with variety for humane and decent ends. No theory gives us these ends: they are the much discussed virtues that have been with us from the time of Aristotle, and prominent among these is Justice.

Secondly, I think it is crucial, the very crux or crossing point of the problem of inquiry in the human realm, that we recover the true and grounding meaning of 'theory'. Our job is not to force the human world into archaic mechanistic forms, but to provide illuminating description that allows that which was concealed before to shine forth in the light of the human presence. And now we hear the older meaning of *theoria*. *Thea* is the appearance that shows itself, the root we retain in our *theater*, and *horao* is to look closely. If we snatch back the old Greek meaning of theory from the arrogant Roman templating, it is the close looking upon that which appears. But it is also more. *Thea* is the goddess who appeared to Parmenides as Truth, and *ora* is respect and honor. Theory, its meaning retrieved yet more deeply, is the honoring of Truth, and in the human world that can only be limpid, clear-seeing description that illuminates the darkness. And that is why the human presence has the capacity to negate the concealing darkness of *Lethe*, the underworld, and so make Truth *a-letheia*, unconcealment. Notice that a body of well-tested and coherent generalizations from the physical sciences is well described by such a meaning of Truth. But notice equally, that an untested and untestable set of speculations, pretentiously clothed in the word theory, bears little relation to such a grounding meaning. I do not think that this requires a radical and sharp change in direction for geographic inquiry, but it does mean that we regard our own descriptive endeavors as honorable and appropriate achievements. We should be proud and forthright to conduct human inquiry in ways that are appropriate to the human realm, and understand science itself as a human endeavor.

References

Apel K-O, 1987 "Global ethics" *Man and World* **20** 3-40
Atkin R, 1965 "Abstract physics" *Il Nuevo Cimento* **38** 496-517
Atkin R, 1974 *Mathematical Structure in Human Affairs* (Heinemann Educational Books, London)
Atkin R, 1981 "A theory of surprises" *Environment and Planning B* **8** 359-365
Beer S, 1984 *Brain of the Firm* Second Edition (John Wiley, New York)
Berlinski D, 1986 *Black Mischief: The Mechanics of Modern Science* (William Morrow, New York)
Brown G, 1957 *Probability and Scientific Inference* (Longman Green, London)
Casti J, Karlqvist A, 1986 *Complexity, Language and Life: Mathematical Approaches* (Springer-Verlag, Berlin)
Chaitin G, 1974 "Information-theoretic computational complexity" *IEEE Transactions on Information Theory* **IT-14** 662-664
Chapman G, 1982 *The Green Revolution* (Marginal Context, Cambridge)
Crutchfield J, Farmer J, Packard N, Shaw R, 1986 "Chaos," *Scientific American* **255** 46-57
Forrester J, 1973 "Counterintuitive Behavior of Social Systems" in *Towards Global Equilibrium* Eds D Meadows, D Meadows, (Wright-Allen Press, Cambridge, Massachusetts) pp 5-30
Gripps J, Alibhai S, Gurnell J, Krebs C, 1986 "A plague of voles: a search for a cure" *New Scientist* **1516** 48-51
Gould P, 1985a "The present and future being of geography as a human science" *Geoforum* **16** 99-107
Gould P, 1985b *The Geographer At Work* (Routledge and Kegan Paul, London)
Gould P, 1986a "Purpose and possibility I: to illuminate our world" *Environment and Planning A* **18** 1421-1422
Gould P, 1986b "Purpose and possibility II: is the human world maximally complex?" *Environment and Planning A* **18** 1556-1558
Gould P, 1987a "Purpose and possibility III: what does 'theory' mean in the human sciences?" *Environment and Planning A* **19** 1-2
Gould P, 1987b "Pensiamentos sobra geografia" *GeoCritica*
Gould P, 1987c "A critique of dissipative structures in the human realm" *European Journal of Operational Research* **30** 211-221
Gould P, 1987d "Review of on human geography" *Progress in Human Geography*
Habermas J, 1968 "Knowledge and human interests: a general perspective" inaugural address Frankfurt, June, 1965 contained in *Knowledge and Human Interests* (Beacon Press, Boston) pp 301-317
Heidegger M, 1962 *Being and Time* (Harper and Row, New York)
Heidegger M, 1967 *What Is A Thing?* (Gateway Editions, South Bend, Indiana)
Heidegger M, 1977 "Science and reflection" in *The Question Concerning Technology and Other Essays* (Harper and Row, New York) pp 155-182
Heidegger M, 1979 *Nietzsche. Volume I: The Will to Power* (Harper and Row, New York)
Heidegger M, 1985 *History of the Concept of Time* (Indiana University Press, Bloomington, Indiana)
Johnston R, 1986 *On Human Geography* (Basil Blackwell, Oxford)

Kolmogorov A, 1974 "Logical basis for information theory and probability
    theory" *IEEE Transactions on Information Theory* **IT-20** 10-15
Källén A, Arcuri P, Murray J, 1985 "A simple model for the spread and control
    of rabies" *Journal of Theoretical Biology* **116** 377-393
Linhart J, 1973 "Uncertainty epidemics among interacting particles" *Il Nuevo
    Cimento* **13A** 355-372
Lorenz E, 1969 "The approaches to atmospheric predictability" *Bulletin of the
    American Meteorological Society* **50** 345-349
Lovelock J, 1979 *Gaia* (Oxford University Press, Oxford)
MacIntyre A, 1984 *After Virtue* (University of Notre Dame Press, Notre Dame,
    Indiana)
Mandelbrot B, 1977 *Fractals: Form, Chance and Dimension* (W. H. Freeman,
    San Francisco)
Peterson I, 1987 "Zeroing in on chaos" *Science News* **131** 137-139
Petit-Maire N, 1984 "Le Sahara, de la steppe en desert" *La Recherche* **15** 1372-
    1383
Prigogine I, Stengers I, 1984 *Order Out of Chaos* (Bantam Books, New York)
Stegmuller W, 1976 *The Structure and Dynamics of Theories* (Springer Verlag,
    Berlin)
Stensteth N, 1986 "Darwinian evolution in ecosystems: a survey of some ideas
    and difficulties together with some possible solutions" in *Complexity,
    Language and Life* Eds J Casti, A Karlqvist (Springer Verlag, Berlin) pp
    105-145
Thom R, 1975 *Structural Stability and Morphogenesis: An Outline of a General
    Theory of Models* (W.A. Benjamin, Reading, Massachusetts)
Zeeman C, 1976 "Catastrophe theory" *Scientific American* **234** 65-83
Zeeman C,1987 "Quantum chaos?" *Scientific American* **256** 62, 64

Struggles over land, struggles over meaning: some thoughts on naming, peasant resistance and the politics of place *

Michael Watts

"There are no facts as such. We must always begin by introducing a meaning in order for there to be a fact."

Friederich Nietzsche

Men and women make their own History but not under conditions of their own choosing. Men and women also experience historical conditions and interpret History; they make and remake meanings, they simultaneously represent, contest and invent the past. Men and women reclaim History by naming; by naming they locate or call something from memory, it is rescued and kept for thought. Years come and go, years of peace and war, years of what men and women call History. Men and women also write stories in order to live, and since the Enlightenment they have been called Histories. Sometimes the stories tell themselves.[1]

How do we approach the history of people - peasants, workers, artisans - and the places in which their histories are deposited? How do we, as Gramsci[2] said, know people as a product of the historical process to date which has left within them an infinity of traces but no inventory? How do we tell the story of peasants and capitalism, people on whom the wave of modernity has just broken?

Culture, politics and place

"The individual is best defined by his social geography."

Diana Trilling[3]

For those of us who study the Great Arch of capitalist development, and the lesser reaches of the agrarian question, there are two compelling narratives. The first is the history of the commodity; it is the story of how use values become exchange values, of how commodities such as sugar and rubber enter the circuits of world trade, of the relentless search for profit, the complex puzzles of the market and the genesis of quite radically new ways of producing things.[4] If the story has as a subtext the tale of Third World agriculture, the narrative relates the fortunes of peasants, the rise of plantations, estates and free labor and how, to use Kautsky's dramatic language, capital takes hold of the point of production, shaking it loose from its pre-capitalist fetters.[5] The moral of the story is the deep structure of production and politics.

---

* The field work for this paper was conducted with the assistance of John Sutter, Ousainou Baldeh, and Chris Scharffenberger. I am especially dependent on the work of Judith Carney who worked as part of the same project.
[1] With apologies to Karl Marx, Carlo Levi, Michel Foucault, Martin Heidegger, Roland Barthes and Joan Didion.
[2] Gramsci, cited in Said, 1979, page 25.
[3] Trilling, cited in Amis, 1986, page 56.
[4] See, for example, Mintz, 1985.
[5] Kautsky, 1979.

But there is another history, the history of commodity fetishism; it illuminates the other face of the commodity, problematizing the commodity-form itself.[6] This narrative broached, of course, by Marx himself, but more powerfully by Benjamin,[7] leads to the question of how the phantom objectivity of capitalist culture is created. It is about fragmentation and modernity, and about how all that is solid melts into air. If we tell the tale of Third World agriculture, the other face of the commodity is pursued dialectically through the Other, perhaps peasants and workers, and specifically *their* cultural reactions to, and representations of, a nascent capitalism and *our* confrontation via the Other with "the phantom objectivity in which capitalist culture enshrouds its social creations" (Taussig 1980, page 4).[8] The moral of this story is meaning, the meanings of capitalism and the semiotic contests between capitalist and precapitalist meanings.

The two Janus-faced stories are enacted in places. This enactment renders place itself an exceptionally dense concept, a keyword for social theory and an icon for no less a person than Michel Foucault whose entire canon resonates with the vocabulary of place and space. Insofar as most people live their lives locally, then to the same extent their experience and popular consciousness is forged in specific places. This is especially apparent if one examines the politics of the periphery. Place is the crucible in which experience and style is forged. But lived conditions are differentially experienced and articulated, and one must be sensitive, as Raymond Williams and Edward Thompson[9] have constantly asserted, to the meanings and values which arise among distinctive social groups and how these meanings both embody, express and interpret given historical conditions. Place is thus the crucible within which *experiences* are contested, a contest that is fundamentally cultural in an active sense:

"The cultural does not simply mark, or in some simple sense live out wider social contradictions. It works upon them with its own resources to achieve partial resolutions, recombinations ... and limited transformations."[10]

To approach these resolutions, contradictions and transformations - the politics of place - is to see place as a local archipelago, saturated with "tactics and strategies deployed through implantations, distributions, demarcations, control of territories and organization of domains which make up a sort of geopolitics."[11] Exploring this micro-physics of power, the strategies and the interpretive struggles, recouplings and reclassifications that accompany them is, in my opinion, to uncover the grammar of place.

A tale

"Perhaps it is precisely the petit-bourgeoisie who has the presentiment of a new heroism both enormous and collective, on the model of ants."

Robert Musil[12]

John Mulholland, the harried Director of the Wallikunda Irrigation Project (Figure 1), returning to Central Gambia from a well-earned home leave in late

---

[6] Taussig, 1980.

[7] Benjamin, 1969.

[8] Taussig, 1980, chapter 1.

[9] For an excellent review, see Hall's "Cultural Studies" in Bennett 1981, pages 19-38.

[10] Willis, 1987, page 124.

[11] Foucault, 1980, page 251.

[12] Musil, 1979, page 21.

1952 discovered that a substantial slice of his project rice harvest, some 400 bags of paddy all told, had mysteriously disappeared. Petty theft and popular appropriation by tenants had hardly been a rarity since the scheme was hatched in 1949 by the Colonial Development Corporation (CDC), but this recent pilferage was of a wholly new order for it implied, at the very least, a sinister collusion by local chiefs. The Wallikunda enterprise was incubated by a postwar West African Rice Mission rather taken by the heady vision of introducing mechanized double-cropping of rice into the middle-river districts of The Gambia, an area in which female-controlled swamp and tidal rice production was of some antiquity.[13] Wallikunda actually linked two adjacent swamps - Jahaly and Pacharr - and in its original blueprint proposed extensive bund and canal construction designed to bring 10,880 acres under irrigation.[14] It proved to be an expensive disaster - the CDC alone was in hock to the tune of over U.S. $500,000 - plagued by a Chaplinesque fiasco of design flaws.[15] Rice theft by ornery tenants following close on the heels of extensive flooding, inadequate surveying and leveling, canal collapse and rumors of exploitation of child labor and wild debauchery by the British construction crew, quite literally brought the project to its knees. "If these Gothic predations are to continue" the Director noted of the rice speculation, "we may as well pack the whole thing up."[16] Indeed, they did.

The Gothic predations sprouted in the fertile soil of colonial folly and byzantine ineptitude. The appropriation and seizure of rice lands by the CDC on a thirty year lease from the Native Authority which they quite wrongly designated "uncultivated," initiated a flood of land claims and disputes; indeed, it was the belief of the Mandinka peasants on the Wallikunda scheme that "they were taking the rice because the whites had taken their land."[17] The CDC debacle - followed shortly after by another, the nightmarish failure of the Gambian Poultry Scheme near Banjul - was superceded in 1953 by direct government control and the creation, on a much more modest scale, of the Gambian Rice Farm, in essence a state-farm with limited water control employing wage labor for all non-mechanized farm operations, weeding and harvesting in particular. Peasant orneriness again proved intractable. Wage workers were, it turned out, almost impossible to recruit and discipline because rice labor-demand conflicted directly with the primary labor bottlenecks on rainfed upland crops (groundnuts, millet and sorghum)[18]; the output of hired labor was in any case shockingly low, and pilferage was rampant. In desperation in 1954, the farm management introduced sharecropping on the farm for women operators - many of whom had lost, and were then contesting, their prior

---

[13] Swamp rice refers to several distinctive (non-irrigated) rice ecologies shaped by daily or seasonal tides and salinity. Lower swamps experiencing daily tidal inundations (*bafaro*) by usually year-round fresh water are typical of the Wallikunda area. Upper swamps (*leofaro*) occasionally inundated by high spring tides and by rainy season run-off may also be used for rice production. For a discussion, see Haswell, 1975; Weil, 1973, Carney, 1984.

[14] See the National Archives (NAG), The Gambia, File 84/175S3087, Volume 1. Rice Project at Wallikunda.

[15] For a discussion of the CDC and its early failures, see Cowen, 1983.

[16] National Archives (NAG), File 2/3313, no pagination.

[17] Ibid, no pagination.

[18] The rice production systems are simply one part of a complex, gendered production system embracing individually and collectively owned upland and lowland fields devoted to mixtures of rainfed cereals (millet, sorghum, maize) and groundnuts. The latter is a solely male crop and rice, until the introduction of irrigation, primarily the domain of women. Food crops are traditionally jointly cultivated on family, i.e., collective fields. See Dunsmore, et al., 1976.

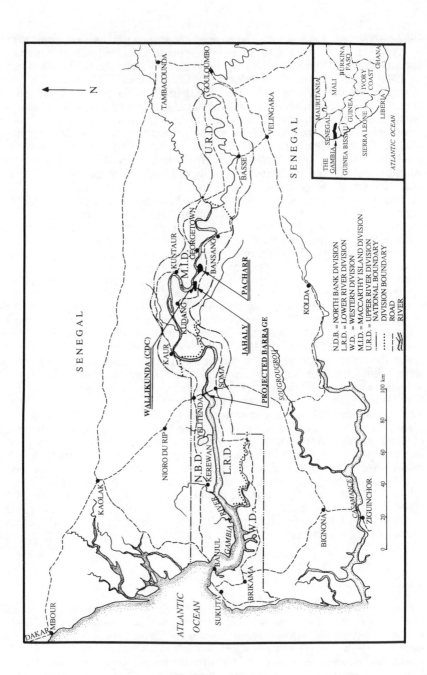

Figure 1. Location of Jahaly and Pacharr Swamps

claims on swamplands in the wake of the CDC lease - but extensive under-reporting and the retention of too much paddy by recalcitrant tenants led to its dissolution after only two years. A half-hearted return to direct cash rental persisted until 1958 by which time the explosive growth of farm-debt owed by the women tenants to the Department of Agriculture for tractor ploughing and other services, determined that the Gambia Rice Farm would be, once more, a casualty of peasant subversion.[19]

Irrigated rice production, this time armed with small 8 inch diesel pumps, was again back on the agenda in 1966, and the Wallikunda area - indeed most of the Upper and Middle river Divisions in The Gambia T- found itself successively invaded by battalions of "development" troops of strikingly different political hue. Phalanxes of Taiwanese (1966-74), World Bank (1973-76) and People's Republic of China (1975-79) personnel invaded, some might say ran amok in, The Gambia, ostensibly to level or rehabilitate some 311 small-scale (ca. 30 acres) community-based rice perimeters covering nearly 2,900 hectares.[20] If the organization of these rice perimeters was distinguished above all by inconsistency,[21] the broad purpose was clear; to re-introduce, in the wake of the CDC fiasco and spiraling rice imports, the double-cropping of rice among peasant producers who would assist in land clearance and leveling. By 1980 the annual cropping intensity of these perimeters was 0.36 - only 18 percent of the total wet and dry season acreage was cultivated - and the outstanding peasant debt on production credit (water costs, tilling, ploughing etc.) in MacCarthy Division alone over the period 1979-1983 was one million dalasis, excluding incidentally the enormous sums accounted for by the 74-83 percent subsidies for water and service provision.[22] Debt recovery by the Gambian authorities consistently ran at less than 20 percent, and by 1984 most peasant irrigation associations steadfastly, and as it turned out, successfully, refused to even countenance repayment. The rice sales to the state marketing agencies were embarrassingly slight. The state it seemed was, in good Gothic fashion, fully captured by the low intensity predation of peasants.

In 1982 a new irrigation vessel was launched into the stormy waters of Gambian rice development. The Jahaly-Pacharr project[23] represents a return to the CDC model in a variety of senses. Not only is the new advanced perimeter located on the site of the failed CDC scheme, but it also operates on a leased land-tenancy basis; it is a large - one in eight of all Gambian households will ultimately be affected by it - pump-irrigated system under centralized management using labor intensive farm-operations, and resting on the bedrock of the household economy. Unlike all past efforts, however, the project management subordinates, or rather it attempts to subordinate, producers to

---

[19] See Carney, 1986.

[20] See Brautigam, 1984; Dey, 1980; The Gambia Food Strategy Report: Part I, 1981, mimeographed (Review of Food and Nutrition, Banjul, The Gambia.

[21] Walking through a Gambian perimeter is a mechanic's nightmare, littered with pumps from Shanghai, rototillers from Bremen, threshers from Seuol, and small tractors from Britain. See The Gambia, Irrigated Rice Development Project: Seasonal Rice Cropping Reports, 1977-1982. (Sapu, The Gambia, 1981).

[22] Department of Agriculture, Irrigated Rice Program Reports, 1980-84. The current exchange rate (1987) is dalasis 7.4 = U.S. $1.00. This debt refers to approximately 4000 cultivators (ca. 250 dalasis per head) and is roughly equal to 50 percent of annual per capita income. See Watts, forthcoming.

[23] A multi-donor funded (U.S. $16.53 million) project to develop 1500 hectares, 560 hectares for pump-irrigation double cropping of Green Revolution rice varieties. The scheme will also improve 700 acres of tidal-swamps. IFAD has a major role in project management. See "The Jahaly-Pacharr Project: A Fact Sheet", unpublished manuscript, Banjul, no date; Webb, 1984; Carney, 1987.

grow rice under contract in a rigid work routine, appropriating paddy in payment for advanced production "credit" (covering water and land preparation costs). By 1985 the double-cropping regime appeared to be firmly in place; yields for both seasons averaged in excess of 5 tons per hectare and loan repayment was 98 percent. Had the labor and technical problems that had so immobilized the CDC project been eclipsed by Jahaly-Pacharr? Apparently not, if one considers increasing militancy by many women rice cultivators, a spectacular escalation in conflicts over land claims and crop rights, and unsettling signs of domestic violence centered on the withdrawal of female labor power for household farm operations.

A moral, or two or three

"Many indisputable truths, which could save men, go unspoken for reasons of this kind; those who could utter them cannot formulate them, and those who could formulate them could not utter them. If politics were taken seriously, finding a remedy for this would be one of its more urgent problems."

Simone Weil[24]

First, over a forty year period Mandinka family farms have confronted a series of systematic efforts to expand and control marketable surpluses of rice - a long standing staple in the region - through double-cropping and mechanized water control. Second, colonial and post-colonial states, usually in league with various agents of international finance capital, have discovered that the control of the labor process of millions of decentralized smallholders is wholly problematic. This is especially so where labor is at a premium and divisions of labor deeply sedimented by work rhythms segmented by gender. The relative autonomy of household production, and the internal logic and solidity of pre-capitalist property relations,[25] have spawned a variety of efforts to increase the yield and marketable surpluses of rice by tapping (and by definition amplifying demand for) the reservoir of unpaid household labor. The Jahaly-Pacharr project is simply the most recent, and the most elaborate and complex, in a sequence of technological innovations aimed at peasant subordination and especially *discipline*. And third, the narrowly technical history of irrigation has a social guise revealed in the "low-subversion" of Mandinka peasants themselves, the everyday resistance "between passivity and open, collective defiance."[26]
I wish to suggest that the example of the Jahaly-Pacharr project throws an intriguing light on the polyp-like quality of peasant microtactics and on the politics of place. The project contracts Mandinka producers to grow rice under a regimented, supervised labor regime which vastly expands intrahousehold labor demands. Labor amplification has acted to perturb a deeply entrenched nexus of crop and property rights and reciprocal claims on household labor, such that this new labor process converts the domestic arena, and its multiple-claim property system,[27] into a terrain of struggle. The fulcrum of these ideological, symbolic and material struggles is gender, and specifically the conjugal contract.

---

[24] Weil, cited in Daniels, 1985, page xi.

[25] Brenner in Roemer, 1986, pages 23-53.

[26] Scott, 1985.

[27] See Okali, 1983.

The unique qualities of family farms as contract producers - the unity of labor and property[28] - has inscribed production politics and family politics within the same domestic sphere. The collapsing of two discrete political domains can be seen as an internalization of 'small arms warfare' within the household, articulated as struggle over access to land and interpretive conflicts over *how resources are named* - what Bourdieu calls legitimate naming - and hence who can activate labor and crop rights. A new production routine/technology is not simply reproducing social relations - manufacturing consent in Burawoy's[29] lexicon - but rather *manufacturing discontent*. Many of the "minute warren of individual ... tactics and strategies ... which inflect the ... overall domination"[30] are enacted on the household stage as the popular politics of women, a politics in which land is ideologically central.

By illuminating the black box of the household and shedding light on its circuits of economic, symbolic and cultural capital, I believe one can appreciate how peasant resistance as part of the politics of place is fundamentally about *interpretive struggles over rights, over naming and over customary meaning*. These struggles are fundamentally part of the seamless web of normal resistance, but they highlight some of the contradictory qualities, the twists and turns, of what is often postulated to be a unitary small-arms arsenal pointed toward the heavy artillery of the state or predatory landlords. One should not underestimate this domestic 'network of antidiscipline' as Michel de Certeau[31] called it, which actually threatens the system of dispositions - the causality of the probable - that leads individuals to act in a way that reproduces social structure without transforming it.[32]

Households' rights and pre-capitalist property

"[P]roperty rights do not represent rights over material objects; rather they represent rights with respect to people ... to alter property rights is to redefine social relationships."

Robert Bates[33]

If we view Mandinka family farms as forms of simple commodity production,[34] they can be analyzed along two axes: relations *of* production, and relations *in* production.[35] The former - generally to be understood as systems of property relations and rights[36] - posit family farms as types of enterprise imbricated in the market and which entail a contradictory unity of labor and property.[37] As direct producers they hold direct access to their means of production, yet they may

---

[28] Friedmann, 1986, pages 186-193.

[29] Burawoy, 1985.

[30] Foucault, 1980, page 251.

[31] de Certeau, 1984.

[32] Bourdieu, 1987.

[33] Bates, 1987, page 19.

[34] Individualized production units, usually organized through family labor in which property and labor are combined, and reproduction occurs in the context of the market. See Friedmann, 1986b. I differ from Friedmann in that I do not take *generalized* circulation as an absolute prerequisite for simple commodity production.

[35] Burawoy, 1985, pages 13-14.

[36] "The relationship among the direct producers, among the class of exploiters (if any exist), and between the exploiters and producers which specify and determine the regular and systematic access of individual economic actors ... to the means of production and to the economic product." Brenner, 1986, page 26.

[37] Friedmann, 1979, pages 159-183.

also buy and sell labor; but neither as workers by virtue of their connections to property, nor as capitalists since they themselves labor. The relations in production, or labor process, are distinctively "domestic", by virtue of the dominance of kinship and gender. While relations within the household may be influenced by the market calculus, they remain non-commodified. The labor process (i.e., the social organization of work) is therefore fundamentally inseparable from the empirically diverse social relations (conjugal ties, life-cycle, inter-generational, and gender responsibilities) of the domestic unit in peasant society. These social relations have alongside them "distinctive political and ideological ap-paratuses of production"[38] which regulate - that is to say reproduce - the house-hold form of production.

Implicit in my remarks is the idea that peasant politics and the structures of resistance associated with family farms must address the organization of the household economy and most especially the internal architecture of the domestic unit.[39] This is so because of the collapsing of social and economic relations: marriage or age-sets, for example, can function as relations of production. It is precisely household social processes that have been a central point of debate in the study of African agrarian systems over the last decade.[40] What has become clear is that the household is not a "natural" unit, neither is it a solitary entity (*contra* Chayanov) in which production, consumption and investment are somehow all magically isomorphic. The neo-classical approach to the household, resting on exogenously given joint-utility functions and a heavy infusion of altruism, has been exposed by feminist research for its neglect of inequality, patterns of property ownership and internal bargaining.[41] It is the porosity of household boundaries, the tensions between the enterprise and the individual, the complexity and fluidity of internal social processes, and the constitutive role of 'external' political economy that has stimulated a revisionism in which the African household "is a variable structure: It is both outcome and channel of broader social processes ... and it is the site of separable, often competing, interests, rights and responsibilities."[42]

There are two aspects of household dynamics I seek to emphasize. The first is the segmented and balkanized structure of internal organization, and specifically gender segmentation. The links between patriarchy and property relations are quite basic to the "conjugal contract,"[43] that is to say the terms on which claims on goods, services, labor, and income can be made between husbands and wives. And second, what I refer to as the multi-valency of household social structure.[44] This goes beyond the important recognition of competing rights, interests and obligations or the sexual division of labor and is perhaps closer to Bourdieu's notion of a social field as "a multi-dimensional space of positions."[45] It is the fact that there are a plethora of nested and overlapping claims which are multi-valent; claims on labor which constitute the

---

[38] Burawoy, 1985, page 8.

[39] Post, 1982.

[40] See, for example, Guyer and Peters, 1987a; Moock, 1986.

[41] Folbre, 1986.

[42] Guyer and Peters, 1987b.

[43] Whitehead, 1984.

[44] "[L]abor has been added, multiplied, substituted, decomposed and recomposed in patterns whose configurational form and directions of change are ... not captured [by the division of labor]", Guyer, 1987.

[45] Bourdieu, 1987, page 724. "A given agent within the social space can thus be defined by the position he (sic) occupies in the different fields, that is in the distribution of the powers [economic, cultural and symbolic capitals] that are active within each of them."

scaffolding of work routines may be tied to specific property rights, and such rights have to be culturally and ideologically validated. It is the density and simultaneity of this social, economic and cultural field-of-force which I shall return to later.

The Mandinka farming system illustrates perfectly the complex intersection of household social organization and production dynamics. Cropping patterns are markedly seasonal, reflecting a relatively short (June-October) growing season and geographically segmented agro-ecology: upland rainfed (*tendako*) cereals and groundnuts are linked with lowland riverine swamps or hydro-morphic depressions rice systems (*barfaro, bantafaro*). Labor mobilization in the context of balkanized labor demands, labor intensive work routines, and overlapping crop regimes, presents an unusually complex scheduling problem for the domestic unit. The basic residential unit (*suo*) is the compound, a patrilineal and patriarchal kin group, usually polygamous and inter-generational, which may on occasion contain over 100 persons.

While the long-term usufructory rights to land inhere within the compound, the *suo* is functionally disaggregated into flexible sub-units for productive and consumptive purposes. The basic unit of consumption is the *sinkiro* (a word which refers to women who rotate cooking duties as well as those who eat from the same pot) which may also be the basis for labor mobilization since all members must contribute labor for "communal" food production. Conversely, those who farm together form a discrete *dabada*. It is entirely possible that these two entities may be isomorphic but increasingly compounds split into several constellations of work and labor units (see Figure 2). It is commonplace for brothers of the same parentage to form a *dabada* and brothers of different mothers to establish their own *dabada*. The number of *sinkirolu* (pl.) within a *dabada* will depend in large measure on inter-wife co-operation. The *sinkiro* is generally subordinate to the *dabada* and status (and hence land or crop claims) within each is determined by gender, marital status, age, and seniority.

The *dabada* head (usually male) who presides over those who labor for subsistence crops is also responsible for allocating land among *dabada* members and for negotiating additional land from the compound head. Land used for subsistence crops, always under the jurisdiction of the *dabada* head, is referred to as *maruo* and is, by definition, used solely within the *sinkiro*, not for sale. All *sinkiro* members are obliged to work on *maruo* fields - indeed, *maruo* fields have prior claims on labor - and hence *maruo* property simultaneously refers to labor claims associated with collective food production (whether upland or swamp). Male *maruo* obligations are generally met through upland millet cultivation and through swamp rice production by women. Customarily, both men and women therefore cultivate wet-season *maruo*, but since dry-season production was only introduced in 1966 there is no customary right for a husband or *dabada* head to claim dependent labor for dry-season communal production.

In contradistinction to communal land which secures household reproduction and is inalienable, there are individually owned farms (*kamanyango*) which are part of personal circuits of accumulation.[46] *Kamanyango* refers to two discrete phenomena, however; first, fields which confer individual crop rights and are allocated by the *dabada* head from the pool of compound-land to any "paid-up"

---

[46] In theory, land resided in District Authorities and by extension land-holding lineages, but all cultivators rightly maintain that land (and not usufructory rights) is owned by individuals or compounds. There are no written titles and land cannot be sold, but individuals claiming land through inheritance, gift or clearance have an undisputed right to give away or pass on the land. See Haswell, 1975.

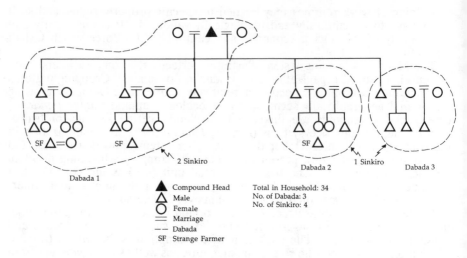

Figure 2. Mandinka Residence: Internal Structure

dependent (*dimbaya*) for the duration of their residence in the compound.[47] And second, to a field either cleared by the owner or acquired through inheritance.[48] In spite of male claims to the contrary, many women own rice fields which are frequently inherited *inter vivos* through the agnatic line. Personal rice fields are an important source of autonomy for women and confer a measure of independence from household labor claims. Individually owned farms are regularly borrowed or rented - though rarely sold - but cannot lay claim to *dabada* or *sinkiro* labor. Women accordingly mobilize labor through age-grade, reciprocal (*julo*) or communal labor groups (*kafo*), but most notably through their daughters, and deploy these holdings as strategic assets for their female offspring who may marry into resource-poor households.[49]

Compound land-assets vary considerably between farm families, but land holding differentiation is framed by descent, specifically whether a compound has membership in a founder or settler lineage.[50] Nonetheless, it is clear that ranking senior males play a determinant role in the distribution of *maruo* and *kamanyango* rights, allocations and obligations. Exogamous marriage and virilocal residence ensure that women are doubly dependent upon the conjugal contract for access to rice plots, while the explosive growth of groundnut production over the last two hundred years has further deepened sex-specific crop production.

Against the historic backdrop of the interdigitation of crop rights, labor obligations and engendered production systems, it is to be expected that conflicts over land claims are of some antiquity. The colonial project to double tidal rice production through large scale mangrove clearance in the 1940s

---

[47] See Dey, 1982.

[48] Strictly speaking, this is individual usufructory rights on communal (*maruo*) property.

[49] According to Dey, 1980, page 264, almost one third of all rice lands in Saruja village were individually owned prior to the Jahaly-Pacharr project.

[50] Settler lineages are often of slave descent, whereas founder lineages, by virtue of length of residence, have long-standing claims to larger rice acreages. See Dey, 1981.

opened up new rice lands to female cultivators who, on the basis of clearance, claimed individual ownership. Men resisted privatization on the grounds that the high incidence of divorce in a polygamous culture and virilocal residence would circulate valuable land resources out of the household.[51] As the case of the CDC project in Wallikunda in the 1950s also vividly illustrated, cleared land - in spite of prior female land claims or clearance of virgin swamps by women - was ultimately returned to land-holding descent segments (*kabilos*) whose ranking males naturally conferred *maruo* status. The genesis of the small-scale irrigation perimeters in the 1960s only served to exacerbate the land disputes. Female rice lands leveled under Taiwanese or World Bank auspices were either granted to male *kamanyango* or as *maruo* inherited solely by male agnatic kin. In either case, 1) additional claims could be made on female labor, 2) female land-use and crop rights were systematically eroded, 3) and the differential commodification of male and female budgets was further enforced.[52]

Of contracts, gender and production politics

"Family enterprise is a battleground over patriarchy where property is immediately at stake."

Harriet Friedmann[53]

The Jahaly-Pacharr project (Figure 1) builds upon and departs from the previous practice of irrigation in the Gambia. Land is leased - and hence cultivators are strictly speaking tenants - and most of the farm operations rely on household labor. To ensure double cropping and a marketable surplus,[54] the project ties usufruct, however, to a "contract" that demands full repayment of production loans (for water delivery, land preparation and infrastructure maintenance) at harvest.[55] Jahaly-Pacharr is, therefore, a form of contract farming[56] in which households provide labor and receive Green Revolution inputs, services, and tight surveillance in a specific crop routine in return for a harvest share.[57] Sharecropping is not unknown in The Gambia and generally serves to facilitate the devolution of property within or between households.[58] Jahaly-

---

[51] In the words of one male farmer, "if women mark the land ... it will become women's property ... Women must not own land." Rahman, 1949 cited in Dey, 1982, page 389. Cross-cousin marriage in any case limits the social space in which female inherited rice land actually circulates.

[52] For a similar argument, see Whitehead, 1984, ff 92-101.

[53] Friedmann, 1986, page 192.

[54] In 1984, The Gambia imported 55,000 tons of milled rice, certainly more than 50 percent of total rice consumption.

[55] The project has a tripartite agreement between management which provides water delivery, extension and land preparation, tenants who cover all hand operations from nursery preparation to threshing and canal maintenance, and the Gambian Co-operative Union which undertakes input supply, rice storage and record keeping.

[56] Contract farming is a form of vertical integration between growers and buyer/processors which directly shapes the production process. It has three aspects: a future or forward market, the linkage of factor and product markets, and the differential allocation of production and market risk. The formality of the "contract" varies widely, but contract farming has been important in U.S. agriculture since the 1930s, especially in commodities with high perishability or quality standards. See Watts, 1986.

[57] In the first three years of operation (1984-1986) the management share approximated on average, one third of the household harvest. Only three of 387 farmers defaulted in the first year. In 1986, dry season production costs were 672 dalasis per plot (i.e., approx. one metric ton of rice). See Carney, 1987, page 12.

[58] Some of the small scale rice perimeters in Serrahuli communities in Upper River Division are sharecropped, and the long-standing Gambian institution of "strange farmers" - migrant labor residing in farming households and working on

Pacharr constitutes a quite different share contract most particularly in terms of formality and the regimented and supervized labor process. It rests, however, on the principle that the contract offers a mechanism for gaining access to labor in the absence of a landless class because "the peasant producer has access to parts of the labor market which capitalists cannot reach".[59]

Water delivery is organized through ten hectare blocks divided into the basic field units of 0.5 hectares each. Project management determines the cropping calendar and the carefully regimented water-distribution schedule. Each rice cycle covers approximately 120 days: from early January to May for the dry season crop and from June to November-December in the case of the wet season. Inter-season scheduling is critical and dramatizes the issue of labor mobilization in the context of amplified household labor demands initiated by double cropping (Figure 3). A delay in the wet season rice preparation and planting runs the grave danger of low temperatures at the point of crop maturity in November-December, while a tardy dry season rice harvest generates a tight labor bottleneck in conflict with the male priority granted to upland groundnut planting.[60]

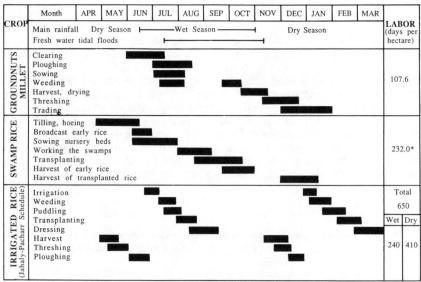

*Transplanted swamp rice without tractor ploughing

Figure 3. Work Patterns by Crop Complex

The Jahaly-Pacharr project was controversial from the outset and the lightning rod was, of course, land. Local male skepticism over long-term land lease was assuaged by Land Committees constituted largely by persuasive

---

male groundnuts fields for specified periods in return for a small groundnut plot and maintenance - rests on a share contract. See Robertson, 1987. Also, Watts, forthcoming.

[59] Lehmann, 1986, page 337. Lehmann is referring quite directly to the mobilization of labor power through non-market (social structural) means.

[60] See Watts and Carney, forthcoming. Also, Hobson, 1984.

political elites and lineage gerontocrats who sought to guarantee access to plots for 1) influential founder lineages and 2) male compound or *dabada* heads. The latter was legitimated on the grounds of virilocal marriage and the entirely fallacious argument that double-cropping exceeded the labor capacity of one person and individual women precisely lacked the capacity to mobilize labor.[61] During the first land allocation of 220 hectares in 1984, 87 percent of the plots were registered by men in spite of the fact that dependent women provided the appropriated rice lands in both swamps. Mandinka women, in other words, had practically lost their *kamanyango* rights (and independent income), but inherited new labor obligations.[62]

Amidst considerable resistance by both men and women, including deputations by Jahaly women to the capital city and pressure on the Gambian project manager, the major donor IFAD (the International Fund for Agricultural Development) intervened directly in the allocation process and an additional distribution of 340 hectares. As a consequence, two thirds of Pacharr plots and 99 percent of Jahaly plots were registered in women's names by 1985[63], although some 110 original tillers remained without any plot. While the redistribution was hailed as a feminist victory and a vote for equity,[64] the management decision simply formalized household heads' claim on irrigated plots as *maruo* property.

During the first year pumped plots were designated *maruo* and women provided virtually all of the farm labor. By the second season, women, faced with the erosion of *kamanyango* rights, pressured the management to grant them individual plots in the non-irrigated tidal zone. According to project data, 80 percent of the most labor demanding tasks - transplanting, land preparation, and weeding - are undertaken by women.[65] At the same time, the very status of irrigated plots as *maruo* was self-evidently contradicted by the fact of crop sale, both to the project under contract and for private male gain. Indeed, in 1984-1985 in seven project villages surveyed, between 27 and 43 percent of irrigated rice was sold.[66] Further, from the inception it has been the male household head who markets and sells the rice and who individually appropriates all rice revenues.[67] Even with sub-optimal yields, the surpluses generated for individual accumulation and investment from irrigated rice are substantial, perhaps two to three times the pre-project per capita income (U.S. $130).[68]

Among Mandinka households, technological innovation and a restructuring of the labor process had fundamental consequences for the micro-politics of the household. Male heads apparently expanded their hegemony through a manipulation and centralization of crop and labor rights. Dependent women, conversely, faced attenuated land claims or actual loss of individual rice fields, while men appropriated, in the guise of communal food production, large

---

[61] According to Euroconsult, the Dutch feasibility team, one plot required 358 person days per year.

[62] There was also a significant influx of outsiders - bureaucrats, traders, military - who had exceedingly tenuous claims on swamp land and failed to meet the household labor prerequisite for rice land.

[63] See Herzog, 1984.

[64] See *Africa Business*, January 23, 1986, page 22.

[65] See von Braun and Puetz, 1986.

[66] Ibid., page 14.

[67] In this regard von Braun and Webb are entirely mistaken when they say that the new irrigated rice fields are "communal" (page 19). They then go on to argue that the expansion of communal fields (the addition of irrigated rice as (*maruo*) has reduced the ability of individuals to maximize individual welfare (page 28). But obviously not ranking males! von Braun and Webb, 1987.

[68] Carney, 1987, page 32.

investible surpluses. This recomposition of labor and the reclassification of property rights naturally manufactured considerable stresses within, and simply overloaded, the social architecture of the Mandinka household. In short, many of the new claims, new rights and new obligations were contested on a variety of material, symbolic and ideological terrains. Emotion and material interest arose, then, from the same social - in this case household - matrix and this matrix is deeply embedded in "property relations, working processes and the structure of domination."[69]

Struggles over land, struggles over meaning

"The issue is rather one of the on-going struggle over meaning. The struggle is formed in the context of the social relations of individuals, groups, classes and cultures which at the same time are constituted by the struggle. Reciprocity, dependency and resistance ... are not 'structurally given' ... they come into being only in the struggle for meaning."

Hans Medick[70]

What capillary forms of struggle are thrown up within the Mandinka household? An infinity of particular conflicts and outcomes are shaped by household wealth, familial dynamics, ethnicity, and much else. Some relatively well-to-do households in land surplus have actually granted irrigated plots to wives, and sometimes daughters and sisters, as individual fields, but it should be emphasized that, even in these limited cases, other women's plots in the same unit have been converted into "communal property". But the broad social pattern is quite different, three facets stand out. The first is the emergence of sharecropping between man and women (and particularly between husbands and wives) on purportedly communal irrigated plots. That is to say, the social (project) form of labor subordination has been internalized within the household. This has been achieved through complex and occasionally violent bargaining and negotiation. In Wellingara village, where almost one quarter of households sharecropped in this way, the female share was on average 10-25 percent of the rice harvest.[71]

Second, and this is notably the case in either land poor or rigidly patriarchal households, women have withdrawn their household labor outright for irrigated plots. Men, who have in any case been compelled to assume some labor responsibilities for dry season rice fields, face labor shortages now regularly covered by wage labor, not unusually by their wives or other females organized into collective work groups. In effect, there is a proletarianization of the conjugal contract, a dispossession of dependent women, and the conversion of traditional communal women's work groups (usually, non-wage, reciprocal labor exchange) into proletarianized "companies", that is to say, gang-labor. Since less than 25 percent of all households participating in the scheme are self-sufficient in family labor, moreover, between one-quarter and one-half of all production costs is accounted for by wet-season wage labor. Women's gang labor remunerates individuals in excess of the local daily wage and hence women are simultaneously challenging not only household patriarchy, but also the nascent (and formerly deeply segmented) labor market. Contract farming rather than

---

[69] Medick and Sabean, 1984.

[70] Medick, 1987.

[71] See Carney, 1978, page 34.

irrigating from a subterranean, non-commodified source of labor has *de facto* created a labor market mediated by local social structure.

Third and finally is the explosion of essentially juridical and strategic conflicts over land claims. Women, rightly fearing a contagious growth of irrigation-privatization in the wake of the extraordinarily high yields in the first season of Jahaly-Pacharr, are aggressively asserting claims outside of the project area. Marketing and delimitation of what is known locally as self-help fields are cases of cultural offense being the best form of defense. One Mandinka farmer, Maiama Koita, who has become active among local women work groups put it quite explicitly:

"When you're born, you're given land by your mother. It becomes your land. You can get compound land from your husband, but if you marry a man who has no land to give you as his own, your mother's land is always there for you to support yourself. Even the village headman hasn't the right to take the land away from you."

The undercurrents of legal ambiguity in light of allocation terminology - plots are "registered" but not owned - has not lessened the vigilance of the likes of Maiama Koita and many land disputes have seeped through to the local courts. In 1985 a Pacharr divorce settlement, in which the household head claimed the entire irrigated plot for himself, awarded the plot jointly (divided equally) to both parties, apparently with the support of the District Chief. In another case, a Pacharr man divorced his wife and claimed a swamp plot, but was contested by the wife on the grounds that the project had claimed usufructory rights could be retained through village residence. The woman won the case amidst considerable debate among a Land Allocation Committee which, significantly, had female representation, but the plot remained as communal property within the husband's compound.

These struggles over labor and the conditions of work have three other important aspects. The first pertains to the considerable surpluses controlled largely by senior men. In many cases, the investible rice revenues are not, as the project would wish, being channeled into the advertised production package, but rather, as one might anticipate, into women. The growth of polygamy is locally quite striking. Almost half of all project farmers stated that surpluses were used to acquire more wives, but this has served to inflate marriage costs and to enhance the bargaining power of eligible women. Secondly, conjugal and gender based conflicts have erupted, in some cases into explicit domestic violence, and a mushrooming of potential or actual divorce claims. And finally, the feminization of the labor force has conferred a certain strategic power on women, reflected in the fact that many Mandinka households, faced with labor withdrawal, have been incapable of meeting the exacting demands of the regimented labor schedule set by project management.

The Mandinka domestic struggles over labor are clearly material, but they are also cultural and symbolic because "any work context involves [the] ... production of things ... [the] production of social relations and [the] ... production of an experience of those relations."[72] The two moral axes of Mandinka domestic life - *badingya* and *fadingya* - have been in some fundamental sense realigned. *Badingya* represents co-operation, obligation and harmony, and *fadingya* connotes ambition, selfishness, conflict and at the limit a domestic or community anomie. The oscillation between these poles naturally

[72] Burawoy, 1985, page 39.

carries a strong cultural current - behavior must be culturally validated - but also an interpretive one; that is to say, what is normal or just or simply "tradition" is established through discursive practice. This war of worlds is similar in form to that described by Scott in relation to inter-household poverty and wealth, but in this case revolves around proper and expected behavior within the conjugal contract.[73] As one women in Kerewan Samba Sire put it, "it is our custom that men should provide, but you cannot always depend on men." If husbands are seen to appropriate women's lands without adequate compensation or lay non-customary claims on women's labor, it can elicit accusations of selfishness, greed and poor family leadership. In a nominally Muslim society such as Mandinka, reciprocal gift giving is ideologically central and, at the very least, women whose individual farms have been reinterpreted as communal property expect, and in some cases receive, recompense. But a refusal on the husband's part is in effect a profound abrogation of the conjugal contract. Indeed, it is grounds for divorce. Furthermore, such conflict and negotiation is conducted publicly within the compound and is contagious, creating friction and animosity within the other domestic segments. Such disharmony carries an especially heavy cultural premium in Mandinka society. In a not unusual case in Wellingara village, for example, a conjugal struggle over adequate compensation resulted in the wife refusing to cook for the consumption unit. This particular form of withdrawal is ideologically charged and the most explosive consequence of interpretive struggles over custom. It is seen locally to constitute grounds for violence. In the Wellingara instance, the wife was severely beaten and fled to her mother's compound in a nearby village.

The bargaining and negotiation over just rewards and just claims is reflected in two other sorts of cultural struggles. First, the fact that women in losing individual property necessarily lose a major source of personal income, escalates the possibility of infidelity. "There are some married women who take lovers" said one woman, "it's all based on economics." The crisis the material basis of women's personal budgets naturally sustains, in these sorts of cases, enormous tension and conflict. And second, the withdrawal of female communal labor on irrigated fields also charges the antagonisms between husbands and wives as they bargain over the wage at which the wife is prepared to work on project plots. Mandinka females see rice as "women's sweat" which, if projected onto the larger ideological screen of domestic struggle, makes for quite volatile wage bargaining. A consequence of the synthesis of contract farming with household production is that one has a type of incipient trade unionism within the family, a development which adds some irony to the comment of the project manager at the onset of production in 1985: "frankly, we expect a lot ... from women, more so than from men."

The Jahaly-Pacharr project has animated this discursive realm; it has manufactured symbolic discontent. This is not surprising, because every field is the site of a struggle over the definition of legitimate principles of the division of the field:

"In the symbolic struggle over the production of common sense, or more precisely, legitimate naming, ... agents engage the symbolic capital they have acquired in previous struggles ... [that is] all power they posses over instituted taxonomies."[74]

---

[73] Scott, 1985, chapter 1.

[74] Bourdieu, 1985, page 734.

It is largely through language that local practices are instituted, but meanings are never fixed and outside forces can often determine what is to be endowed with meaning. In the context of naming and the power to name - "the speakers of truth" - one can appreciate why debate over the naming of irrigated plots is, in Mandinka society, so charged and so political. While it is within the language of everyday life that meaning is mobilized in the defense of domination, the outcome of struggles such as those initiated within Mandinka farming households is far from overdetermined. This is not only to suggest that the wage relation may have liberating consequences for women, but more generally, that culture contributes toward the creative, tense, and uncertain social reproduction of diverse kinds of relationship, that "cultural reproduction always carries with it the possibility of producing ... alternative outcomes."[75] Maiama Koita, a second wife and mother of seven, put the matter succinctly: "I am prepared to change tradition if I have the power and the money."

The discontent manufactured by the Jahaly-Pacharr project suggests that one might have the beginnings of a transgression which threatens the discipline of everyday domination.[76] The politicization of women's communal labor groups, the presence of women on Land Allocation Committees, the rumblings of juridical change, female deputations to government ministers and the like, all suggest that, to use the words of a women rice farmer from Wellingara:

"It seems this project is just like the Chinese one when we suffered before. We aren't going to put up with that again ... I have this to say to you men. We women aren't going to accept the way we have been treated in the past. We were asleep then. Now we are awake."

The change in consciousness which this statement implies, arising out of the ashes of previous conflicts over women's land, is suggestive of how profound the internal resistance - in this case to "normal" patriarchal exploitation - and its consequences have been.

Politics of place

"Everyday life invents itself by poaching in countless ways on the property of others ... [T]he goal ... is to bring to light the clandestine forms taken by dispersed, tactical and makeshift creativity of groups or individuals already caught in nets of 'discipline'."

Michel de Certeau[77]

Place is, as John Agnew[78] suggests, a contested concept. But places are themselves contested. It is this contest, a contest conducted on many terrains, which constitutes the politics of place. I have tried to suggest that for peasants experiencing, to use Walter Benjamin's term,[79] the "shock" of modernity, struggles over access to resources become struggles over cultural modalities. These struggles are inscribed in various spheres - family, workplace, conjugal relations - but they all bear the hallmark of contests over meaning in asymmetrically structured social contexts. In the example I have described, land

---

[75] Willis, 1981, page 172. I have also been deeply influenced in this regard by Taussig, 1987.

[76] See Stallybrass and White, 1984.

[77] de Certeau, 1984, pages xii-xiv.

[78] Agnew, 1987.

[79] See Wolin, 1982.

was ideologically central - a sort of icon or condensation of deeply sedimented rights, meanings and values - and shaped the local politics of place.

Subaltern societies are engaged in a dialectical struggle between active and passive, acceptance and resistance, coercion and consent, segmentation and cohesion. The case I have described is, at a prosaic level, about large capital confronting small producers, and about the unanticipated and contradictory struggles which ensue, but perhaps more profoundly, it demonstrates what is being crushed is not rural purity, authenticity or populist production, but, to use Jean Franco's expression, "heterogeneity ... [Those] practices which are obstacles to modernity."[80]

References

Agnew J, 1987 *Place and Politics* (Allen and Unwin, London)

Amis M, 1986 *The Moronic Inferno* (Penguin, London)

Bates R, 1987 "The agrarian origins of Mau Mau" *Agricultural History* **61** (1) 1-28

Benjamin W, 1969 *Illuminations* (Schrocken, New York)

Bourdieu P, 1987 "The social space and the genesis of groups" *Theory and Society* **14** (6) 1-28

Brautigam D, 1984 "The Peoples Republic of China irrigated rice project in The Gambia" Working Document #42, University of Michigan, Gambia River Basin Studies, Ann Arbor

Brenner R, 1986 "The social basis of economic development" in *Analytical Marxism* (Cambridge University Press, Cambridge) pp 23-53

Burawoy M, 1985 *The Politics of Production* (Verso, London)

Carney J, 1984 "Socio-economic and environmental considerations relative to the antisalinity barrage on the Gambia River" Working Document #46, University of Michigan, Gambia River Basin Studies, Ann Arbor

Carney J, 1986 "The social history of Gambian rice production" Ph.D. dissertation, University of California, Berkeley

Carney J, 1987 "Contract farming in irrigated rice production" Working paper #9, Institute for Development Anthropology, Binghampton

Cowen M, 1983 "Early years of the Colonial Development Corporation" paper delivered to the Institute of Commonwealth Studies, University of London

de Certeau M, 1984 *The Practice of Everyday Life* (University of California Press, Berkeley)

Daniels J, 1985 *Place/Everyone* (University of Wisconsin Press, Madison)

Dey J, 1980 "Women and rice in The Gambia" Ph.D. dissertation, University of Reading

Dey J, 1981 "The socio-economic organization of farming in The Gambia, Agricultural Administration Network Papers #7 (London Overseas Development Administration)

Dey J, 1982 "Development planning in The Gambia *World Development* **10** (5) 377-396

Dunsmore J, et al., 1976 "The agricultural development of The Gambia" Land Resource Study #22, Ministry of Overseas Development, Land Resources Division, London

Folbre N, 1986 "Hearts and spades: paradigms of household economics" *World Development* **14** (2) 245-256

Foucault M, 1980 *Power/Knowledge* (Harvester Press, Brighton)

---

[80] Franco, 1986, page 6.

Franco J, 1986 "Death camp confessions and resistance to violence in Latin America" *Socialism and Democracy* **1** (1) 5-17

Friedmann H, 1979 "Household production and the national economy" *Journal of Peasant Studies* **7** (2) 159-183

Friedmann H, 1986a "Patriarchy and property" *Sociologia Rualis,* **XXVI** (2), 186-193

Friedmann H, 1986b "Postscript" *Labour, Capital and Society* **19** (1) 117-126

Guyer J, 1987 "The multiplication of labor, gender and agricultural change in Africa" unpublished manuscript, Boston University

Guyer J, Peters P, Eds 1987a Special Issue on "Conceptualizing the Household" *Development and Change* **18** (2)

Guyer J, Peters P, 1987b "Introduction" *Development and Change* **18** (2) 210

Hall S, 1981 "Cultural studies" in *Culture, Ideology and Social Process* Ed T. Bennett (Open University, London) pp 19-38

Haswell M, 1975 *The Nature of Poverty* (MacMillan, London)

Herzog V, 1984 "Progress report on a second mission to the Jahaly Pacharr smallholder project" (IFAD, Rome)

Hobson S, 1984 "Bitter Rice" *International Agricultural Development* March 5-6

Kautsky K, 1979 *La Question Agraire* (Maspero, Paris)

Lehmann D, 1986 "Sharecropping and the Capitalist Transition in Agriculture *Journal of Development Economics* **23** (4) 333-354

Medick H, 1987 "Missionaries in a row boat" *Comparative Studies in Society and History* **29** (1) 76-98

Medick H, Sabean D, 1984 "Introduction" in *Interest and Emotion* Eds H Medick, D Sabean (Cambridge University Press, Cambridge) pp 1-18

Mintz S, 1985 *Sweetness and Power* (Harper, New York)

Moock J, 1986 *Understanding Rural Africa's Household and Farming Systems* (Westview, Boulder)

Musil R, 1979 *A Man Without Qualities Volume 1* (Avon, London)

Okali C, 1983 *Cocoa and Kinship in Ghana* (Routledge and Kegan Paul, London)

Post K, 1982 "Everyday forms of peasant resistance: some notes on theoretical issues" unpublished manuscript, The Hague

Robertson A, 1987 *The Dynamics of Productive Relationships: African Share Contacts in Comparative Perspective* (Cambridge University Press, Cambridge)

Said E, 1979 *Orientalism* (Vintage, New York)

Scott J, 1985 *Weapons of the Weak: Everyday Forms of Peasant Resistance* (Yale University Press, New Haven)

Stallybrass P, White A, 1984 *The Politics and Poetics of Transgression* (Cornell University Press, Ithica)

Taussig M, 1980 *The Devil and Commodity Fetishism in Latin America* (University of North Carolina Press, Chapel Hill)

Taussig M, 1987 "History as commodity" unpublished manuscript, Institute of Ethnography, Bogota

von Braun J, Puetz D, 1986 "Preliminary results of IFPRI-PPMU survey, Jahaly-Pacharr Project (Round I Survey) Washington, D.C.

von Braun J, Webb, P, 1987 "Effects of new agricultural technology and commercialization on women farmers in a West African setting" Paper prepared for the Conference of the Association of Women Development, IFPRI, Washington, D.C.

Watts M, 1986 "Contract farming in Africa" Working Paper #1, Institute of Development Anthropology, Binghampton, New York

Watts M, *A Peasantry Triumphant?: Production Politics Among Gambian Farmers*, forthcoming

Watts M, Carney J, "Struggles over meaning, struggles over land" forthcoming

Webb P, 1984 "Of rice and men: the story behind The Gambia's decision to dam its river" in *The Social and Environmental Effects of Large Dams* Eds E Goldsmith, N Hildyard (Wadebridge Ecological Centre, Wadebridge)

Weil P, 1973 "Wet rice, women and adaptation in The Gambia" *Rural Africana* **19** 20-29

Whitehead A, 1984 "I'm hungry Mum: the politics of domestic budgeting" in *Of Marriage and the Market* Eds K Young, C Wolkowitz, R McCullagh (Institute for International Development, Cambridge, Mass) pp 88-111

Willis P, 1981 *Learning to Labor* (Columbia University Press, New York)

Wolin R, 1982 *Walter Benjamin: An Aesthetic of Redemption* (Columbia University Press, New York)

The resurrection of local uniqueness

Barney Warf

This paper offers a realist approach to regional change that integrates notions of uneven development with those pertaining to everyday life and social reproduction. To do so, it draws upon two bodies of social theory, one concerned with the inter-relations between consciousness and social structures, primarily as found in Giddens' theory of structuration (1977, 1979, 1981, 1984), and the other pertaining to the literature on the regional dimensions of business cycles and the spatial division of labor, especially as theorized in the works of Massey (1979, 1983, 1984). While the intersections between these two approaches have remained unarticulated by their respective proponents, their synthesis offers a means of examining regional change in a substantively new manner. Since it is clearly impossible to review these topics in full detail, only a brief overview will be attempted in this paper.

The contours of the analysis offered here may be summarized as follows:

1. Any critique of the political economy of regional change must incorporate a role, however limited, for human consciousness, a view long voiced by humanistic geographers (e.g., Buttimer, 1976) but rarely taken seriously among economic geographers. Unlike most positivist, empiricist and structural Marxist views, structuration theory does not dismiss human agency as ephemeral, yet unlike most behavioral or phenomenological approaches, it emphatically recognizes the boundedness of individual thought and action, i.e., its location within specific historical contexts. The theory thus offers the possibility of incorporating everyday life as a fundamental moment in the dissection of regional structures.

2. The second analytical foundation of this paper asserts that regional and inter-regional change are inseparable, i.e., the dynamics of local growth, transformation and decay are never self-contained but are inescapably interwoven with broader rotations of political and economic structures. Thus the sequence of events which shape the identity of particular places cannot be divorced from the wider spatial division of labor. This notion, well expressed in the early export-base theories of regional growth (e.g., North, 1955; Tiebout, 1956; Stabler, 1968), has seen little integration with the body of theory concerned with human agency, social reproduction, and the like. A notable exception is Pred (1984a, 1985a), who has portrayed places as "historically contingent processes."

The paper examines these themes in light of the possibility of an analytically reconstituted regional geography, one which appropriates the local uniqueness of place and the rich detail of the historical record in theoretically meaningful terms. Ontologically, this approach leads to an integration of a broad theory of the labor process, technological change and uneven development in space and time with an understanding of culture, intentionality and everyday life. Epistemologically, such a project entails the sacrifice of "general laws" of explanation and the revival of the idiographic as a legitimate object of inquiry.

1. The political economy of the labor process: A brief synopsis

The analysis begins within the broad conception of labor as both the medium and the outcome of everyday life, as the process which allows human beings to exist and, simultaneously, as the product of that existence. Through labor, people change their natural environment, objectify knowledge, and reproduce their social relations. This is not to lapse into economism, in which production is upheld as the sole determinant of social action; it is only to emphasize the enormously influential role of work in the constitution of social and built environments.

The model of the "deep structure" of commodity production invoked here (Figure 1) is borrowed from Roweis and Scott (1981). It begins with the sphere of production - the workplace - in which firms combine labor and capital to produce tangible commodities, which are then sold on the sphere of exchange - the market - resulting in their conversion to intangible capital. In the process, a gross surplus is generated, from which firms deduct the amount necessary to recover the costs of their capital inputs.

The remaining net surplus is then divided into profits and wages. It follows that there exists a structural "collision" between wages and profits, a necessarily inverse relation specific to any given level of surplus. The determination of these "returns to factor inputs," however, unlike neoclassical economic notions of equilibrium, is not made *a priori*, but reflects the ability of firms and workers to advance their interests at the workplace. Marx noted in *Capital* (1981, page 443) that the issue "is only settled by the continuous struggle between capital and labor, the capitalist tending to reduce wages to the physical minimum and to extend the working day to its maximum, while the working man constantly presses in the opposite direction. The matter resolves itself into a question of the relative powers of the combatants." For example, to the extent that wage rates exceed gains in labor productivity, *ceterus paribus*, firms will experience a "profit squeeze." Hence, far from constituting purely market phenomena, wages and profits are pregnant with political tensions.

This model allows for a rather unorthodox view of technological change, which mediates the combination of capital and labor at the workplace and deeply affects the returns to each. Clearly, firms, under the lure of profits and threat of ruin, will strive to introduce new production methods when possible. Yet unlike mechanistic approaches (e.g., input-output analysis) which tend to portray technological change as politically "neutral" or the old liberal assumption that such change is inherently progressive, this conception situates new technologies within the context of the wage-profit struggle. As a long labor history from the Luddites onwards illustrates, the introduction of new technologies can be dramatically affected by the ways in which workers perceive their probable impacts on their jobs and livelihoods; thus the issues of the adoption of new production methods is rarely, if ever, unproblematically determined simply by competition in the marketplace.

Appended to this conception is a role for the State as the institution which stabilizes the overall conditions of production and reproduction, controlling market failures and mobilizing social resources against actors which disturb the smooth operation of commodity production (see Roweis and Scott, 1981; Clark and Dear, 1984). While State intervention politicizes this issue even further, it is by no means guaranteed: like firms and unions, it is an organization (albeit a unique one), possessed of an ideology, rife with contradictions, and a producer of unintended consequences to action.

The structure of the commodity production system sketched out here varies widely over time and space, for it has no predetermined form: it is contingent, arising from and given its shape by the people who live and create it daily. As Sayer (1982) put it, such systems are "determined," in the sense that some order to them is observable, but they are not predetermined, in the sense of exhibiting a given outcome for any defined set of circumstances. It is this characteristic which is responsible for much of the uniqueness of places historically and

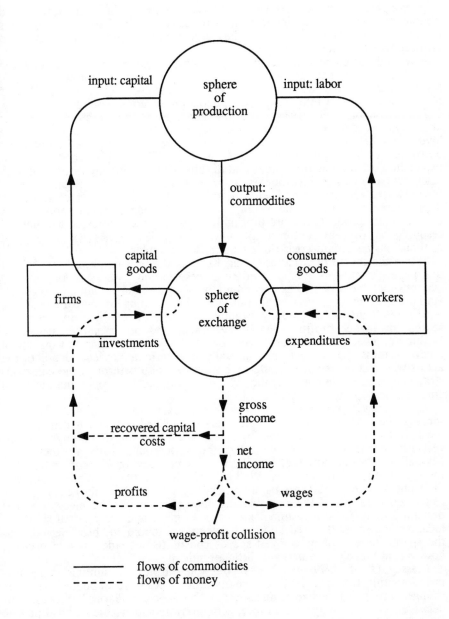

Source: Roweis and Scott, 1981

Figure 1. Schematic model of the "deep structure" of commodity production

geographically. It may also be noted that an analysis which integrates broad notions of uneven development, technological change, and so forth, confronts precisely those issues for which the structurationist perspective has been criticized for ignoring.

The study of uneven development over time, of course, reflects a long and rich literature, including Kondratief "long waves" (Rothwell, 1982), technological change (Schumpeter, 1939), business cycles (Kuznets, 1953) and recent investigations into the political economy of crises (Boddy and Crotty, 1975; O'Connor, 1981, 1984). As the neoclassical "accelerator" hypothesis argues, much of the causes of business cycles can be traced to the competitive investment behavior of firms; they are, so to speak, themselves unintended outcomes of attempts to maximize profits. These episodic "rounds of production" of varying amplitudes and durations are frequently associated with significant changes in investments, searches for new markets, fluctuations in prices, wages and profits, and relocations of capital and labor. Recessions and depressions, therefore, are not simply obstacles to production, but opportunities to restructure production more profitably; because crises represent a structural resource as well as a constraint, O'Connor (1981, 1984) concludes that capitalism is not simply crisis-ridden, but crisis-dependent.

While the theme of Kondratief and Kuznets waves is employed throughout this paper, it must be emphasized that these various "waves of production" cannot simply be accepted as uncontentious historical and economic categories. Rather, they express very real, but also very contingent outcomes of the "structural logic" of commodity production, itself driven by firms' constant search for higher profits through investment and other market strategies. Within any given epoch and any given region, the detailed timing and spacing of a new business cycle is never mechanically predetermined independently of the actors whose circumstances it affects, but instead results through the conscious strategies of actors in everyday life, who unintentionally generate unanticipated consequences in time and space.

Uneven development in space likewise has generated a great deal of interest through the manner in which it engenders specialized productive structures in local areas, a theme theorized by neoclassical economists through various versions of the Heckscher-Ohlin hypothesis of comparative advantage, by Myrdal's celebrated notion of cumulative causation, and by Marxists in terms of the spatial division of labor (cf. Walker, 1978; Smith, 1984). While significant differences underlie the various approaches to this question, they need not be reiterated here; all of them, to varying degrees, focus on the mechanics and outcomes of regional investment and disinvestment and the repercussions for local communities. The crucial fact that temporal "boom and bust" periods and the spatial mosaic of parcellized spaces constitute two sides of one process, however, has received remarkably little attention.

Massey (1978, 1979, 1984) has gone the farthest in uniting these two traditions, illustrating that as the comparative advantage of individual areas changes through successive business cycles, the associated "layers" of investment decisively come to shape the history, geography and social life of local places. Each "wave" of production alters the form of the labor process, prices, profits, wage levels and standards of living, spatial structures of home and work, and, more subtly, patterns of State intervention, local ideological and cultural climates, and so forth. Through the actions of actors (e.g., firms and workers), each "round of production" becomes indelibly etched into local social and physical landscapes. The spatial division of labor is thus reproduced through successive cycles of investment overlain upon, responding to, and modifying earlier patterns of uneven development. It follows that individual locales within this wider system reflect the imprints of a whole series of different phases of production (Urry, 1981), a notion described as palimpsests by an earlier generation of cultural geographers (e.g., Sauer, 1925) and advanced more systematically later in the paper.

2. Structuration, everyday life and regional change

What the literature broadly concerned with social reproduction and everyday life has made abundantly clear is that processes such as regional growth and decay do not simply "occur" without reference to the way in which people experience and interpret their world. Some account of intentionality, culture, ideology, and social reproduction - in short, everyday life, a great vacuum in current regional science - is mandatory if regional change is to be comprehended not as some mechanical outcome of "forces" devoid of people, but as the products of human action. Duncan and Ley (1982) argue that such a consideration is needed if social science is to view people as authors of their worlds, and not as simply finders of a world already made. As Lukes (1977, page 127) put it,

> "Social life can only be properly understood as a dialectic of power and structure, a web of possibilities for agents, whose nature is both active and structured, to make certain choices and pursue strategies within given limits, which in consequence expand and contract over time. Any standpoint or methodology which reduces that dialectic to a one sided consideration of agents without (internal or external) limits, or structures without agents, or which does not address the problems of their inter-relations will be unsatisfactory."

On the one hand, everyday life cannot be divorced from the production process (the error of most behavioralists and phenomenologists) because work is the central determinant of incomes, socioeconomic status, opportunities and even the subjective perspectives of workers themselves. Conversely, however, neither can the labor process be fully comprehended without some understanding of "lived experience" and social reproduction (the error of most structural Marxists). Because firms constantly require an adequately socialized labor supply in order for production to proceed smoothly, every production system, in one form or another, reproduces those relations that make production possible.

This theme has been elaborated at length in Giddens' theory of structuration (1977, 1979, 1981, 1984), which concerns itself with the interpenetration of social forms and individual life. Because the theory has seen a rapid widening of its popularity among several disciplines recently, and because numerous insightful critiques of Giddens' project are readily available (cf. Carlstein, 1981; Gane, 1983; Soja, 1983; Wright, 1983; Moos and Dear, 1986), this paper offers only a skeletal summary of its most important facets, deliberately sidestepping some important issues found in his works (time-space distanciation, social and system integration, structures of legitimation, domination and signification). For a fuller explication of a rather subtle, but highly rewarding body of literature, the reader is also referred to the works of Bourdieu (1977), Bhaskar (1979) and Schmidt (1985).

In abbreviated form, the structurationist perspective affirms that social structures exist only as the rules and resources which respectively constrain and allow the intentional actions of individuals in daily life. In order for any social formation to exist, individuals within in must possess large stocks of deeply internalized knowledge, that is, they must construct a "taken-for-granted world" which defines the "intuitively obvious." Ideology or "common sense" is thus not incidental to the functioning of society, but a necessary condition for its operation: knowledge is not simply descriptive of social reality, but *constitutive* as well (Sayer, 1982). Unlike structural Marxist conceptions, therefore, this approach immediately raises the broader issues of intentionality and social reproduction as analytically pressing moments in the comprehension of social and spatial change.

If prying apart social structures opens a necessary space for consciousness, however, that agency is always and everywhere bounded by its milieu, for each "lifeworld" is built through intentions superimposed over an extensive system of taken-for-granted presuppositions. The constant acquisition of ideology is central to social reproduction, for the continuity of social existence involves a constant "regrooving" of established perceptions and ideologies. As Gregory (1978b, page 71) notes, "If men make history they do not do so entirely under conditions of their own choosing - hence the significance of boundedness, which ensures that the production of social life coincides with the reproduction of social structures."

It follows that the intentional actions of daily life do indeed reproduce the "deep structure" of social formations, but largely *unintentionally*. The organization of society simultaneously forms the "unacknowledged preconditions" to action as well as the unintended consequences to action, or as Bhaskar (1979, page 43) puts it, society is "the ever-present 'condition' (material cause) and the continually reproduced 'outcome' of human agency." These unacknowledged preconditions and unintended consequences of action - the very core of structuration theory - are tied together by the purposeful nature of behavior which is a routine feature of human conduct. In constructing their own biographies, people reconstruct - unwittingly - their social contexts. Hence, social and geographic relations are neither directly produced by, nor independent of the consciousness of their inhabitants, and neither immediately express, nor bluntly determine the intentionality of social actors. Social reality is neither deducible from a formal analysis of structures (as structural Marxism held possible), nor reducible to an analysis of individual behavior (the perspective implicitly advocated by most behavioral and phenomenological approaches).

Gregory (1985, page 27) notes that "The task of structuration theory is to explicate the space-time interconnection of routinized and repetitive strategic conduct between actors or groups of actors with long term, large-scale institutional development." Following Layder (1981), it may be argued that it is *organizations* which primarily mediate individual actions with the collective pursuit of interests, for through them the strategic conduct of actors reflects and affects institutional development through time and space. Organizations (e.g., firms, labor unions, the State) serve as primary vehicles for the translation of intentional actions into unanticipated consequences, although to individuals it often appears as if it is organizations which act. An enormous and rich sociological literature exists concerned with collective action, the strategic conduct of workers' movements and the importance of local time-space coordinates in the organization of domination and subordination (see Oberschall, 1973; Gamson, 1975; Tilly, 1981; Calhoun, 1982), little of it appropriated by either geographers or participants in the structuration debate.

A growing body of literature has sought to integrate analyses of production system dynamics with historical narratives of the complexity of working class experience. E.P. Thompson's (1966) enormously influential analysis of the English working class inaugurated a tradition which transformed the idea of "culture" from a static "superstructure" to a shifting formation of attitudes and practices that constantly interacts with class and power relations. Derek

Gregory employed it for his analysis of the British woollen industry during the Industrial Revolution (1982, 1984). Other empirical applications are found in Pred's reviews of nineteenth century port formation (1984b) and Swedish agrarian change (1985b), Christopherson's (1983) study of family and class in Ciudad Juarez, Mexico, Smith's (1983) investigation of the beef industry, Penn's (1985) work on British cotton workers, and Moos and Dear's (1986) analysis of psychiatric patients in Ontario. These contributions illustrate that structuration theory has become something of a "sensitizing device," advancing the recognition that, while the frames of meaning employed by actors are not simply reducible to their structural contexts, such meanings are always bounded by those contexts. In so doing, this literature has served to make it clear that any social science concerned with the textures of everyday life must explicate the origins, boundaries and consequences of intentional action through time and space, and thus comprehend the simultaneously nondeterminate (i.e., contingent) and nonreductionist nature of social life.

Within the context of "waves of production" as described above, it may be seen that the preconditions to action are periodically rewoven, for new forms of production generate new conditions of work and life, new resources and constraints to action. More subtly, such changes redefine the unquestioned assumptions of daily life (what type of work to expect, the degree of upward mobility, the necessity for unionization, when to rely on the State, etc.), and are powerful because they define what is "normal" (and what is not) in the routines of everyday life.

3. Conclusion: The recovery of local uniqueness

"Ever since regional geography was declared to be dead - most frequently by those who had never been much good at it anyway - geographers, to their credit, have kept trying to revivify it in one form or another. ... This is a vital task: objections to the comfortable pinhead perch of neoclassical economics are familiar enough, but they also apply to the rest of political economy and social science. We need to know about the constitution of regional social formations, of regional articulations and regional transformations."

(Gregory, 1978, page 171).

Contemporary debates among social theorists have grasped the fundamentally temporal nature of social life. But much of current thought, while acknowledging the historical specificity of social structures and change, has failed to acknowledge a parallel geographical specificity. The topic was largely abandoned in the search for "general laws" of explanation and the rejection of the idiographic as mere curiosity or unexplainable abberation.

Traditional chorology, of course, expressed an abiding concern for the site-specific nature of regions, but in a manner which precluded embedding notions of regional structure within any wider conception of historical process. As essentially inductive description, it became reduced to ahistorical collections of facts which jettisoned from the domain of theory any recognition that both local uniqueness and the commonalities of places were socially created.

The dilemma was not solved by the frozen geometries of positivism, in which a geography of "regions without theories" quickly became a geography of "theories without regions." At best, local areas became reduced to vehicles for the testing of theories; at worst, they were dismissed altogether as pointless distractions. The effort to make geography "scientific" was predicated upon the insistent rejection of uniqueness in order to sustain the legitimacy of general laws with universal applicability. "Laws," by definition, could not be valid for some places and not others. Yet in obliterating the unique, geography became increasingly divorced from the world of human experience and questions of daily life "in all its uncouth complexity" (Giddens, 1976, page 23). Simultaneously, and not coincidentally, such a geography became a stranger to the general public.

Under post-positivist epistemologies there has emerged a renewed concern with regionalism (cf. Holland, 1976; Massey, 1978; Urry, 1981; Hart, 1982; Markusen, 1983; Hebbert, 1984; Pred, 1984a, 1985; Soja, 1985). While far from constituting a homogeneous whole, such perspectives tend to share the view that regions must be subjected to an historically informed, "case by case" analysis. Thrift (1983, page 39) stated the nature of the "new" regional geography succinctly:

"No doubt, any reconstituted regional geography can start conventionally enough with a compositional account of 'the regional setting.' This involves, first of all, all those geographical determinations that can be grouped under the general heading of topography; such things as geology, hydrology, and climatic conditions which have likely been changed already by the impacts of the societies over the years. An account of the organization of production in a region is then needed, which involves ascertaining the level of the productive forces and the form of the productive relations, concentrating on the labor process. This emphasis leads, under capitalism in particular, to an outline of the class structure of a region and to the history of the prevailing sexual division of labor, of course, but also ethnic, racial, and religious divisions. Finally, the local form of the State must be taken into account. Already written into such a compositional analysis is the possibility of quite dramatic interactions along the boundaries of one or all of these divides."

Yet, the recent literature on regionalism has offered little analytical guidance for the reappropriation of regions. What is needed is a movement through the incisions made by structuration theory toward a social science sensitive to the highly particularized nature of local places, one which views intentional action and its unintended consequences as practices whose rhythms both reveal deeper structures of power and economy and simultaneously lend to areas their distinctiveness and identity.

Toward this end, the broad outlines of the approach employed in this analysis may be rehearsed briefly. A regionally reconstituted social science may theorize local uniqueness - the irreducible specificity of regional structures - to emerge from two intertwined sources. On the one hand, regions may be seen as part of and emerging from a system of regions in constant flux. Under a system of commodity production, this flux generally assumes the form of business cycles and the changing spatial division of labor, which present to actors in local places a changing network of political and economic (and hence ideological) possibilities. On the other hand, because such successive "rounds" alter only the *preconditions* to action, the matrix of opportunities and constraints in the division of the surplus product, the specific outcomes to action are never mechanically predetermined, but are always contingent.

Because local political economies and social life necessarily involve the means by which ordinary people comprehend and change their world, the outcomes to local actions (e.g., the wage-profit conflict) are never fully predictable, nor are they but rarely anticipated by the people who participate in them. This condition exists, as Sayer (1982) notes, because social reality is determined, but not *pre*determined. Further, because individual regions play different "roles" (that is, enjoy different comparative advantages) within the national and international division of labor at different times (and so are subject to different "vintages" of technological and political innovation), and because local firms, workers, and State officials behave problematically within each such "wave" of production, the structure and evolution of different places is fundamentally unique. It is precisely this uniqueness which was obliterated in the frenzied search for commonalities, and it is uniqueness, not similarities, which emerges from the behavior of different groups of actors unintentionally recreating different local contexts. This theme suggests that regional problems, regional structures (rules and resources to action), regional politics, and regional ideologies are not simply the products of abstract "universal laws" divorced from the historical process, and that a social science sensitive to the pervasive regionalism of social life must acknowledge what is, fundamentally, a deep incomparability of analyses of different regions.

Such a contextual approach to regional change entails a tacit admission that the idiographic details of local places are not being captured by models and theories designed to fit all areas. Yet reappropriating the earthy realm of everyday life also allows for significant analytical advances. If much of the simplicity and certainty of mechanical explanations is lost, then gained is a rich view of the world as a multi-layered ontology, "as it really is" and not as overly abstracted models paint it to be. For example, a focus upon human action stretched over irregularly textured landscapes rather than isotropic planes reveals the interpenetration of the social and physical worlds, providing an opportunity to re-establish a unity between two parts of the spatial sciences whose relations remain marked by mutual indifference. Making geography concrete, consequently, entails a focus upon absolute rather than relative location, a focus upon the people who create and inhabit places rather than upon "space" *per se*. Such a perspective would also allow the field to gain much needed public exposure by taking seriously the popular description of regions, a task long since abandoned to non-geographers (see for example, Garreau, 1981).

Upon giving up what is, essentially, a fruitless search for "general laws" of social science and the quest for predictive capability (both holdovers of the positivist legacy), the unique once again becomes a significant and interesting problem for analysis. To grasp regions thus, as historically constituted periods and places, is to build upon the rich sense of context exemplified by traditional cultural geography. The evolution of local landscapes as palimpsests, for example, was captured in the literature on sequent occupance (Sauer, 1925; Whittlesey, 1926). Unlike earlier chorologies, however, a restructured regional geography cannot comprehend regions as predefined individual units, but as the product of local actors (e.g., firms, workers, the State) situated within a wider division of labor. Such a project avoids such illusive polarities as nomothetic-idiographic, structure and agent, or synchronic and diachronic abstraction, all of which can be maintained only at enormous costs of distortion. In the resuscitation of uniqueness, the wearisome opposition between "general laws" and idiographic particularities is rendered altogether false: general laws are not revealed except in specific circumstances, and one may do more with the unique than contemplate it.

References

Baker A, 1982 "On ideology and historical geography" in *Period and Place: Research Methods in Historical Geography* Eds A Baker and M Billinge (Cambridge University Press, Cambridge)
Bhaskar R, 1979 *The Possibility of Naturalism* (Harvester, Brighton)

Billinge M. 1977 "In search of negativism: phenomenology and historical geography" *Journal of Historical Geography* **3** 55-67

Billinge M. 1982 "Reconstructing societies of the past: The collective biography of local communities" in *Period and Place: Research Methods in Historical Geography* Eds A Baker and M Billinge (Cambridge University Press, Cambridge)

Boddy R, Crotty J, 1975 "Class conflict and macro-policy: The political business cycle" *Review of Radical Political Economics* **7** 1-19

Bourdieu P, 1977 *Outline of a Theory of Practice* (Cambridge University Press, Cambridge)

Buttimer A, 1976 "Grasping the dynamism of lifeworld" *Annals of the Association of American Geographers* **66** 277-292

Calhoun C, 1982 *The Question of Class Struggle: Social Foundations of Popular Radicalism during the Industrial Revolution* (University of Chicago Press, Chicago)

Christopherson S, 1983 "The household and class formation: determinants of residential mobility in Ciudad Juarez" *Environment and Planning D: Society and Space* **1** 323-328

Clark G, Dear M, 1984 *State Apparatus: Structures and Language of Legitimacy* (Allen & Unwin, Boston)

Dear M, Moos A, 1986 "Structuration theory in urban analysis: 2. Empirical application" *Environment and Planning A* **18** 351-373

Duncan J, Ley D, 1982 "Structural Marxism and human geography: A critical assessment" *Annals of the Association of American Geographers* **72** 30-59

Edwards R, 1979 *Contested Terrain: The Transformation of the Workplace in the Twentieth Century* (Basic Books, New York)

Gamson W, 1975 *The Strategy of Social Protest* (Dorsey, Homewood, Ill)

Gane M. 1983 "Anthony Giddens and the crisis of social theory" *Economy and Society* **12** 369-398

Garreau J, 1981 *The Nine Nations of North America* (Avon, New York)

Giddens A, 1977 *Studies in Social and Political Theory* (Hutchinson, London)

Giddens A, 1979 *Central Problems in Social Theory* (Hutchinson, London)

Giddens A, 1981 *A Contemporary Critique of Historical Materialism* (University of California Press, Berkeley)

Giddens A, 1984 *The Constitution of Society: Outline of the Theory of Structuration* (University of California Press, Berkeley)

Gordon D, Edwards R, Reich M, 1982 *Segmented Work, Divided Workers: The Historical Transformation of Labor in the United States* (Cambridge University Press, Cambridge)

Gregory D, 1978a "The discourse of the past: phenomenology, structuralism and historical geography" *Journal of Historical Geography* **4** 161-173

Gregory D, 1978b *Ideology, Science and Human Geography* (St. Martin's Press, New York)

Gregory D, 1982 *Regional Transformation and Industrial Revolution: A Geography of the Yorkshire Wollen Industry* (University of Minnesota Press, Minneapolis)

Gregory D, 1984 "Contours of crisis? Sketches for a geography of class struggle in the early industrial revolution in England" in *Explanations in Historical Geography* Eds A Baker, D Gregory (Cambridge University Press, Cambridge)

Gregory D, 1985 *Space and Time in Social Life* (Clark University Press, Worcester, Mass)

Gutman H, 1966 *Work, Culture and Society in Industrializing America* (Vintage Books, New York)

Hart J, 1982 "The highest form of the geographer's art" *Annals of the Association of American Geographers* **72** 1-29

Hebbert M, 1984 "Regionalism versus Realism" *Environment and Planning D: Society and Space* **2** 133-150

Holland S, 1976 *Capital Versus the Regions* (MacMillan, London)

Kuznets S, 1953 *Economic Change: Selected Essays in Business Cycles, National Income and Economic Growth* (Norton, New York)

Layder D, 1981 *Structure, Interaction and Social Theory* (Routledge & Kegan Paul, London)

Lukes S, 1977 *Essays in Social Theory* (MacMillan, London)

Markusen A, 1983 "Regions and regionalism" in *Regional Analysis and the New International Division of Labor* Eds F Moulaert, P Salinas (Nijhoff, The Hague)

Marx K, 1981 *Capital Volume 2* (Vintage Books, New York)

Massey D, 1978 "Regionalism: some current issues" *Capital and Class* **6** 106-125

Massey D, 1979 "In what sense a regional problem?" *Regional Studies* **13** 233-243

Massey D, 1983 "Industrial restructuring as class restructuring: Production decentralization and local uniqueness" *Regional Studies* **17** 73-89

Massey D, 1984 *Spatial Divisions of Labor* (MacMillan, London)

Moos A, and Dear M, 1986 "Structuration theory in urban analysis: 1. Theoretical exegesis" *Environment and Planning A* **18** 231-252

North D, 1955 "Location theory and regional economic growth" *Journal of Political Economy* **63** 243-58

Oberschall A, 1973 *Social Conflict and Social Movements* (Prentice Hall, Engelwood Cliffs, N.J.)

O'Connor J, 1981 "The meaning of crisis" *International Journal of Urban and Regional Research* **5** 301-329

O'Connor J, 1984 *Accumulation Crisis* (Basil Blackwell, London)

Penn R, 1985 *Skilled Workers in the Class Structure* (Cambridge University Press, Cambridge)

Pred A, 1984a "Place as historically contingent process: structuration and the time-geography of becoming places" *Annals of the Association of American Geographers* **74** 279-97

Pred A, 1984b "Structuration, biography formation, and knowledge: observations on port growth during the late mercantile period" *Environment and Planning D: Society and Space* **2** 251-275

Pred A, 1985a "Interpenetrating processes: Human agency and the becoming of regional spatial and social structures" *Papers of the Regional Science Association* **57** 7-18

Pred A, 1985b *Place, Practice and Structure: Social and Spatial Transformation in Southern Sweden, 1750-1850* (Polity Press, Cambridge)

Rothwell R, 1982 "The role of technology in industrial change: implications for regional policy" *Regional Studies* **16** 361-370

Roweis S, Scott A, 1981 "The urban land question" in *Urbanization and Urban Planning in Capitalist Society* Eds M Dear, A Scott (Methuen, London)

Sauer C, 1925 "The morphology of landscape" *University of California Publications in Geography* **2** 19-53

Sayer A, 1982 "Explanation in Economic Geography" *Progress in Human Geography* **6** 68-88

Schmidt J, 1985 *Maurice Merleau-Ponty: Between Phenomenology and Structuralism* (St. Martin's Press, New York)

Schumpeter J, 1939 *Business Cycles* (McGraw Hill, New York)

Smith C, 1983 "A case study of structuration: the pure-bred beef business" *Journal for the Theory of Social Behavior* **13** 3-17

Smith N, 1984 *Uneven Development* (Basil Blackwell, New York)

Soja E, 1983 "Redoubling the helix: space-time and the critical theory of Anthony Giddens" *Environment and Planning A* **15** 1267-1272

Soja E, 1985 "Regions in context: spatiality, periodicity, and the historical geography of the regional question" *Environment and Planning D: Society and Space* **3** 175-190

Stabler J, 1968 "Exports and evolution: the process of regional change" *Land Economics* **4** 11-23

Thompson E, 1966 *The Making of the English Working Class* (Vintage Books, New York)

Thrift, N. 1983 "On the determination of social action in space and time" *Environment and Planning D: Society and Space* **1** 23-57

Tiebout C, "Exports and Regional Economic Growth" *Journal of Political Economy* **64** 160-169

Tilly C, *As Sociology Meets History* (Academic Press, New York)

Urry J, 1981 "Localities, regions and social class" *International Journal of Urban and Regional Research* **5** 455-474

Walker R, 1978 "Two sources of uneven development under advanced capitalism: Spatial differentiation and capital mobility" *Review of Radical Political Economies* **10** 28-37

Wallerstein I, 1979 *The Capitalist World-Economy* (Cambridge University Press, Cambridge)

Whittlesey D, 1926 "Sequent occupance" *Annals of the Association of American Geographers* **19** 163-165

Wright E, 1983 "Giddens' critique of Marxism" *New Left Review* **138** 11-36

Science and humanism in geography: multiple languages in multiple realities

Reginald G. Golledge

"The first great judgment of God on the ambition of man was the confusion of tongues whereby the open trade and intercourse of learning and knowledge was chiefly imbarred."

Sir Francis Bacon, *The Advancement of Learning*

A cynical look at lions and unicorns

Imagine multiple realities, each existing as a different level in a universe of different realities. Imagine further that these realities can be successively ordered. The ordering begins with one that contains predominantly unique elements, such as life-forms, things, events, processes and languages, and ends with a perfectly ordered reality with no unknowns or uncertainties. Thus, anchoring one end of the continuum is a reality of individual uniquely differentiated things, linked only by forces of nature or the creative physical and mental activities of its inhabitants - a population of uniquely different unicorns. Anchoring the other end is a holistic, highly integrated and generalized reality populated by a set of remarkably similar lions. Between the two extremes are a multitude of realities with more or less uniqueness or more or less generality. Now imagine a pride of lions complete with a body of tested, secure and accepted knowledge, and an understanding of their reality couched in an appropriate language, setting off to circumnavigate the universe of realities of which they know they are a part. Simultaneously, a number of unicorns set out from their reality on a similar quest. But while each lion speaks a common lion language, each unicorn has many idiosyncratic expressions consistent with the degree of uniqueness of its knowledge base. Assume further that unicorns travel independently to explore different realities. Realizing the immense number of realities to be explored, the lions split into smaller groups which travel at different rates through the various levels.

At the first meeting of a group of lions and a unicorn, unfamiliarity produces a natural antagonism, exacerbated by the fact that they could not communicate well. However, by assiduous open-minded efforts on the part of both, a means of communication developed. The lions tell of their world of identifiable things and commonly observable events. The unicorn tells of a uniquely experienced world where each of his kind saw or experienced things in many different ways. Both marveled at the other's reality, but could not quite comprehend how it could possibly exist. Not sure whether the other was real or a passing figment of imagination, they parted and went their separate ways. Neither was sure if he had understood what the other thought about or experienced in the present or the "home" reality.

Within a short time, both entered other levels and experienced other realities. When the unicorn met another lion, he found it easier to communicate because of his prior experiences with lion concepts and lion language, but he soon became bored with lions who all seemed the same to him. As a lion met each new unicorn, his frustration level rose because communication had to start again almost from ground zero. In fact, at times the lion was unsure that the creature with whom he was communicating was really a unicorn at all! Because of the constant need to make such a fresh start, each lion was able to cumulate very little information about unicorns, the reality they experienced, and the realities and levels that they had visited. At each meeting lions tried to convince each unicorn to adopt lion symbols, concepts, language, axioms, generalizations, and guidelines for recording what was in a given reality so that degrees of similarity or difference between each one and the respective home universe could be determined. Being interested in experiencing each reality from a unique perspective, the unicorns resisted these attempts to confine their experience and to limit their sensory activity. More meetings produced more conflicts, incompatibilities and frustrations, and less real communication until both sets of creatures wandered through the same realities, no longer bothering to interact. Each suffered from an increased inability to comprehend the different levels of reality that appeared to be further and further from their home base. Unicorns feared the conformity of those realities closest to lionland and became increasingly unable or unwilling to try to comprehend the language spoken by the ever-increasing quantities of lions. A similar aversion faced even the most adventurous lions as they approached unicornland..

In geography there has been somewhat of a tendency for humanist unicorns and scientific lions to wander past each other throughout a growing variety of realities. Despite continued good intentions on both sides, *the* possibility for interaction has, as Gunnar Olsson so eloquently put it, frequently "bumped its head on the ceiling of language". Many of our 'unicorns' endorse Wittgenstein's dictum that "even if lions could talk, we could not understand them"; and so think many of the lions about the discipline's unicorns.

This tragedy necessitates concern for finding an intervening reality - a common ground- where not only lion and unicorn, but also other beasts of natural or mythical origin may roam together. Which reality defines the ground for the common search for ways to communicate, to exist harmoniously, and to provide the stuff from which common understanding is made?

In a very real sense, when one becomes immersed in one level of reality, one acquires an understanding of the signs, symbols and the languages in which the components of that reality are communally expressed. The transition from the currently occupied reality to any other reality may cause complete reconstitutioning of elements and restructuring or reordering of knowledge of components in the new state. Departing from a known level involves not only a search for a new understanding of the nature of the reality existing at another level, but also a search for an understanding of the ways of speaking or communicating about it and the processes and mechanisms by which one can acquire information relating to that reality. To paraphrase Wittgenstein, even if we experienced a different reality, we may not be able to talk about it because our language may not encompass its components or processes! Thus, as one moves up and down through various levels of this universe, one obtains more or less *general* understanding of each reality, more or less *specific* understanding of isolated components, more or less of an ability to modify one's internal knowledge structure and communication skills so that interaction can take place with other occupants and components of a given level of reality. Thus, when the inhabitants of one level of reality attempt communication and conversation with inhabitants of a different reality, the closer together the two realities lie in their ordered universe, the greater the chance of some type of understanding developing. The further they are apart, the less likely they are even to realize that a language is being used or that communication is being attempted.

For many years it was posited that scientists and humanist spoke the equivalent of "lion" and "unicorn". Even when the science lion spoke, the humanist unicorn exhibited either a real or feigned lack of understanding (and vice versa). Despite vigorous attempts by both sides to articulate the axioms and rules of their language and elaborate the schemes by which concepts and constructs could be imagined, developed, and communicated, there was a noticeable mismatch. Thus, even when the science lion and the humanist unicorn found themselves coincidentally in the same physical reality, their attempts to communicate in a meaningful way frequently rebounded against impermeable barriers that had their roots at the most fundamental level of thought and experience. It was in this context that the schism between science and humanism in geography developed. The inability to comprehend not only the language, but the essence of different realities and, indeed, the constitution of the realities themselves, produced distrust, isolationism, outspoken criticism, and at times, rejection of the existence of one by the other. Thus, a lack of understanding fostered suspicion, suspicion fostered hostility, and hostility fostered rejection.

For three decades the discipline of geography has enfolded this schism within (at times) maternal and unifying arms. But more often than not, inflammatory discourse has erupted based on different percepts, concepts and constructs. Often the ignorance from which emotional criticism erupted resulted from language barriers - some humanists being confounded by arguments expressed using scientific language (such as logic and mathematics), while some scientists repudiated as largely irrelevant the beauty and subtlety of thought expressed in prose as being esoteric, unreliable, unverifiable, or uninterpretable. Pure prose was considered an art form and like many artists' renditions, it was seen as open to a myriad of interpretations. The languages of science, although robust in terms of their manipulative ability, were not generally as rich in terms of idiosyncratic interpretability. It was argued that the language of data, symbol, logic, and clear structure, was incompatible with the language of subjective imagery and beliefs, and varying degrees of richness of meaning.

The situation outlined above parallels that described earlier: the tenet of the occupants of one reality leaping into a distant reality, and in so doing bypassing an understanding of the intervening stages that facilitate the ultimate merging of the separate knowledge structures into a coherent whole. Without the intervening experience, it is quite possible that such a transition could only occur if all the accumulated baggage of knowledge were left behind and there was instantaneous rebirth into a different reality; which would of course mean that one becomes a new tenant of the destination without prior knowledge of the former origin.

The system of realities and the question of aggregation
Although the lions and unicorns examined above did not successfully integrate, there is an underlying assumption they could have. It was implied that physically their respective realities were compatible, but the percepts, concepts, structures and languages differed so greatly that integration proved impossible. Even in intervening realities, the structures, habits and culture of the original realities proved too powerful and unbending for successful interaction and integration.

In some ways, the question of reality interface posed in the fable can be treated as a problem of aggregation develops. In the classic aggregation situation, individual identity merges into group or common identity as people, things, events and processes are pooled according to set criteria. Problems arose in situations where a unicorn looked for individual trees, but lions wandered through forests; whereas each unicorn was seen as a distinct entity, lions saw themselves as a population of animate beings. In the intervening realities, lions may have experienced aggregates of like trees still definable as "forests", but perhaps with other qualifiers (e.g., deciduous, non-deciduous). Unicorns may also have experienced tree clusters but may have used different qualifiers to describe them (e.g., pine, oak, beech). Conceptually both may have been able to accept the concept of clustering, but were not able to grasp the logic or criteria for the other's clustering process. With experience of other realities, both might be capable of conceptualizing new or partly new structures based on general principles of aggregation or disaggregation, but be unable to articulate the rules used in a way conducive to understanding by others. The language that necessarily emerged to handle new concepts could potentially have slowly become more similar, but in fact lion language in successive realities became more lion-like because of the tie between new concepts and their closest antecedent and so too for the unicorn language developed to handle those intervening realities.

The above process often holds true for aggregation or disaggregation processes. Clearly identifiable individual elements lose their identity when lumped together, and in fact often form new things that are unlike any single element of the original members (Hubert et al., 1981). We all know what an "average" is, conceptually, but few have observed or experienced the existence of one. The reverse often holds true for disaggregation - the concept of a "herd" is difficult to grasp if only a single entity is ever experienced.

In this context, the transition from one type of reality to another can be envisaged as a process of aggregation/disaggregation. Fundamentally, there are two different types of aggregation, cross-sectional (static) and longitudinal (dynamic). Cross sectional aggregation is in many cases undertaken so that we can build a picture of the state of existence at any particular point in time. We do this both to increase the amount of knowledge about ourselves and the environments in which we live, and as part of a procedure designed to help us understand the ongoing process of existence. This cross-sectional aggregation is accomplished by taking the equivalent of a Dedekind cut through the general flux of existence at a particular point in time. Lee (1973) explains the logical relation between continuous and discrete series in terms of a "Dedekind" cut. The explanation is embedded in the theory of linear continuity and is specifically concerned with the relationship between the series of real numbers and the series of rational numbers. The series of real numbers is usually regarded as a linear continuum in which each element is an infinite class, having no last member, but approaching a bounding limit. This upper bounding limit is described as a "Dedekind" cut. The cut is basically "a division of a set into two exhaustive parts such that every element in one part is less than every element in the other." (Lee, 1973, page 6). In practice, the Dedekind cut can be made at uniform or irregular intervals chosen so that an idea of how a process works may be obtained. In the context of our continuum of realities, arbitrary separation can be achieved using this notion of a Dedekind cut. Since all the elements of one reality thus defined are less than (or greater than) those in the immediately adjoining realities, a loose parallel can be drawn between this procedure and a procedure of aggregation in which each reality embeds within its boundaries not only all elements of preceding realities, but also new elements formed by combining elements from one or more lower ordered realities.

In making a Dedekind cut, we immediately make the assumption that the world is made up of objects that exist in space and time and that these objects are both discrete and relatively permanent. They can be distinguished one from the other by the unique property of location and they have an unbroken, continuous existence over some substantial time period. Simply put, it is assumed that something is there and that different humans interact with different subsets of what *is* there.

Since we are aware that, for the most part, things are changing and events are occurring in a continuous interactive process, we have followed the advice of philosophers from Plato to Wittgenstein, who have pointed out that the only way to grasp a continuous process is to stop it. Such processes are stopped conceptually, not actually, for by stopping a process, one kills it.

To understand a reality or some subset of it, one must "stop" the ongoing process of existence. By doing this, events in space-time can be defined and a picture of a moment of existence (i.e., a reality) can be constructed. As we cut the continuous space-time process at different places, it is possible that different sets of facts can be observed to be in existence at each particular place. Natural phenomena, or things that exist in the everyday external environment, can be interpreted as objects or events that exist in space and time and are perceivable in principle. They are delineated by concepts and their contents are the intuitive data that are the concepts of perception. Natural phenomena are, therefore, considered to be episodes in the flux of being.

The elements of objective reality are, in essence, facts in space-time. But facts about space are physically conditioned by the frame of reference to which they relate and by the conceptual frame by which they become known (i.e., by characteristics of the reality in which they are grounded). Recognition of the existence of such facts is a product of the way mind reacts to the flux outside its boundary and makes its Dedekind cuts (Lee, 1973). Thus, knowledge of space and the elements or things and events of space result from the reaction between mind and the external universe, and the content of knowledge is composed of selections from this flux which mind orders and builds into a structure. When undertaking a cross-sectional analysis, therefore, we stop a process, and assume that the state of being and the state of affairs existing at that point of cutting space-time are invariant and repetitive. We then attribute particular characteristics or states to the elements of space-time that are observable during that cut, and finally, by a process of aggregation, begin the search for statements of generality about the nature of being and the nature of things in that reality. Each "cut" thus allows definition of the state of existence at the time of the cut, and further allows identification of similarities and differences between what exists each time a cut is made. Identification of similarities and difference in the structure and/or composition of things so exposed, allows inferences to be made about the existence and nature of processes such as growth, change, development, evolution and so on. Definitions of elements that remain unaltered and elements that differ provides the basis for categorization. In turn this implies a conceptual ability to group according to specified criteria, and a perceptual ability to recognize and mentally aggregate things so that an economical and general language term can be used to describe them. Thus meaning becomes attached to related descriptors such as common identity, location, magnitude, temporal existence, and so on.

Aggregation can also be longitudinal, dynamic, and process-oriented. This is both a temporal and somewhat speculative approach in that the goal of the investigation is to lay bare certain elements of the general structure of knowledge. This approach assumes that the world is a world of process and argues that in the course of obtaining knowledge and understanding, things are abstracted from events. What happens is more fundamental than what is, because what happens gives rise to what is. Thus, if we give an emphasis to events rather than things, time and continuity are given an importance beyond what normally accrues to them in the cross-sectional approach. *Events*, then, are defined as selections from the continuous, ongoing flux of process, but *things* are static and discrete.   While it would seem reasonable using the cross-sectional approach to concentrate on things, and consequently to aggregate them, it is much more problematic that a process of aggregation can take place if one concentrates on events. Since space, like time, is a continuum, it would seem that to acquire knowledge about space, it is only reasonable to concentrate on processes and events related to space rather than on the things of space (Golledge, 1979).

In essence, the above argument lays the foundation for an epistemological justification for the aggregation of things: it allows, for example, the accumulation of "households" (or houses) to make up a residential sector of a city: it allows quantities of goods to be accumulated to make a national product: it allows trees to be cumulated to account for a forest. If we "thingify" people, it allows people to be cumulated to form populations, subsets of a population, or societies and social groups. Consequently, it is feasible to imagine models of individuals treated like things to be successively cumulated or aggregated into a single model that accounts for the activities of a population.

This procedure of aggregation is not, however, so easily justified when we concentrate on events or processes. Each time we cut the ongoing flux of process, we build a picture which when viewed as a series of cuts over time, allows us by interpolation to deduce "what is going on". The process of change itself, however, allows us to make only the grossest links between our cuts, or cross-sectional pictures, because we cannot justify the existence of the same sets of assumptions over the entire course of the process. Theoretically, this would demand being able to observe from all possible positions in space-time all the phenomena and relations existing during a given cut. This is necessary, for simply by introducing space into our framework, we change the system of things: we change the relation between individuals and individuals, individuals and things, and things and things, and consequently can never be sure that the same events are proceeding in all directions equally at the same point in time.

As geographers, therefore, we are faced with some fundamental problems. If we confine ourselves to determining what is outside of us, we are in effect concentrating only on a procedure of external validation of a segment of a single external objective reality. Even if we are capable of establishing what exactly exists in the external environment at a particular point in time, at the most, we establish its presence for only a fleeting moment. While this fleeting period of time may be enough for us as individuals to obtain a generalized picture of how the objects in an external reality are associated with each other, and while the gaining of such knowledge may help us in coordinating our activities with each other and with the object relationships that we can determine, it is doubtful whether we can make any generalizations for any other period of time (or for other realities) unless we rigidly define the sets of assumptions concerning the invariance and continuity of the things and events observed at the time of our cut through space-time.

The stability of realities

Many of the "regularities", "certainties", or "generalizations" for which we search are those that simply establish the permanence or impermanence, the transitive nature or the stability of elements in whatever reality in which we place ourselves. Because of the complexity of each reality, we place different constructions on them in an attempt to help our information-gathering process and our selection and everyday use of this information. So, to remove ourselves from the realm of uncertainty or chaos in which we are bombarded with an infinite number of bits of information at each successive point in time, we impose many different structures on environments, and even more structure on the activity relationship between ourselves and those environments. These structures are solidified in culture, and help to identify permanent and temporary components of life space, such as the institutions (real and imagined) within which we largely agree to exist (or within which we of necessity exist). These structures are the permanencies which allow us to obtain comprehension and allow us to infer that order and generality exists in the flux of being. So we have as well as sets of objective realities a series of constructions (or alternate realities). These constructions limit human ability to interact with the external environment and partly condition or constrain possible behaviors. The success with which we can recognize and with which we are consequently able to use elements of reality are highly dependent on the transformations that are made at the individual level from objective reality to the world inside our heads. This transformation process is, of course, mediated by the constructions identified with any reality - they are limited by language, by cumulated knowledge, and by our state of knowing at any given point in time. Together, these define the degree of stability in any identified reality.

Some further thoughts about realities, lions, and unicorns
If each individual accepted every level of existence as unique, there would be no such thing as communal knowing. Only when bits of information are joined together into groups or clusters that are identified by a percept or concept embedded in a language, can there be said to be any accumulation of knowledge. Because spatial information is so abundant, it is particularly important to be able to categorize, and consequently generalize, from bits of spatial data. Thus, the partitioning of space can be seen as part of a general categorization process that contributes both to the accumulation of knowledge and the development of understanding. Clearly, without at least minimal knowledge of things and events in the constant flux of being, anything as mundane as directed spatial behavior would be impossible.

Given the above it is necessary to assume that it is possible to communicate among beings. To do this it is imperative that there be a sufficient degree of communal agreement among the categories used to order all of what Norbert Wienercalls the "to whom it may concern" messages contained in a reality. This degree of communal agreement is ensured by the development of language and culture - where culture is taken to refer to a combination of transmitted structuring systems and the shared habits of human groups. One of the most fundamental segments of a cultural system is its language, for it forms the basic interpretive framework for constructions of the world. Within each culture, however, there are numerous institutions which constrain individual life experience to various degrees - these include political, legal, social, economic, psychological, and religious systems. Such systems are learned formally and informally in the normal development from birth to adulthood and death, and facilitate communication, interaction, and the giving of meaning to things and events in the ongoing flux of being. Spatial knowledge, in particular, is conditioned by culture-specific structuring systems.

Focusing on the entity "people", it can be shown that changing the level of abstraction with which this entity is dealt sometimes produces incompatibilities at different levels. For example, a level in which the only inhabitants were economically rational beings (with the characteristics of income, needs, intelligence, complete information, selfishness, and so on) cannot simultaneously include psychologically motivated beings (with habits, specific tastes and preferences that are unique, culture, sensitivity, limited understanding, incomplete knowledge, imperfect language, and risky decision-making). The latter would have to occupy a completely different level which may or may not be proximal. Dual occupance by both groups may only occur at an even higher level still. Thus, as we change assumptions about the relevant model of man, we change the role which the human entity has to play, and we change the nature of the reality in which people can exist. At the lowest level we may *allow* the entire mix of roles that the system can support when even lions *are* unicorns! As we move up the system, we successively eliminate alternate roles and successively constrain the individuals into populations that are more uniform, playing more or less the same role in the system. Confusion occurs when attempts are made at cross-breeding - e.g., if we attempt to combine economic man and psychological man into a man of "bounded rationality", the resulting lio-corn may be hopelessly schizoid and paranoid, incapable of comprehensible thought or action, depending on the reality in which we place him!. We may be unsure *where* such a person can exist in the system of things, and how a complete system (or how description of human activity in the system) could proceed with such a behaving unit built into it.

Until such a time as the set of realities facing us is acknowledged, and until such times as geographers are able to identify the necessary components of at least a minimal set of commonly accepted realities, it is hard to believe that our lions and unicorns will ever be capable of sharing a common ground. Yet there *is* hope. Perhaps all that is needed are some generally accepted (ground) rules to ensure that object, person, event and process in worlds of lion and unicorn alike are dealt with in a language modified enough to aid communication. Instead of lions writing for and talking only to lions, and instead of unicorns writing for and talking largely to themselves, such rules would help define sets of realities in which communal understanding might develop. Definition of those rules is a matter of some importance and, in fact, provides the theme for this and other attempts (Olsson, 1980; Gale and Olsson, 1979; Gould and Olsson, 1982; Couclelis, 1984) to provide suggestions for linking the multiplicity of realities through which we still rather aimlessly wander. I hope that by highlighting the problems of multiple realities, future discussions of the nature of the science-humanist interaction controversy can be more profitably pursued.

> "To have the true testimonies of learning better heard without the interruption of tacit objections I think good to have it delivered from the discredits and disgraces that it hath received all from ignorance severally disguised appearing sometimes in the zeal and jealousy of divines sometimes in the severity and arrogance of politiques and sometimes in the errors and imperfections of learned men themselves."
>
> Sir Francis Bacon, *The Advancement of Learning*

References

Couclelis H, 1980 "Philosophy in the construction of geographic reality" Ph.D. dissertation, University of Cambridge, England

Couclelis H, 1984a "The notion of prior structure in urban modeling" *Environment and Planning A* **16** 319-338

Couclelis H, 1984b "A theoretical framework for alternative models of spatial decision-making and behavior" *Annals of the Association of American Geographers* **76** (1) 95-113

Dedekind R, 1901 "Continuity and irrational numbers" *Essays in the Theory of Numbers* Translator W. Berman (Oak Court Publishing Co, Lasalle, Ill)

Dorrigo G, Tobler W, 1983 "Push-pull migration laws" *Annals of the Association of American Geographers* **73** (1) 1-18

Gale S, Olsson G, Eds 1979 *Philosophy in Geography* (D. Reidel Publishing Co., Boston)

Golledge R, 1978 "Learning about urban environments" in *Timing Space and Spacing Time* Eds T Carlstein, D Parkes, N Thrift (Edward Arnold, London) pp 76-98

Golledge R, 1979 "Reality, process, and the dialectical relation between man and environment" in *Philosophy in Geography* Eds S Gale, G Olsson (Dodrecht, Holland)

Gould P, Olsson G, 1982 *A Search for Common Ground* (Pion, London)

Hubert L, Golledge, R, Kenney T, Costanzo M, 1981 "Aggregation in data tables: implications for evaluating criminal justice statistics" *Geographical Analysis* 13 38-50

Hägerstrand T, 1970 "What about people in regional science?" *Papers of the Regional Science Association* 24 7-21

Lee H, 1973 *Percepts, Concepts and Theoretical Knowledge* (Memphis State University Press, Memphis)

Lowry I, 1964 *A Model of Metropolis* (Rand, Santa Monica)

Moore G, Golledge R, Eds 1976 *Environmental Knowing* (Dowden, Hutchinson and Ross, Stroudsburg)

Olsson G, 1980 *Birds in Eggs/Eggs in Birds* (Pion, London)

Pred A, 1981 "Of paths and projects: individual behavior in its societal context" in *Behavioral problems in Geography Revisited* Eds K Cox, R Golledge (Methuen, Boston) pp 213-255

Woodcock A, Davis M, 1978 *Catastrophe Theory* (Dutton, New York)

Knowledge, theory, and practice: the role of practical reason in geographical theory*

John Pickles

"Posing for discourse the question of power means basically to ask whom does discourse serve?"

(Foucault, 1980, page 115)

"For the world to become philosophic amounts to philosophy's becoming world-order reality; and it means that philosophy, at the same time that it is realized, disappears."

(Marx in his doctoral dissertation, 1839-1841)

Introduction

In part, this essay arises out of frustration with the question often asked of those interested in social theory: but is it practical?, and how do we [when will you] do practical research? More indirectly it is concerned with what Neil Smith (1987) has recently called "the dangers of the empirical turn", in the sense that the problem of balance between theory and empirical research will always exist for a social science which does not re-think its fundamental conception of and relation to practice. By historically reconstructing current usage and redefining "practical science," I hope to show that social theory is inherently *practical*, and conversely that much empirical research has the character of technically applicable knowledge, but is not in any meaningful sense practical.

The paper has three parts. Part I situates the argument I will make in the broader context of science and humanism in geography, and criticizes the oppositional thinking that underpins the distinction between humanism and science. It addresses the confusion in the development of a human science of geography, specifically the confusion over objectivism and subjectivism. Part II focuses on the nature of practical reason and the implication that this has for our understanding of the human sciences and their methods. Part III links practical reason and the human sciences to a different set of interests, in particular to Foucault's notion of the "insurrection of subjugated discourses" (1980, page 81), and thus raises serious questions about the form, content, and broader relations of a re-theorized human geography.

If we accept the powerful and extensive critique of scientism and its relationship to, and fostering of, technocratic and bureaucratic forms of social organization - typified by the Comtean project and modern social engineering - we must ask what alternative forms of inquiry are available to geographers? By concatenating science and humanism under the rubric of science, and then pulling them apart under the rubric of knowledge, I will enter this debate and raise the issue of the relationship between truth and marginalized knowledge forms. The paper concludes by asking what a science would look like which sought to foster the practical knowledge necessary for everyday life and emancipatory social action, or at the very least which sought not to hinder democratic empowerment and participation.

* A preliminary version of this chapter was presented in two parts at the Association of American Geographers Annual Meeting in Minneapolis in May 1986, and at the Santa Barbara Symposium on Humanism and Science in Geography in June 1986.

Conceptually the paper problematizes several crucial issues central to modern geographical theory. The main points I wish to make are: (1) Having seen the development over the past decade of a substantial critique of scientism and objectivism, along with a developing unease about relativism, we must still ask how we can overcome the arrogance of theoretical (or planning) reason which presumes scientific knowledge (conceived in a particular way) to be the only valid knowledge with which to organize a rational, humane society? (2) In overcoming one conception of science, it remains necessary to ask further about the possibility of a rigorous interpretative science with its own sets of methods and principles, founded in a different form of interest. Because social action is interwound with language, communicative contexts, discourse, and distortion (power and domination), it involves a different form of knowledge than the theoretical knowledge of empirical and descriptive science. (3) If we are to have a critical and empowering human science we must show how such a human science is concerned both with the practical understanding of discourse, debate, and communication in communal life AND with the critical evaluation of power and domination which systematically excludes and prevents people from participating in such dialogical communities - with "those systemic features of contemporary society that inhibit, distort, or prevent such dialogue from being concretely embodied in our everyday practices" (Bernstein, 1983, page 224; see also Pickles, 1988). (4) Such an enterprise must map out the ways in which interpretation, understanding, and application inter-relate and are necessary for a "politics of everyday life in which individuals act together to form new specific and local forms of community" (Bernstein, 1983, page 229). If the terrain on which science and humanism has developed is misunderstood, so also is the relationship between theoretical and applied science. The effect of both misspecifications is that the practical knowledge which is necessary for everyday life is denigrated or ignored. We need a means by which we can deal seriously with such knowledge.

PART I

Scientific and humanistic thought in geography
The topic of the symposium for which this essay was written was "The Relationship between Scientific and Humanistic Thought in Geography". This title carries with it a great deal more than a first glance might suggest: the title both presupposes the very understanding of science and humanism that must be brought into question if the relationship is to be made clear, and at the same time the title invites us to reflect critically on both the nature of thinking in geography as it currently stands, caught in the tradition of modernity in which science and humanism must be opposed, as well as on the nature and form of the ideas which will be necessary in moving beyond such thinking. In this light, by transposing the title into a question, is there a relationship between scientific and humanistic thought in geography?, we can begin to address a central issue for the human sciences.

Following the internecine skirmishes between empiricists and humanists in the discipline, and in the social sciences generally, an important issue is whether any meaningful relationship between the two exists, or whether any re-unification of geographical discourse is possible. If any re-unification is to be achieved, then two issues must be clarified. The first is what we mean by science, and the second is what is the central project of humanism? How are we to understand a science of human action without at the same time losing what is human about action, and without reducing action to behavior or consciousness?

Can science and humanity be wedded together, or as Peter Gould has asked "is human science an oxymoron?"

Science and humanity - two attitudes with which few sensible people would take issue - have become scientism and humanism. The two have buffeted geographical discourse from side to side. The "isms" suggest that in each case an EITHER/OR position has been adopted. Scientism argued that the world can and must be explained empirically or mathematically and that this form of knowledge has priority over other forms of experience - experience which since the time of Descartes no longer seemed appropriately called "knowledge". Under humanism, and in response to the reductionistic tendencies of scientism, the attempt has been to regain some sense of humanity - as Downs (1970) argued "to include more realistic models of man" or as Ley (1980) argued to resituate - to replace - human beings at the very center of our project. But in placing human beings at the center of the discipline, humanists generally selected a partial model of what is human, emphasizing the individual and it consciousness. Under this model and its existentialist interpretation, some humanists and their critics sought to deny science and scientific method as appropriate means to gain any knowledge of humanity. But in this way the intersubjectivity necessary to the practice of all research seemed to be denied a unattainable. For this reason, humanism in geography flirted and still flirts with relativism.

On the one hand, the lifeworld of practical experience has been reduced to a system problem. The lifeworld and the communicative nature of social interaction are either operationalized or ignored in the process of formalization. As the formal relationships thus derived from system problems are then applied to the world of social interaction, they change it. The result is a lifeworld increasingly dominated by technological science: the colonization of the lifeworld to which Habermas (1985) refers[1], and the domination of subjugated knowledges and regimes of truth to which Foucault (1980) refers. On the other hand, the humanist reaction to the application of scientific reason has resulted in the reduction of system problems to lifeworld problems. Here the lifeworld is seen to be the foundation for understanding all problems of social interaction. Deep structural constraints, inter-group, or class dynamics are thus reduced to psychological description of individual attitudes, beliefs, and feelings. On the one side we have objectivism, on the other side subjectivism and psychologism.

In order to transcend such dualisms, we need to retrieve science from the "scientific" and clarify the way in which the subjectivization of everyday experience has occurred along with, and through, the formalization of the methods of modern science.

Retrieving positive science from positivism

Elsewhere (Pickles, 1985a) I have argued *first* that all empirical science involve procedures of distanciation and objectification, thematization formalization, and possibly, but not necessarily, functionalization and mathematization. These procedures posit a framework of meaning (physical biological, social) within which relationships between objects can be examined. *Second*, this process of thematization requires a corresponding descriptive science which clarifies the way in which the world is taken (constituted) as a

---

[1] By the "colonization of the lifeworld" Habermas (1985, page 20) means: "the impoverishment of expressive an communicative possibilities which ... remain necessary even in complex societies. These are the possibilities that enable individuals to find themselves, to deal with their personal conflicts, and to save their common problems communally by means of collective will-formation."

object for each of the domains of the empirical sciences (the regional ontologies of space, time, Nature, life, psyche, etc.). Without such a descriptive science empirical science gradually loses its claim to be a rational enterprise and becomes ideology. *Third*, method in modern science has the character of exactitude, but this seems to imply a reduction. The insistence on exactitude has produced an insurmountable barrier to alternative methodologies which are not exact in the same way. In attempting to avoid reductionism, humanists have avoided careful discussion of method, and consequently have at times dabbled with the trivial - with what Husserl (1970, page 328) referred to as "the empty understanding of the others and their experiential situation." In such geographical humanisms only the relativities of the everyday world have been described, and not the idealizations and abstractive processes necessary to thematize and typify that world.[2] Thus, while empiricism forgets that facts are a product of a complex process of abstraction and idealization (what Whitehead (1948) called the fallacy of misplaced concreteness), humanism in rejecting empiricism in the way that it has, denies abstraction and reverts instead to naïve, personalistic description bereft of critical vision or rigorous method. The relativities of the everyday lifeworld and the idealizations and abstractive processes necessary to thematize and typify that world are either ignored under empiricism, or concatenated and treated as one under humanism.

This empiricist narrowing of the concept of "science" AND the humanist emphasis on the subjective and personal are both to be challenged. On the one hand, the objectivism of modern science is to be overcome. On the other hand, the subjectivism (and attendant voluntarism and relativism) of responses to that empiricism are to be shown to be mistaken. We need, then, to show how the schism arose between objectivism/subjectivism, science/humanism, general/individual, etc. Second, we need to clarify the broader conception of science with which we will work henceforth.

The subjectivizing of experience and modern science

The project of *modernity* has been the attempt to put human beings at the center of the world. But in placing human beings at the center, Cartesian science and method separated the objective world from the subjective world. Prior to the rise of modern science the opposition between objectivity and subjectivity had no meaning. It is with Cartesian or modern science that subjectivity is unbottled as an issue for modern man as the other side of the coin of exact science. Modernity is thus predicated on the power of science, and with it the technological use of science. It arises as David Harvey (1985) has shown with the conflict between modernity and tradition - between science and sentiment. Modernity is thus, in part, the "historical context within which the Enlightenment problematic developed: [that is] how to create a new world free from the constraints of monarchy, the church, and superstition. Positivism was one answer to such an enlightened future" (Harvey, 1985).

Modernism thus seeks to overcome tradition; to free itself from myth and superstition. A consequence has been the subjectivizing of tradition and experience to the extent that Bernstein (1983, page 126) has argued that subjectivism pervades all modern thought as a reflection of the modern obsession with objectivism. The unhappy consequence of this modern view is that the human sciences have to model themselves on the natural sciences if

---

[2] Even the interpretation of phenomenology in geography has served to extend this view of method: the immediacy of the lifeworld has been taken as the main focus of attention, while the abstractive and idealizing processes necessary for all science have been ignored (see Pickles, 1985a).

they are to provide us with exact, objective knowledge, or they must give up any claim to objective knowledge and be resigned to dealing with what is left over merely subjective impressions and private feelings. Since they model the idea of science and knowledge on the natural sciences, the human sciences are seen to be different only in that they deal with an artistic element (artistic feeling, intuition, empathy, artistic induction). From the nineteenth century to the present, one consequence has been the elaboration of a new concept of experience - inner experience (*Erlebnis*), and a concept of psychological empathy. Here the aim of understanding is to grasp the subjective intentions of the author of a work of art, a text (Rose, 1980), of historical agents (Guelke, 1982), or of human behaviour (behavioralism). The result is that meaning is subjectivized and treated as a psychological rather than an historical and social concept. Meaning within social systems is reduced to the contents of cultural tradition or to individual meaning.

One of the great tragedies of the human sciences and recent humanisms has been that in the attempt to demonstrate their legitimacy, the human sciences have implicitly accepted this dichotomy between the subjective and objective. But in so doing, their acceptance of a role which deals with the subjective has, in turn, correctly been used to question the legitimacy and rigor of such inquiry as scientific (Bernstein, 1983, page 126).

Thus, until recently, geographers have sought to develop a theoretically directed analysis which has (a) "dissolved the intelligibility of actions into the datum of conscious willing" (voluntarism and subjectivism) or (b) dissolved the intelligibility of actions into the domain of observable movements (behaviour) (Apel, 1984, page 32). These approaches presuppose natural science methodology (or some variant of it) in which the relation between subject and object takes a theoretical form. Such a view abandons the epistemology of participating observer in favour of the epistemology of non-participating observer. Furthermore, as Apel (1984, page 32) argues, it also abandons any claim to deal with "the reciprocity between practical self-understanding and the understanding of the actions of other human beings, a reciprocity presupposed in every action and linguistic communication."

Apel (1984) has illustrated how this issue becomes a problem through Kant's treatment of theoretical and practical reason. In the *Critique of Pure Reason* Kant limits the idea of knowledge to modern natural science. In so doing, he confirms the Cartesian elimination of "internal" understanding from the object of scientific experience, in which, according to Descartes, method would overcome the "deception of the senses". This radical scientism was embedded within the self-understanding of the human sciences (especially in geography and history through the direct and indirect influence of the neo-Kantianism of Windelband and Rickert). But it has remained deeply unsatisfying. Under this view the empirical phenomena of the human sciences - intentional actions, speech acts, texts, - were not recognized as part of the domain of empirical science, i.e., of knowledge (Apel, 1984, page 33). The "thing-in itself/appearance" distinction further removed the freedom of will (human agency) from the world of experience (social structure). The social-historical world of practical freedom in action is thus scientistically or phenomenally reduced. The theory of science drew one of two conclusions:

(1) The promotion of social inquiry to the status of a science was contingent on the possibility of reducing the categories to those of a theoretical science, i.e., to the language of causal-analytical, nomological natural science. This was the conclusion drawn by positivism and logical empiricism (see Schaefer, 1953).

(2) The domain of social inquiry must revise the Kantian epistemology that grounds the social sciences and ground them anew in a renewed concept of practical reason: this was the project of Wilhelm Dilthey's "critique of historical reason" (but a project which floundered on the shores of psychologism).

In both positions intentional action and social interaction have been reduced; in one case to mechanistic models of behaviour, in the other case to individual meaning. Social structures, emergent properties, and individual action have been collapsed. Sedimented and objectified social meanings have been denied. The crucial question then is how do we deal with system constraints AND a lifeworld of social interaction without reducing the one to the other?

PART II

Theoretical and practical reason

In the attempt to build a human science which takes seriously the critique of instrumental reason, we must reconsider this issue: what is the relationship between theoretical reason (*techne*) and practical reason (*phronesis*)? To understand why I would make a distinction between practical and theoretical reason - and why I will go on to argue that we can distinguish sciences concerned with practical reason from sciences concerned with theoretical reason - it will be necessary to re-define what we mean by science.

As late as the eighteenth century, philosophy and science were synonymous. But at this time science did not simply mean research grounded on the modern notion of method (Gadamer, 1981, page 89). Thus, when Aristotle referred to practical philosophy, he also meant practical science: that is, he meant knowledge which uses demonstration, but not what the Greeks called theoretical knowledge - the exemplar of which was mathematics.

"This science is called political in contradistinction to theoretical philosophy as comprised by physics (knowledge of nature), mathematics and theology (or first science, or metaphysics) ... In the light of this background the modern opposition between theory and practice seems rather odd, for the classical opposition ultimately was a contrast within knowledge, not an opposition between science and its application."

(Gadamer, 1981, page 89)

Practical science has to do with the manner in which action occurs, and the possibilities for and constraints upon such action. The kind of knowledge to which I refer gives direction to action and is called for by concrete circumstances. Consequently, this practical science is neither theoretical science (as mathematics) nor expert know-how (as in *poiesis* - i.e., the knowledgeable mastery of operational procedures). It is instead a different sort of science. It arises from the practice of constantly changing situations and modes of conduct, and it is related back to such practice (Gadamer, 1981, page 92). Such practical science is certainly a "science", in that it seeks knowledge through common principles and methods in a rigorous manner. It does not constitute its object by positing an abstract theoretical framework, but deals with concrete situations, which may themselves call for the knowledge of a theoretically directed science to be mediated in practical circumstances.

Planning reason

From what we have just said, it is clear that, unlike the natural sciences, the human sciences have retained an ambivalent relation to the Aristotelian separation of theoretical and practical reason (and particularly to its Kantian reformulation) (Apel, 1984, page 32). This difference is illustrated in John Stuart Mill's and more recently Charles Taylor's (1977, page 130) use of the term "moral sciences" to refer to the sciences concerned with practical reason. What has not yet been fully recognized is the fundamentally different epistemology and methodology necessary to articulate this ambivalence. In this view, the human sciences can develop a fundamentally different epistemology only from the standpoint of practical reason.

For our present purposes, the issue revolves around the interpretation of the concept of science and the way in which the relationship between theoretical and practical reason is dealt with. On the one hand, nomological, explanatory natural science which presupposes subject-object differentiation, and which over the long term involves incorporating the biological and social sciences within its purview, requires the overall phenomenal reduction to a scientistic ideal of objectivity. Psychology and economics currently typify this incorporation and reduction most clearly (Figure 1).

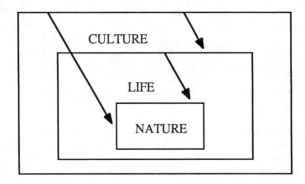

Adoption of Ockham's razor will always result in the eventual reduction of culture to biology, and ultimately to a physical explanation, when Ockham's razor is interpreted to mean that the smallest number of principles possible should be used to explain the phenomenon. The actual claim of Ockham's razor is, however, much more sophisticated and phenomenological. The razor states that the smallest number of principles should be used necessary to capture the phenomenon under investigation. Complex phenomena such as dialogical communities may thus require many explanatory principles. In this context, the first use of the razor would yield exactitude, but would not be rigorous. In the second case, the result may be rigorous, but it would not and could not yield exactitude. Only the second can claim to be scientific.

Figure 1. The reductive impulse of empiricism

On the other hand, some have argued that the human sciences have a special status. These scholars hold the concept of science to be more open, and

---

[3] There is a problem with Mill's and Taylor's claim that the *Geisteswissenschaften* are to be translated as "moral sciences". However misleading this translation may be, it remains suggestive, and indicates the ambiguity in our understanding of the human sciences.

attempt "to adapt methodology to new and different problems rather than to validate the rigid demands of scientific methodology and thereby restrict the area of problems that can be investigated" (Apel, 1984, page 34).   Here, historical-social reality is seen to represent a novel problem which exhibits "a fundamentally different relation to human beings themselves" (Apel, 1984, pages 34-35) - in other words, to practical reason. Much methodological debate in social geography currently typifies this position. But note that in the case of social geography what Gadamer calls "planning reason" is rarely questioned. The underlying intent of such geographies is not a human science of practical reason, but a humane science of social engineering. The rational construction of the built environment is presumed to occur through the expert mediation of social science (and scientists) in the interest of a greater social good; liberal planning reason typified.

The claim that we should move away from planning reason is fundamentally about the type of knowledge that we seek. Both Habermas and Gadamer have suggested that we need a science which provides guidance for practical action, and which deals with the communicative and symbolic nature of social interaction. This is not the form of science that deals with "planning reason", seeking to develop steering mechanisms for controlling complex physical and social systems. Nor is it the counter-response to this objectivism that we find in modern humanism, i.e., subjectivism.

The modern day social sciences sit uncomfortably between these two positions, seeking to address practical matters in a theoretical manner. Certainly they can do this, and do so effectively. The issue has never been whether social science can be carved out in this way. The issue is, what are the implications of so doing, what effects does such a social science have on the way in which we organize society, and what effects does it have on other forms of accounting for social action?

What is practical knowledge?

To develop this argument we must now ask, what do we mean by practice? Fortunately, for our present purposes, the issue has been clarified in some detail in three essays by Gadamer (1981): "What is Practice? The Conditions of Social Reason", "Hermeneutics as Practical Philosophy", and "Hermeneutics as a Theoretical and Practical Task." In this section I will develop Gadamer's ideas insofar as they clarify our own questions in the context of the specific issue of the nature of human science: what do we mean by practice? and, what is practical reason?

In the modern world, practice tends to be defined in opposition to theory as the application of theoretical or scientific knowledge. But in this way of understanding, both theory and practice have been given very limited meaning. "Theory has become a notion instrumental to the investigation of truth and the garnering of new pieces of knowledge" (Gadamer, 1981, page 69). Correspondingly, practice has come to mean the application of this (scientific) knowledge.

This view is already implicit in the origins of modern science. For Galileo the notion of free fall was formulated as a theoretical concept in mathematical terms in a space-time context. The world of experience was reduced through thematization and formalization to those space-time coordinates.   Through experimentation such formal relationships permit the manipulation of initial conditions and subsequent outcomes, and such knowledge can be applied to concrete problems. The relation of such knowledge to practical application has come "to be understood as integral to its modern essence" (page 70). Practice comes to mean the application of science; science and its application in technology are bound together in the very foundations of modern science. The essence of technological science is thus also the essence of modernity in which progressive rationalization, demystification, and demythologization increase the reach of technological science and reduce the scope of practical action to mere application.

As late as the eighteenth century "science" did not have the restricted meaning that we now give to it - i.e., "research grounded on the modern notion of method and deploying mathematics and measurement" (page 89). When Aristotle used "science", he meant by it any knowledge which uses demonstration and generates doctrine. One particular form of this science is the theoretical knowledge of mathematics and physics (science of Nature). Another form is the knowledge of the human world, or political science - that is practical science of political or social action. Thus, the modern distinction between science and its application is not present, and instead we see a *contrast within knowledge itself* between the theoretical and practical sciences (Figure 2).

What, then, distinguishes practical knowledge and the practical sciences? It is the distinction between *phronesis* and *techne*. Phronesis as practical wisdom is "a rational faculty exercised for the attainment of truth in things that are humanly good and bad" (Aristotle, 1955, page 177). Practical knowledge, therefore, does not refer to learnable crafts and skills of production (this is *techne*). Instead, "it has to do with what is each individual's due as a citizen and what constitutes his ... excellence" (Gadamer, 1981, page 92). That is, it is a form of knowledge concerned with how one choice or action is to be preferred to another, be they about environmental, political, social, or community issues. It is a form of knowledge which gives direction to action - Habermas's "social theory with a practical intent" - and it is "called for by concrete situations in which we are to choose the thing to be done" (page 92); a choice which cannot be made for us by technical or empirical knowledge, but one which requires deliberation and decision (Figure 3).

> "As a result, the practical science directed toward this practical knowledge is neither theoretical science in the style of mathematics nor expert know-how in the sense of a knowledgeable mastery of operational procedures (poiesis) but a unique sort of science. It must arise from practice itself and, with all the typical generalizations that it brings to explicit consciousness, be related back to practice."
>
> (Gadamer, 1981, page 93)

- and back to concrete situations. It is knowledge in which action is implicated and required.

> "Practical philosophy, then, certainly is 'science': a knowledge of the universal that as such is teachable. But it is still a science that needs certain conditions to be fulfilled .... to this extent, it does have a certain proximity to the expert knowledge proper to technique, but what separates it fundamentally from technical expertise is that it expressly asks the question of the good too - for example, about the best way of life or about the best constitution of the state."
>
> (Gadamer, 1981, page 93)

What, then, is this practical knowledge, and its corresponding practical science?

Theoretical knowledge	Poetic knowledge of techne	Practical rationality (Phronesis)
Mathematics	Poesis - production based on knowledge that provides the economic basis for the life of the polis.	Knowledge that guides action (Aristotle) Sensus communis (Vico) Moral sciences (Mill, Taylor) Local detail/global structure (Geertz)
Mathematical physics, chemistry, geology, biology	Technai -- productive sciences	

Methods

Distanciation -objectification -thematization -formalization -functionalization -mathematization	Technology	
		Hermeneutics Rhetoric Dialectical
Nomological		

Interests

Certainty Exactitude Predictability	Exactitude Predictability "Application" Control	Speaking Understanding Application Critique Action

* There is increasing "porosity" between techne and theoretical knowledge with the development of technological science -- according to Heidegger, this is the essence and destiny of modern science.

Figure 2. Science, method and interests: articulating the structure of the rigorous sciences

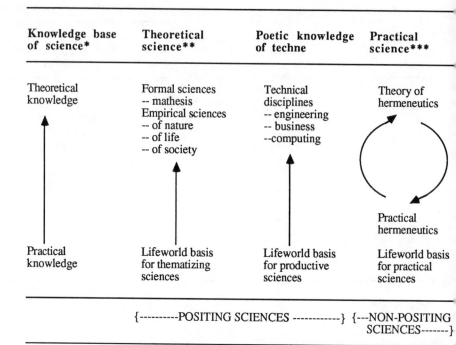

Knowledge base of science*	Theoretical science**	Poetic knowledge of techne	Practical science***
Theoretical knowledge	Formal sciences -- mathesis Empirical sciences -- of nature -- of life -- of society	Technical disciplines -- engineering -- business --computing	Theory of hermeneutics
Practical knowledge	Lifeworld basis for thematizing sciences	Lifeworld basis for productive sciences	Practical hermeneutics Lifeworld basis for practical sciences

{----------POSITING SCIENCES ------------} {---NON-POSITING SCIENCES-------}

* Theory is the highest form of practical knowledge (Aristotle)

** Parts-whole relation is one of subsuming a particular case under a general law (nomological)

*** Practical hermeneutics is not the application of a theoretical hermeneutics, but the concretization of universal claims; a parts-whole relationship in which the particular and the general are surds of each other.

Figure 3. Knowledge and the division of the sciences

Understanding, Interpretation, and Application
The modern mathematical social sciences have restricted the notion of acceptable method and confined the possibilities of "application" to the application of scientific knowledge. The foregoing has begun to peel away some of the prejudices of this perspective, but none is more important in unveiling practical reason than the retrieval of the notion of "application". In our understanding of "application" lies the interpretation of the relation between science and practical reason.

The single most important challenge to positivism has been the recognition that interpretation "is not an occasional additional act subsequent to understanding, but rather understanding is always an interpretation, and hence interpretation is the explicit form of understanding" (Gadamer, 1975, page 274). One effect of this is that the problem of language has been moved from a peripheral to a central position in philosophy and science. A second effect has been the re-thinking of the notion of "application".

In two exemplars of the practical sciences - in this case the hermeneutic sciences of jurisprudence and scriptural interpretation - "understanding always involves something like the application of the text to be understood to the present situation of the interpreter" (Gadamer, 1975, page 274). Understanding, interpretation and application comprise a unified process.

"As the analysis of phronesis shows, the general cannot be understood in advance, and application to the particular cannot be subsequent, because not only is the particular subsumed under the general, but also the general under the particular. Thus, the general is not a pre-given universal that could be pre-known, because it is continually determined by the particular even as it determines the particular. Application is not reductive but productive - precisely because it is not unilateral. If we want to know whether the interpreter applies himself to the text or applies the text to himself, the answer is always each to the other."

(Weinsheimer, 1985, page 192)

PART III

Practical reason, human science, and public action

When Gadamer (1975, page 278) describes understanding as "a particular case of the application of something universal to a particular situation" he also describes a central problematic of modern geography. That is:

"Their object is man and what he knows of himself. But he knows himself as an acting being, and this kind of knowledge that he has of himself does not seek to establish what exists. An active being, rather is concerned with what is not always the same as it is, but can also be different. In it he can discover the point at which he has to act. The purpose of his knowledge is to govern his action."

(Gadamer, 1975, page 280)

Consequently we must begin not with the concept of method - of exactitude or replicability - in modern geography, but with an entirely different issue - the practical knowledge that founds community and social action. Practical knowledge should be of interest to the geographer for it is primarily directed towards the concrete situation in which circumstances must be grasped in their variety. Furthermore, it extends the claims of contemporary geographic theory, which calls for situating research and teaching about the contexts of people's lives within the wider analysis of the forces that shape and affect those lives. Derek Gregory (1983, page 1) has previously argued that modern human geography must be based on "our willingness to reinstate people and places as the touchstones of a genuinely human geography". Reinstating people as actors in the production and reproduction of social life and places recognizes that the contexts for these "daily lives" is no longer bound by mere proximity (as an earlier regional geography would have it) but is a product of global, rather than purely local processes (Lee, 1984, note 44, page 104), in which patterns of communication and discourse are affected by structures of distortion. Thus, any human science of geography must be capable of situating research and teaching about the contexts of peoples' lives within the wider analysis of the forces that shape and affect those lives (see Pickles, 1985b; 1986b).

For Clifford Geertz, this translates into a back and forth motion between local detail and global structures. He seeks "a continuous dialectical tacking between the most local of local detail and the most global of global structure in such a way as to bring both into view simultaneously" (Geertz, 1983, page 239). This is precisely the project of David Harvey's *Consciousness and the Urban*

Experience. Through a historical geography of Paris, Harvey alternates betwee the material conditions and structures of nineteenth century Paris and thei relationship with the consciousness of those involved in the commune and th insurrection. Feyerabend has even suggested that empirical science itself ha the type of understanding that constantly moves back and forth between th "parts" and the "whole" we seek to understand, a form of understanding tha Charles Taylor argues involves the unavoidable problem of interpretatior This, then, presents a severe challenge to the empiricist demand that metho permit definitive empirical verification in testing hypotheses.

> "We cannot hide from ourselves how greatly this option breaks with certai commonly held notions about our scientific tradition. We cannot measur such sciences against the requirements of a science of verification: we cannc judge them by their predictive capacity ... these sciences cannot be "wertfrei' they are moral sciences ... To say this is not to say anything new: Aristotl makes a similar point in Book I of the *Ethics*. But it is still radically shockin and unassimilable to the mainstream of modern science."
>
> (Taylor, 1977, page 130

Having said this, it is not only our conception of method which must underg radical change, but our conception of knowledge. In particular, in recognizin that we are arguing for the explicit articulation of alternative forms c knowledge production, we must ask: which form of knowledge, for what end: and under whose control? For Habermas this is the question of how w develop a social theory of action with practical intent, or as Harvey (1974) aske over twelve years ago: what kind of geography for what kind of public policy?

Here we are faced with a difficult methodological problem: how do we tak the world of practical reason (the lifeworld) as a theme of universal scienc without at the same time losing its character as practical? The problem i evident in the debates between scientism and humanism in geography. Wher the approach to the world of practical reason has been through abstractiv methodologies of empiricism, the formalizing and idealizing procedures hav transformed practical reason into theoretical reason: the production an exchange of commodities become rational optimizing or satisfying economi behaviour; engagement with the world becomes space searching behavioui social action becomes individual behaviour.

Where the abstractive methodologies of empiricism have been rejected i favor of contextual investigation, many results have been little more than naïve albeit detailed, description. But in being detailed, these descriptions are no necessarily rich nor explanatory. In being naïve, they have largely bee uncritical, and have failed to situate the apparent immediacy of naïve everyda experience within the equally immediate hidden everyday experience: unequa exchange relationships, the legislative framework which constantly mediate action; structures of legitimation, the masks of ideology, and the relationshij between knowledge and power.

Such concerns are central to Giddens' structuration project. For Gidden (1984, page 327) social research involves four levels of analysis: (1) th hermeneutic elucidation of the frames of meaning or mutual knowledge tha researcher and researched inhabit in their common cultural milieu; (2) th investigation of the content and form of practical consciousness; (3 identification of the bounds of agents' knowledgeability; and (4) the analysis o the conditions of social and system integration in the institutional systems.

This hierarchy of projects has much in common with the necessary element of a research agenda for practical science laid out above, and on the face of it

Giddens seems to be arguing for precisely the kind of consideration of practical reason for which I have argued. Indeed, any critical social science must come to terms with the levels of analysis that Giddens lays out for us. Having said this, it remains an open question for us whether Giddens' scheme does not incorporate practical reason as an object of study for a theoretically motivated social science. Practical knowledge is here treated as the object of ethnographic analysis, and not a fundamental challenge to a theoretically motivated social science, and practical science is not theorized within an altered relation between theory and practice, science and society, knowledge and power.

In such ethnographic endeavors, how hermeneutically informed social science also will be a practically critical science remains unclear. Such a hermeneutically informed science maps out the experiences and discourses of a social group and context, and it develops an intricate web between actors and the structures which mediate their actions. In so doing, such ethnographies direct our attention to both the contents and limits of social life. But how is such knowledge practically critical? It is so only to the extent that understanding and application are moments of the endeavor. But how are understanding and application brought together other than for the scholarly community in which the research is conducted? The problem has been resolved in part by artificial attempts to present the findings of research to the subjects as part of the interpretative design. Through a series of iterations between research and its subjects, interpretation and application are brought together. But far from producing a critical science with practical intent, this procedure seems destined less to change the understanding of the researcher and more to 'socialize' the understanding of the subjects into the categories, languages, and concepts of the research findings. At root it is not critical in one important sense - it is what Foucault calls a totalizing form of knowledge, which seeks to colonize a prior understanding and in so doing to raise the stature of science (and the scientist). If our goal is to broaden the possibilities for democratic control over knowledge production, which reorients knowledge production away from a totalizing knowledge predicated on a community of "experts" and towards practically oriented social theory and practical science, we must question the very relationship between knowledge and power.

Let me illustrate the concrete applicability of the notion of practical reason by turning to an unusual application of the concept: Foucault's discussion of local knowledge. Foucault (1980) begins his discussion of local knowledges by reflecting on the past 10-15 years, during which time the dominion of science and the colonization of the lifeworld have become particularly noticeable. Accepted institutions, practices, and discourses have, during this period, become increasingly vulnerable, and "global, totalitarian theories" have been questioned. In their place, he argues, "the local character of criticism" has led to the "insurrection of subjugated knowledges" - on the one hand, knowledges that have been buried and disguised, on the other hand, knowledges that have been disqualified as inadequate, inappropriate or outmoded.

Criticism and genealogy "entertain the claims to attention of local, discontinuous, disqualified, illegitimate knowledges against the claims of a unitary body of theory which would filter, hierarchize and order them in the name of some true knowledge and some arbitrary idea of what constitutes a science and its objects" (page 83). This reactivation of local knowledges resembles an archaeology, and counters the institutions and effects of the knowledge and power of theoretical reason[4].

---

[4] For reasons of space I am unable to develop this further here, but the elaboration of such an archaeology can be found

PART IV

Conclusions

In concluding, let me try to deal more concretely with the claim that human science is concerned with the practical knowledge that founds community and social interaction, and that this knowledge has the practical intent of guiding action. The critique of instrumental reason has brought about four principle changes in our approach to the human sciences. Each of these changes is fundamental and substantial.

(1) Reductionism and scientism have been challenged, and with that challenge has begun a re-thinking of the relationship between science and society, particularly insofar as science contributes towards the development of a technocracy (Mercer, 1983; Pickles, 1986b).

(2) Conceptual confusion and "crazy dualisms" have been clarified. The result has been a change in the nature of discourse about the social realm and about science. The idiographic/nomothetic distinction, and its conceptual underpinnings in subject/object, fact/opinion, mind/body, belief/fact oppositions have been shown to be mistaken (Sayer, 1984; Pickles, 1986a). Each of these oppositions has its own problems. Each has been misunderstood in various ways, and each misunderstanding lies at the heart of one or other debates within geography. The result has been a confusing array of interpretations of the social world, ranging from the naturalistic to the voluntaristic and subjectivistic.

(3) As reductionism has been overcome, and as the conceptual confusion of oppositional thinking has been challenged, a strong critique of voluntarism and subjectivism has been developed. This, in turn, has redefined the basic nature of geography as science, and has opened debate on the relationship between lifeworld and system, or between social interaction and social structure.

(4) The critique of reductionism and voluntarism, or in other words, the rejection of the determinism-freedom poles, has led directly to the current on-going debate between agency and structure, or about local knowledge, i.e., between what Geertz has referred to as the most local of local detail and the most global of global structure. This debate is now in place.

The critique of objectivism (as positivism) and the overemphasis on system has been well developed, but the attempts to develop humanistic approaches to science also fail on several counts: (1) From the beginning these approaches have accepted the discourse of modern science, in particular the Cartesian split between subjective and objective in which the subjective was consigned to the realm of "unscientific" as the "deception of the senses". Thus, it is with Cartesian or modern science that subjectivity is unbottled as an issue for modern man. Subjectivity is the other side of the coin of objective science, an opposition which had no meaning prior to the rise of modern science. (2) These

---

in Foucault (1972, 1973, 1975, 1980). At some point, however, it will be necessary to ask about the implications of following Foucault's project, particularly in regard to the institutional arrangements which would be appropriate for a fully developed practical science of social action. Are we to be bound by the institutional arrangements of nineteenth century university departments and the intellectual division of labor which produced them, or is practical knowledge a wedge which breaks apart the collusion of disciplinary boundaries, and opens up the possibilities of new forms of institutional arrangement? Here I am thinking, in particular, of the ways in which the relationship between knowledge production and formal institutions is rethought in the work of Paulo Freire in the context of the education of a Third World peasantry (Freire, 1973, 1985; Misgeld, 1985).

humanistic approaches have accepted their role to be the sciences of *Erlebnis* - inner experience - a role which consigns humanism to a forever non-rigorous, methodless science. This subjectivisation of experience occurs along with the objectivizing of the world in the project of Cartesian science (Pickles, 1986c). The unhappy consequence is that the human sciences have had either to model themselves on the natural sciences, if they are to provide us with objective knowledge, or they must give up any claim to objective knowledge and be resigned to deal with what is left over - merely subjective impressions and private feeling. One of the great tragedies of the human sciences and the recent humanisms has been that attempts to demonstrate the legitimacy of the human sciences have implicitly accepted the very dichotomy of the subjective and objective (and its corollary dualisms, particularly the idiographic-nomothetic), which is then correctly criticized on methodological grounds as to its legitimacy and rigor. (3) In attempting to develop a theoretical science of interpretative action, geographers have not given up what Gadamer calls "planning reason". They have failed to step out of the technocratic mindset, and to consider the possibility that interpretative science implicates an entirely different form of knowledge and concepts of practice and application.

Modern social geography and much *verstehende* sociology and geography are ambiguous in this regard. In following the methodologies of sociology, they have accepted interpretative methods (participant observation, empathy, thick description, in-depth interviews, etc.,) as sophisticated tools in the pursuit of an adapted empiricism. But such an interpretative science is misconceived when it is seen to be merely an adjunct to or a honing of empirical science. Interpretative sciences of understanding also implicate application (Gadamer, 1981). They are practical sciences concerned with a different way of knowing than the theoretical sciences typified by mathematics and the sciences of Nature. They direct us towards a very different conception of human science.

When we ask, what is the central issue concerning the human sciences, in part we must answer that the knowledge of the human sciences provides us with an understanding of the forces which are of importance for living. For Vico this is the *sensus communis*, common sense or the sense which founds community. Practical knowledge (*phronesis*) seeks to address this knowledge to concrete situations. The *sensus communis* is acquired by living in the community and mediating its structures and aims - producing continuity and change through such mediation.

But now we perhaps recognize a major difficulty for the claims of human science to be a science of practical reason. As I have argued elsewhere (Pickles, 1986b) the current attempt to extend the hold of geography on the American school system runs counter to the historical tendency for Americans to lose control over the production and reproduction of their own environments, built or otherwise. The divorce of public, educative, scientific, and work places from each other creates a severe barrier to any practical endeavor that seeks to unite them through public action. The divorce of educative practices from the public domain and their concentration in formal spheres of education, the divorce of educative practices from the workplace, the divorce of science from the community, ... each of these presents very serious "practical" difficulties to a practical science whose intent is to guide social action in the formation of community and places. The retrieval of practical knowledge and subjugated discourses implicates a much broader project, namely the democratization of social and public action. Practical science is potentially democratic since it provides us with the knowledge and understanding necessary for the creation of our own worlds (see Gregory, 1980; Mercer, 1983) and it does so in a way which empowers those re-excavated discourses. But by very dint of it being inherently

democratic, in encouraging participation in the production and reproduction o
community and place, such practical knowledge will undoubtedly have a
difficult path to acceptance in the face of the "practice" of "planning reason.
The claim that practical science makes on the scientific community is not a
straightforward one. A human science which takes seriously practical reason
will not be achieved merely by a reframing of our methodological vision, no
will it be critical merely because we ask questions about particular aspects o
social life or from particular political standpoints. Practical science will be
scientific, but it will place demands on and require fundamental change in the
modern university and our present understanding of social organization.

The recognition of the rigor and viability of the practical science o
geography will cause us to re-think our present understanding of "science" and
its "application", and it will force us to recognize that the ways in which we
struggle to produce and reproduce our knowledge of the world have a great dea
in common with the ways in which we struggle to produce and reproduce the
social and material relationships in specific places. The debate about science
and knowledge is not a disembodied discourse about method, but an ongoing
debate about how we live in places and about who controls the places and
commonplaces of our lives. To this extent, it is *doubly geographical*, concerning
itself with the creation of places and the creation of geographies of places. Both
implicate practical reason and demand practical science.

Acknowledgements. I would like to thank Reg Golledge and Helen Couclelis
for organizing both aforementioned symposia, the University of California at
Santa Barbara and West Virginia University for providing funds, and
participants in the symposia for their comments and questions. I would also like
to thank Will Mallett and Lynn Pickles for their comments on earlier versions of
this chapter.

References
Apel K, 1984 *Understanding and Explanation: A Transcendental-Pragmatic
    Perspective* Translator G Warnke (The MIT Press, Cambridge, Mass)
Aristotle 1955 *Nicomachean Ethics* Translator J Thomson (Penguin Books,
    London)
Bernstein R, 1983 *Beyond Objectivism and Relativism: Science, Hermeneutics,
    and Praxis* (University of Pennsylvania Press, Philadelphia)
Downs R, 1970 "Geographic space perception: past approaches and future
    prospects" *Progress in Geography* 2 65-108 (St. Martin's Press, New York)
Foucault M, 1972 *The Archaeology of Knowledge and the Discourse on Language*
    (Harper and Row, New York)
Foucault M, 1973 *The Order of Things. An Archaeology of the Human Sciences*
    (Random House, New York)
Foucault M, 1975 *The Birth of the Clinic. An Archaeology of Medical Perception*
    Random House, New York)
Foucault M, 1980 "Two Lectures" in *Power/Knowledge: Selected Interviews and
    Other Writings 1972-1977* Ed C Gordon, Translators C Gordon, L Marshall,
    J Mepham, K Soper (Pantheon Books, New York) pp 78-108
Freire P, 1973 *Pedagogy of the Oppressed* Translator M B Ramos Seabury Press,
    New York)
Freire P, 1985 *The Politics of Education: Culture, Power and Liberation*
    Translator D Macedo (Bergin and Garvey Publishers, Mass)
Gadamer H, 1975 *Truth and Method* (Continuum, New York)

Gadamer H, 1981 "What is practice? The conditions of social reason" *Reason in the Age of Science* Translator F Lawrence (The MIT Press, Cambridge, Mass) pp 69-87

Gadamer H, 1981 "Hermeneutics as practical philosophy" *Reason in the Age of Science* Translator F Lawrence (The MIT Press, Cambridge, Mass) pp 88-112

Gadamer H, 1981 "Hermeneutics as a theoretical and practical task " *Reason in the Age of Science* Translator F G Lawrence (The MIT Press, Cambridge, Mass) pp 113-138

Geertz C, 1983 "From the natives point of view: on the nature of anthropological understanding" *Local Knowledge: Further Essays on Interpretive Anthropology* (Basic Books, New York) pp 55-70

Giddens A, 1984 *The Constitution of Society: Outline of the Theory of Structuration* (University of California Press, Berkeley and Los Angeles)

Gregory D, 1980 "The ideology of control--systems theory in geography" *Tijdschrift voor Economische en Sociale Geografie* **71** 327-47

Gregory D, 1983 "People, places and practices: the future of human geography" Mimeo (Sidney Sussex College, Cambridge)

Guelke L, 1982 *Historical Understanding in Geography: An Idealist Approach* (Cambridge University Press, Cambridge)

Habermas J, 1985 *Observations on "The Spiritual Situation of the Age"* (MIT Press, Cambridge, Mass)

Harvey D, 1974 "What kind of geography for what kind of public policy?" *Transactions of the Institute of British Geographers* **63** 18-24

Harvey D, 1984 "On the history and present condition of geography: an historical materialist mainfesto" *The Professional Geographer* **36** 1-10

Harvey D, 1985 *Consciousness and the Urban Experience* (Johns Hopkins University Press, Baltimore)

Husserl E, 1970 *The Crisis of the European Sciences and Transcendental Phenomenology: An Introduction to Phenomenological Philosophy* (Northwestern University Press, Evanston)

Kant I, 1788 *Critique of Pure Reason* Translator L W Beck in 1956 (Bobbs Merrill, Indianapolis)

Lee R, 1984 "Process and region in the A-level syllabus" *Geography* 69-105

Ley D, 1980 "Geography without man: a humanistic critique" University of Oxford School of Geography Research Paper 24

Mercer D, 1983 "Unmasking technocratic geography" in *Recollections of a Revolution: Geography as Spatial Science* Eds M Billinge, D Gregory, R Martin (St. Martin's Press, New York) pp 153-199

Misgeld D, 1985 "Education and cultural invasion: critical social theory, education as instruction, and the 'pedagogy of the oppressed'" in *Critical Theory and Public Life* Ed J Forrester (The MIT Press, Cambridge, Mass) pp 77-118

Pickles J, 1985a *Phenomenology, Science and Geography: Spatiality and the Human Sciences* (Cambridge University Press, Cambridge)

Pickles J, 1985b "The role of place and commonplaces in democratic empowerment" *Issues in Education* **3** 232-241

Pickles J, 1986a "Crazy dualisms and conceptual leakage: or how we continue to misunderstand human geography" *Ohio Geographers* **14** 75-84

Pickles J, 1986b "Geographic theory and educating for democracy" *Antipode* **18** 136-154

Pickles J, 1986c "Human science and the confusion over method: searching for practical understanding" Presented at the Association of American Geographers Annual Meeting Minneapolis, Minn

Pickles J, 1988 "From fact-world to life-world: the phenomenological method
    and social science research" in *Qualitative Methods in Human Geography*
    Eds J Eyles, D Smith (Polity Press)
Rose C, 1980 "Human geography as text interpretation" in *The Human
    Experience of Space and Place* Eds A Buttimer, D Seamon (St. Martin's
    Press, New York) pp 123-134
Sayer A, 1984 *Method in Social Science: A Realist Approach* (Hutchinson,
    London)
Schaefer F 1953 "Exceptionalism in geography: a methodological examination"
    Annals of the Association of American Geographers **43** 226-249
Smith N, 1987 "Dangers of the empirical turn: some comments on the CURS
    initiative" *Antipode* **19** 59-68
Taylor C, 1977 "Interpretation and the science of man" in *Understanding and
    Social Inquiry* Eds F Dallmayr, T McCarthy (University of Notre Dame
    Press, Notre Dame, Indiana) pp 101-131
Vico G, 1744 *The New Science of Giambattista Vico* Translator T Bergin and M
    Fisch, 1970 (Cornell University Press, Ithaca)
Weinsheimer J, 1985 *Gadamer's Hermeneutics: A Reading of "Truth and Method"*
    (Yale University Press, New Haven)
Whitehead A, 1948 *Science and the Modern World* (Free Press, New York)

Nine graffiti in the corridor of pragmatic geography

Pierre Walther

I am confident about the idea that geographers are on the move again. It seems that a renewed sense of discovery is emerging in some of the departments and that traditional preconceptions and boundaries are being shaken. Some German geographers, for example, have liberated themselves from absolute and essentialist conceptions of the subject matter of the discipline. The concept of landscape which dominated German geography for a century appears to have had a rather weak ontology (Hard, 1982), and the pure geography of a spatial science has been criticized from a European perspective (Eisel, 1980). It seems that geographers are moving closer to the dynamism of the world, but the direction of this movement is not yet clear. You know the situation: When you join a colleague on her visit to the library, you are not sure whether she will lead you to the poetry, physics, philosophy or computer science periodicals. Bartels (1968) argued that after the fall of the discipline's essentialist clamps, there could no longer be a common direction for search in geography because physical and social sciences have fundamentally different subject matters. From his point of view, the project of geography is falling apart and has no theoretical basis. Well, I relegate the cause of the current lack of direction less to the theoretical than to the metaphysical level. Current emphasis on first things, universal principles, laws, and theories on which one can rest and which answer the world's enigma has made geography a hospitable department for discussing the absolutes in a cozy atmosphere. The current dynamism, however, reminds me more of the attitude of pragmatism which is a criticism of the absolute (James, 1909) and a turn away from fixed principles, closed systems, and dogmatism towards an evolutionary conception of the world. To use a metaphor of Papini (cit. in James, 1909): pragmatism lies in the midst of our departments like a corridor through which all must pass who want a practicable way of getting into, respectively out of, their rooms. Who wants to join my exploration into this interspace between necessities? Open your door to the corridor of pragmatic geography, and you may notice some grafitti on the walls which form no coherent system but rather a collage of reflections which all point to metaphysical attitude, the consequences of which I attempt to interpret in a broader framework than Smith (1984) has done for a group of humanistic geographers. Some of the grafitti seems to be rather fresh, some could be well over fifty years old. One feels confident that this corridor has a history because this sustains the belief that geography is still on its way to becoming a normal science.

1 Multiversica

Pragmatists have analyzed many assumptions of the sciences critically, but how can one destruct the illusion of the universe which is still persistent among geographers and could well be the most significant barrier to truth. Pragmatist worked hard to dissolve the notion that there is something like an absolute reality towards which the sciences are traveling (Rorty, 1982). Every object and idea has an environment. The only escape from the mystery of the universe was for James (1909) to become a pluralist and to let things stay in their each-form. In the togetherness nothing is necessarily connected to or dominated by anything absolute. This sounds like old geography and may remind one of new approaches in environmental modeling as well (Hollings, 1978). Stachowiak (1983) argues that modeling theory in general is based on pragmatic metaphysics. The multiverse is *a priori* to the universe, order *a posteriori* to chaos. Imagine that the universe is constructed and reality realized into the perceptual chaos through the continuous process of experience. Science is a possible and controlled form of experience by which one plots the whole through which objects and ideas have a magnitude (space) and a beginning, a middle, and an ending (time; Ricouer, 1984). James (1980) argued that everything real is related to one's active and emotional life. Did he support naive constructivism or subjectivism? Schuetz and Luckmann (1979) maintained that reality is not constituted by the ontological structure of objects, but emphasized the constitutive role of one's attention to life and the tension of experience, both of which are intersubjective. They proposed a plausible model of multiple realities, true by definition: (1) The reality of being awake and in a natural, prescientific tension to life is the paramount reality of man, defined by the need for action and interaction and the persistence of pragmatic motives, purposes. (2) The reality of dreams is passively experienced, a reality without options and freedom and not bound to space and time constraints, a potential hazard. (3) The fantasy worlds of day dreaming, poetry, or games are separate from the need for action and interaction with objects. (4) .... What is the reality of Gunnar Olsson's geography? There are no theoretical reasons for judgments. Each reality is consistent in its attention to life, and jumping is the only way to transcend the limits of a reality (Schuetz and Luckmann, 1979). Sometimes one jumps with purpose, many times one is forced to jump, and some people may no longer be free to jump - sometimes for practical reasons.

2 Commonepisteme

I tend to believe that geographical inquiry has mostly been concerned with plotting a universe into the space between realities. "Inquiry is the controlled or directed transformation of an indeterminate situation into one that is so determinate in its constituent distinctions and relations as to convert the elements of the original situation into a unified whole" (Dewey, 1938, pages 104-105). It is a major problem for some geographers that the project of synthesis is the project of common sense as well. But is there a difference between the logic of inquiry in common sense and science? Dewey (1938) wanted to show the difference not in form, but in subject matter and purpose. Common sense is concerned with the qualitative for the settlement of issues of use and enjoyment, with the matter which matters for the conduct of life in an environment. What is the subject matter of geography? It is hard to think of it apart from the qualitative. Many geographical phenomena are phenomena of the common sense world - commonplaces. Schuetz and Luckmann (1979) argue that a science which intends to interpret or to explain human behavior has to start with a descriptive base model of how the world is structured for humans in their natural, prescientific attitude. Their base model manifests a formal resemblance to the theories of the common sense world which are proposed by scholars who have a more radical objective in mind. They intend to simulate human behavior on computers (Hobbs and Moore, 1985). What about simulating land-use developments? To be tied up so strongly with common sense seems to be the enigma for the project of a scientific geography. Is there any possibility of escaping this struggle, rather, is this struggle possible at all? Peirce (1877) considered common sense as a rich reservoir of knowledge, and he endorsed Aristotle's argument for the existence of basic knowledge as distinct from nonbasic, or demonstrative knowledge. Anthropologists who work in development projects find increasing use of this endorsement (Brokensha, et al., 1980). Pragmatists got rid of many such preconceptions and this evokes criticism among the metaphysical minds. Is all knowledge basic or is it nonbasic? (Almeder, 1980). Peirce had no use for such inquiries because he believed that the quest for epistemological certainty is misguided. After all, reflective thoughts start in 'media res' (Peirce, 1877).

3 Sambucoscience

Take, for example, Sambuco.   Science is a discourse which is primarily committed to truth and not to beauty (poetry) or to power (rhetoric). It is the problem solving and intelligent mind in its most effective form (Dewey, 1938). But what is truth? Pragmatists doubt whether this is the sort of thing about which one should expect to have a philosophically interesting theory (Rorty, 1982). Truth is something about which we have no doubt, about which we do not believe that the opposite might be true as well. It could be the truth of a plausible model. Peirce conceptualized the we as the community of inquirers, but a true statement should be plausible to commonsense beliefs as well (Smith, 1978). What can humans expect from theories which destroy their most intime beliefs and judgments? Imagine that some geographers would find evidence that human agency is not bound in time and space. Join me now in a discourse about a concrete entity, Sambuco (Figure 1). There is no doubt that a change occurred in Sambuco between 1945 and 1977 - at least in the actual world which can be identified by encounters and which is, by definition, the only one that exists. The processual transformation (land abandonment) seems to correspond to a transformation rule because there is a conceptual relation between a condition (land = abandoned) and the natural process of forest encroachment. It is equally true that the trees might not have grown naturally, but might have been planted. The skeptical argument always escapes. This possibility can be investigated more carefully, but there is no escape from making a reasonable belief statement. One agrees as well with the existential possibility (consistent with background stipulations) that Sambuco 1945 could be restored to its near likeness or that somebody could have developed it to a residential area. These possibilities have not been realized in the actual world, but the discourse about Sambuco is still in the realm of truth. The intellectual space of geography is the space of the nomically possible that accepts the existence of natural laws and is, therefore, narrower than the space of the logically possible. The world of facts is even narrower.   Rescher (1975) argues that the realm of *possibilia* is necessarily linked to the resources and processes of the actual world. Possible worlds are products of the intellectual transformation of actual situations. But, what is the purpose of this boring discourse: reality transformation, reality transcendence, development?   Why should one bother with the realm of *possibilia*? Pragmatists agree: The discourse seems to be useless without an explicit purpose.

4 Logethics

Logic is one of the most powerful instruments which a reasoning being has (Dewey, 1938). It is so powerful that scientists have begun to believe in the absoluteness of their knowledge. Habermas (1968) argued that, after Comte's positivism, scientism could no longer be defeated from the outside, only from the inside by criticism of scientific methodology. This was Peirce's project (cit. in Fann, 1970). He maintained that the function of science is explanation. Logic was for him the science of how we ought to think, not of how we think. His logic was, therefore, embedded in ethics. Both Peirce and Dewey (1938) argued that logic is the theory of inquiry, but Peirce considered it as a science itself and Dewey as pure methodology related to subject matter. What makes Peirce's logic useful again for planners (Blanco, 1985) and computer scientists is his theory of abduction which is a logic of reasoning from data towards hypothesis with some plausibility (Fann, 1970). Rule: all marginal places were abandoned in the 1960s. Result: Sambuco was abandoned in the 1960s. Case: Sambuco was a marginal place. Abduction is the logic of the diagnosis of a case. Peirce considered it as the first step in a research process, the only synthetic logical operation since the conclusions contain information which are not contained in the premises. Deduction, then, is the process of tracing out the necessary and probable consequences of a hypothesis

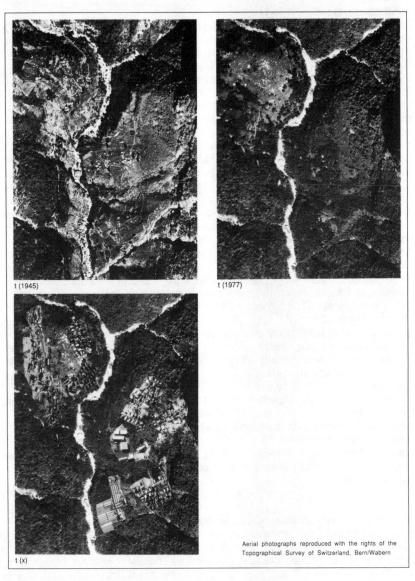

t (1945)

t (1977)

Aerial photographs reproduced with the rights of the
Topographical Survey of Switzerland, Bern/Wabern

t (x)

Figure 1. Transformations of Sambuco (Valle Verzasca, Switzerland) in the
space of possible worlds

and, finally, induction is the classifying process of reasoning from particulars to the
confirmation of a hypothesis with some probability. I wonder how close Peirce's explanatory
hypothesis comes to Davis (1915) 'explanatory description'. Both Peirce and Davis emphasized principles of simplicity and research economy. Peirce proposed a logic of abduction
because he considered the selection of a hypothesis as a conscious, voluntary, and
controlled process and thus open to criticism. A scientist must be able to defend a
hypothesis with reason, and it is the task of the logician to analyze this reason and to discover
methods for investigating and pursuing the truth. Peirce abandoned the idea that general-

izations are suggested by induction (Fann, 1970). Induction can not originate new ideas, but simply confirms what has already been contributed to knowledge. Formalisms? The discipline of logic has made much progress since the 1870s, but the pragmatic approach to the subject still counts.

5 Descriptology

It looks so old fashioned, however, to write about the 'graphei' in geography. One realizes that this prejudice seems to become increasingly old fashioned itself in the face of developments in social theory (Runciman, 1983) and cognitive sciences which both tend to consider descriptions rather as the culmination than the immature beginning of inquiry. Are they signs for the liberation of the descriptive sciences? But how can one write about description and avoid a return to the meaning of Darby's exclamation "Yet everyone - or almost everyone must agree that, amongst other things, geography is concerned with the description of the earth" (1962, page 1)? Bregmann (1977) defined descriptions as compositions of ideals created out of elementary concepts to serve as a map or model of a world situation. It is a search after meaning. To serve makes a difference. The purpose of a description is to derive new descriptions, to calculate expectations and actions and to explain. One may regard it as a means of conceptual organization in relation to a problem or situation at hand. Facts are evidence in this process, but not much else. One has to make a conceptual decision sooner or later. The problem is that geography tends to become more and more a data driven science, and Darby (1962) conceives it as a conceptually driven art form. What reason do I have to suggest that the transformation of Sambuco is caused less by the process of marginalization than by the failure of the land owners to sell the land to people from the city? I have no factual evidence for this suggestion. It is a practical judgment which I dare to make based on familiarity with such situations. One has to settle the disputes in the struggle for truth, and evaluations are the settled outcomes which are based on judgments of practice (Dewey, 1938). Runciman (1983) argued that all descriptions are partial as much as explanations are provisional. I like the instrumentalism of Davis (1915) more than the metaphor 'geographical description is like landscape painting', which seems to secure descriptions and geography to as ends in themselves. But the end for the means has changed since Davis' day.

6 Nogmatism

The reach for the one and only, for the objective true reality, for the ontological and for the absolute meaning is quite persistent. One of the more useless disputes in human geography - at least for physical geographers - is about whether the transformation of Sambuco could be described as a schematic process or ultimately as a narrative. One can identify two sets of geographers: Set A argues that it is suitable to describe Sambuco as a process which proceeds to an end without purpose once it is set in motion. It is a case of the normal process of land abandonment, somehow a bad story whose end or at least whose course is already clear and which can be explained or modeled, for example, with a condition-action-rule. Such a view is acceptable for a physical geographer. Set B claims that Sambuco can never be anything else than a narrative which is the structure of the event chain of experience. Sambuco is a particular case in history which can only be understood by the methodology of interpretation. Narratives are the structure of the dialogue of life in the space of possible actions, and the nucleus of the story leaves room for choices, in particular, the choice to determine the story or to lead it to amelioration, degradation, protection, or frustration of the actors (Bremont, 1980). Pragmatists were determined to show the significance of choices, chances, and potentialities (Dewey, 1958), but liberated themselves as well from the belief in objectivity and the myth that knowledge is a representation of true reality (Rorty, 1982). Why do some geographers assume that the study of natures has to be different from the study of societies or human beings? Rorty (1982) argues that it is the belief that the actor's and human being's own vocabulary is always the best vocabulary for understanding a situation. He interprets hermeneutics not as a special method, but as a way for casting about for a vocabulary that might help. "The only hermeneutical rule is that it's always wise to ask what the subject thinks is up before formulating our own hypothesis. But this is an effort of saving time, not a search for the true meaning of behavior" (Rorty, 1982, page 200). Bang. I still believe that hermeneutics are useful, but one has to avoid the confusion of ontological and moral questions. It might be a mistake to think of one's own interest as privileged, but not a mistake to think of it as morally privileged. The question whether Sambuco is a narrative or a schematic process requires a moral judgment, and moral judgments might be more important in the act of planning than in analysis (e.g., Yeechong, 1984).

7 Dynamisemantics

Pragmatism had its origins in an insecure time plagued by metaphysical disputes (Thayer, 1981). The pragmatic approach to meaning is still the heart of the movement (Peirce, 1878). Is human reasoning different from machine intelligence? Is the transformation of Sambuco a schematic process or a narrative? Peirce's pragmatic maxim was that instead of regarding objects or ideas as possessing sets of static and fixed characters and predicates one has to conceive of them as manifesting these by producing effects in interaction with other things. Pragmatism was meant to be an effective method for settling metaphysical disputes and improving moral judgments by tracing out the consequences of ideas, laws, and policies on the conduct of human life (James, 1907). Peirce (cit. in Smith, 1978) thought of his time as a pedantic age which paid more attention to words than to things. Does it make a difference whether I speak of primary or of secondary forests in Sambuco? It does not in Italy or in Canada. Forests are forests. They are there to be felled. But it makes a difference in Sambuco because the Swiss government issued a law which prohibits cutting of forests which may serve a function (Schweizerischer Bundesrat, 1902). It does not make a difference, however, whether Sambuco is encroached upon by betula or by populus since both tree species have the same function in this case. This certainly is reminiscent of the fatherly advice given by Davis (1915) that geographers should concentrate on the important aspects and that the plot landscape ought to be considered as a functional entity. How can a discipline escape its own history? But pragmatists went beyond Davis. They did not intend to set up a new dogma but they were interested in developing methodologies for settling disputes of the kind 'Is human agency bound in time and space or not?'. It does make a difference, and Peirce (1878) intended to attain this third grade of clarity with the experimental procedures of science. His basic interest was the dynamizing of predicates in search for meaning.

8 Disjuncta

This approach to semantics provides reason for James' (1907) statement that pragmatism moves towards the concrete. Dewey (1938) characterized the concrete as designating immediately experienced qualities, and the abstract as conceptions and relations which are taken without reference to actual applications to things. The filling of an abstract concept with concrete objects is the process of objectification, at least in common sense (Moskovici, 1984). Land abandonment is an abstract concept in economics, and it is objectified in Sambuco, Forno, ... Or, in other terms, the geographic concept of land abandonment is represented by the exemplars of Sambuco, Forno, ... , which do not necessarily share the same properties among themselves and therefore do not form a unitary representation. Diversity? Does anyone suggest moving towards a new class of concepts which are represented by concrete events? It can no longer be claimed that Mexico City better represents the concept of Third World urbanization than Colombo. Such a step can be no more than a thought experiment into a geography liberated from unitary concept representations. Smith and Medin (1981) argue that some classes of concepts might be represented by sets of discrete and qualitative exemplars which develop possibilities for the human mind. For example, (1) concepts can be disjunctive since an item belongs to a concept if it matches this or that exemplar; (2) there is no need that features of one exemplar should be represented in other exemplars as well; and (3) the only necessary relation between the elements in a set is that they point to the same concept. Critics may argue that such formalism fails to specify constraints. What about a set (Sambuco, Mexico City, Mount Everest)? Smith and Medin (1981) promote a contextual model. Constraints might be much looser and less accessible in such a concept representation, and the exemplars remain in the foreground. Discussions are freed from necessities and fixed principles, constraints become subject to critical discourse and change, and concepts might be represented as cells within which the exemplars are allocated. But can there be scientific reasoning with such formalism? Does this lead back to the ideal-typical method of Weber (1949) who considered history as a storehouse of exemplars, or must one fear a return to the Socratic method of teaching geography? The methodology of case analysis is becoming valuable again for social scientists (Mitchell, 1983), and cognitive scientists use sets of primitive operations for reasoning with exemplars (e.g., Holyoak and Glass, 1975; Michalski and Chilanski, 1980; Winston, 1975; Winston, 1980): (A) might be the reasoning with counterexamples to determine the truth of a statement with a quantifier, (B) the induction in order to determine general rules from examples, (C) the search through a set of examples in order to provide a problem description, (D) maps the structural description of one exemplar into another one (reasoning by analogy), and (E) (F) (G) ... . Sambuco is like downtown Edmonton. I realize that I am at the edge of metaphor and, therewith, at the border of science and engineering.

9 Artivector

What is the use of such an engineered approach to concepts? Santayana (1913) commented on the Darwinian influence on pragmatism: pragmatists considered ideas not as mirrors but as weapons which prepare us to meet future events. This metaphor points to Dewey's (1938) instrumental approach to theory in which the realms of the practical and the theoretical collapse into the process of becoming. It could point as well to Simon's (1985) sciences of the artificial in which pure science and engineering seem to be integrated into a broader proposal. The artificial is the man-made which contrasts with the natural, the pure wonder. Simon (1985) developed a science of design in which creativity and engineering penetrate the discussion about how things are and behave. "Since much of design, ..., is concerned with objects or arrangements in real Euclidean two-dimensional or three-dimensional space, the representation of space and things in space will necessarily be a central topic in a science of design" (Simon, 1985, page 153). The realm of artifacts penetrates geography in subject matter, as well as in the never abandoned commitment to synthesis. One can think of 'Sambuco-out-there' as an artifact and propose that 'Sambuco is like downtown Edmonton' is an artifact as well. But it is more difficult to consider 'Sambuco has been encroached upon by trees' or 'Sambuco is a marginal place' as artifacts. All statements are true but the first ones transcend the limits of the factual and have a pointer to the future, the last ones point to the past. Dewey (1938) states that the happening always escapes and that only the happened is recorded. The trust in the value of data is based on the belief that patterns repeat themselves in the passage of events. If there were no patterns, any form of experience (science included) would be difficult. The problem, however, is that the subject matter of geography is potentially in motion within the boundaries of constraints and routines. Most geographers seem to agree that the subject matter of geography is processual (Johnston,

1983), and they are, therefore, part of a metaphysical reorientation which Prigogine and Stengers (1984) summarize for the physical sciences. Dewey (1938) conceptualized inquiry as action and transformation, and emphasized that virtually any form of inquiry takes the form of a controlled experiment. Prigogine and Stengers (1984) interpret experiments as dialogues with nature, as artifacts. The project of designing new and better worlds for human beings (an experimental geography) could be a purer geography than Granö (1929) could have ever dreamt of as an essentialist.

Brr... . A telephone ringing in your room. Maybe you would like to write another graffito on the walls of this corridor (e.g., a critical one), but most of you probably think that this place is too somber and windy. A skylight cannot replace the bright window in your room. But does anyone expect that a metaphysical attitude would provide the security within which research could take place? Throughout this discussion it seemed that the question about the purpose of geography crystalizes as a core problem for those who have moved away from an essentialist conception of the discipline. An academic discipline without purpose is like somebody who visits a library without a goal in mind. The question about the purpose of the project, however, puzzles essentialists as well. A growing group of geographers seems to believe that the purpose of geography is to report facts about the world. A cloud of dogmatic and technological thinking casts its shadow on the colloquia of the scholars who are still committed to science as critical discourse. Another group believes that it is the purpose of geography to broaden human consciousness. I am fascinated by Buttimer's analysis (1974) but find no theoretical reason why she wrote an appendix about phenomenology and existentialism. Still other geographers find no other purpose than their personal interests (personal geography). Has such growing awareness brought us to the edge of an ideological battle? Pragmatists dared to discuss science in such a framework. Dewey (1958) provided the community with hope in the moral importance of science, and he is, in Rorty's terms (1982), waiting at the end of the route which is traveled, for example, by Foucault. From his moral standpoint, science has a positive function for human well-being in problem formulation, as well as in problem solving. The sense of direction, however, seems to be developed on another level. Rescher (1977) argues that the process of science does not proceed along theoretical, but along practical lines. The application of knowledge provides most normal sciences with a direction for search. German geography has long been dominated by the needs of school teachers, but the community of applied geographers is growing. Not surprisingly, applied geographers in my home country, Switzerland, are urging the universities to develop a profile of the discipline. Their goal is to improve the opportunities for geographers in the job market. I do not dare to answer the questions about the purpose of geography. Similar to Rescher (1977) I believe that it lies external to theoretical reasons. Can I be satisfied with a geography which no longer has anything to say about these wicked problems which do not come in disciplinary blocks? Or can I imagine geographers studying consumer behavior in a society which has returned to subsistence farming? One feels tied up with the actuality of past and present worlds and does not expect wonders. Theoretical progress of the discipline for me is basically a methodological progress which helps me to approach the paradox of complex and concrete situations better than I could yesterday.

Acknowledgements. I thank Helen Couclelis (Santa Barbara) for encouragement, Haruko Kishimoto (Zürich) for corrections, and Martin Steinmann (Zürich) for graphical support.

References

Almeder R, 1980 *The Philosophy of Charles S. Peirce: A Critical Introduction* (Blackwell Publishers, Oxford)

Bartels D, 1968 *Zur wissenschaftstheoretischen Grundlegung einer Geographie des Menschen* (Franz Steiner Verlag, Wiesbaden)

Blanco H, 1985 "Pragmatism, abduction and wicked problems" *Berkeley Planning Journal* **1 2** 93-119

Bregmann A, 1977 "Perception and behavior as compositions of ideals" *Cognitive Psychology* **9** 250-292

Bremont C, 1980 "The logic of narrative possibilities" *New Literary Historian 11* **3** 387-411

Brokensha D, Warren D, Werner O, Eds 1980 *Indigenous Knowledge Systems and Development* (University Press of America, Lanham)

Buttimer A, 1974 "Values in geography" *Resource Papers of the Association of American Geographers No. 24* (Washington D.C.)

Darby H, 1962 "The problem of geographical description" *Transact. Inst. British Geogr. 30* **1** 1-14

Davis W, 1915 "The principles of geographical description" *Annals of the Association of American Geographers* **5** 61-105

Dewey J, 1938 *Logic: the Theory of Inquiry* (Henry Holt and Co., New York)

Dewey J, 1958 *Experience and Nature 2nd Edition* (Dover Publications Inc., New York)

Eisel U, 1980 "Die Entwicklung der Anthropogeographie von einer Raumwissenschaft zur Gesellschaftswissenschaft" *Urbs et Regio Volume 17*

Fann K, 1970 *Peirce's Logic of Abduction* (Martinus Nijhoff, The Hague)

Granö J , 1929 "Reine Geographie: eine methodologische Studie" *Acta Geographica* **2** (2) 1-202

Habermas J, 1968 *Erkenntnis und Interesse* (Suhrkamp, Frankfurt)

Hard G, 1982 "Plädoyer für ein besseres Carol-Verständnis" *Geogr. Helvetica 37* **3** 115-166

Hobbs J , Moore R, Eds 1985 *Formal Theories of the Common Sense World* (Ablex Publishers, Norwood N.J.)

Hollings C, 1978 *Adaptive Environmental Assessment and Management* (John Wiley and Sons, New York)

Holyoak K, and Glass A, 1975 "The role of contradictions and counterexamples in the rejection of false sentences" *Journal of Verbal Learning and Behavior* **14 2** 215-239

James W, 1890 *Principles of Psychology Volume 2* (Henry Holt, New York)

James W, 1907 *Pragmatism: A New Word for Some Old Ways of Thinking* (Longmans and Green, New York)

James W, 1909 *A Pluralistic Universe* (Longmans and Green, New York)

Johnston R, 1983 "Resource analysis, resource management, and the integration of physical and human geography" *Progress in Physical Geography 7* **1** 127-146

Michalski R, and Chilanski R, 1980 "Learning by being told and learning from examples: an experimental comparison of the two methods of knowledge acquisition in the context of developing an expert system for soybean disease diagnosis" *Journal of Policy Analysis and Information Systems 4* **2** 125-161

Mitchell J, 1983 "Case and situation analysis" *The Sociological Review* **31** 186-211

Moskovici S, 1984 "The phenomenon of social representations" in *Social Representations* Eds R Farr, S Moskovici (Cambridge University Press, Cambridge) pp 3-70

Peirce C, 1877 "The fixation of belief" *Popular Science Monthly* **12** 1-15

Peirce C, 1878 "How to make our ideas clear" *Popular Science Monthly* **12** 286-302

Prigogine I, Stengers I, 1984 *Order Out of Chaos: Man's New Dialogue With Nature* (Heinemann, London)

Rescher N, 1975 *A Theory of Possibility* (Basil Blackwell, Oxford)

Rescher N, 1977 *Methodological Pragmatism* (Basil Blackwell, Oxford)

Ricouer P, 1984 *Time and Narrative Volume 1* (University of Chicago Press, Chicago)

Rorty R, 1982 *Consequences of Pragmatism* (University of Minnesota Press, Minneapolis)

Runciman W, 1983 *A Treastise on Social Theory Volume 1* (Cambridge University Press, Cambridge)

Santayana G, 1913 *Winds of Doctrine* (Scribner's, New York)

Schütz A, and Luckmann T, 1979 *Strukturen der Lebenswelt Volume 1* (Suhrkamp, Frankfurt)

Simon H, 1985 *The Sciences of the Artificial 4th Edition* (MIT Press, Cambridge Mass)

Smith E, and Medin D L, 1981 *Categories and Concepts* (Harvard University Press, Cambridge Mass)

Smith J, 1978 *Purpose and Thought: The Meaning of Pragmatism* (Hutchinsons, London)

Smith S, 1984 "Practicing humanistic geography" *Annals of the Association of American Geographers* **74** 3 353-374

Stachowiak H, 1983 "Erkenntnisstufen zum systematischen Neopragmatismus und zur allgemeinen Modelltheorie" in *Modelle: Konstruktion der Wirklichkeit* Ed. H Stachowiak (Wilhelm Fink Verlag, München) pp 87-146

Thayer H, 1981 "Pragmatism: a reinterpretation of the origin and consequences" in *Pragmatism: Its Sources and Prospects* Eds R Mulvaney, P Zeltner (University of South Carolina Press, Columbia S.C.) pp 1-20

Weber M, 1949 *The Methodology of the Social Sciences* (The Free Press, Gencoe Ill)

Winston P, 1975 "Learning structural descriptions from examples" in *The Psychology of Computer Vision* Ed. P Winston (McGraw-Hill, New York) pp 157-209

Winston P, 1980 "Learning and reasoning by analogy" *Communic. of the ACM* **23** **12** 689-703

Yeechong W, 1984 "Ideology, tradition and social development: a study in critical and hermeneutical theories of planning" UCB Planning Papers DP 9 University of B.C., Vancouver B.C.

stop here in order not to stumble over the ties of the metaphor, return to geography instead. Let me take up and reconsider the initial proposition:

For the majority of cases we deal with in human geography and the human sciences in general, the assumption of circularity implied in formal logic, conventional mathematics, and statistical models does not hold. There are cases in which the qualitative characteristics of the phenomenon under consideration can neither be assumed to remain unchanged for the time of the inference, nor to remain unaffected by the activity of inferring itself.

It is not simply the significance that change holds for the realm of social phenomena, and not the increasing speed[1] of this change (including the disappearance of time and space that Virilio calls our attention to), that causes this difficulty. The invalidity of the assumption of existential circularity lies in the very nature of the human sciences. The general logic and its consequences were described above. Here, in human geography, subject and object are separate and therefore inseparable. Here human beings reflect on themselves in order to change human life. Based on detailed knowledge of individual/social lives, we think about individual/social lives, thus undermining the moment of stable identity formal logic requires.

Does not human geography's challenge consist of trying to consider both the researchers, as well as the people they describe, as human beings capable of self-reflection? Marked by the fundamental human capacity of self-reference, such a science shows human beings distancing themselves from their selves so as to return to themselves. But the one who comes back is not the same as the one who left. She is another person, although still sufficiently similar to be welcomed as one who returned. *Movement in spirals*, broken circles.

This movement explains the particular situation of a human science, a science whose success consists in its activity of producing self-fulfilling or self-refuting hypotheses.[2] From conventional logic's point of view, such a situation must appear paradoxical. Dialectical reasoning, on the other hand, sees the fundamental dynamics of self-referent thinking expressed in it. These are not the dynamics resulting from the imperfection of our knowledge and the need to examine and revise it constantly. They are not even the consequence of having to keep track of the transformations the object of our investigation goes through. The dynamics of self-referent thinking, the only ones specific for human sciences, stem from this thinking itself. Self-referent thinking leads to changes in what it is thinking about.

It is in this sense that, from dialectical thinking's perspective, human geography, and any human science conceiving man as a self-reflecting human being, must be regarded as a dynamic process. It is dynamic in its social engagement. Far from being reducible to a "context of justification", it does not even consist of a succession of "context of discovery", "-justification", "-eval-

---

[1] It is an increase of speed that cannot be explained simply by increased information or the enlarged horizon we overlook. (See also footnote 47.)

[2] In principle, this peculiarity is not even dependent on the wide public acceptance of hypotheses. It is already there, in the act of reasoning of a scientist who is, has to be, a member of this public.

uation", and "context of utilization".[3] Contexts merge. In the duality of a social science and society, the duality of observer and observed reaches its consequence.

Bound to keep aiming for it, we cannot establish a system of knowledge about the geographies of the concreteness of individual/social life. With the loss of a taken-for-granted, with the raising of a question, and the beginning of reflection, a process has begun which ends in sinking back into a new taken-for-granted. A different one. As a hint in the search for it, our system of knowledge was used up by existence. This is what has to be kept in mind when asking what "theory" means in human geography.[4] It is not only an explanation through identity-relation, but also, necessarily related and incompatible with that, a stimulus for change. It originates in the axioms of its logical system: through the activity of human geography we promote processes. Through it we offer momentary alternatives to be answered for, no lasting answers. Human geography is a science that ends with a question mark, not with a full stop_____.

Writing around circularity and self-reference

Dagmar Reichert

Abstract
Cut into the skin of modernity, marking the body of the human sciences, is a circular scar. One move in the process of dismantling the content and form of research in human geography is my attempt to get to see it.
    When the aim is a circle, the way to describe it cannot be straight. I search for the limits of conventional reasoning, the paradox. Circular structures form

---

[3] This distinction was introduced by Reichenbach in order to separate the logical claim for validity from the social and political circumstances of science. It "leads us to a platonistic interpretation of cognitive validity-claims" (Mittelstrass, 1980, 1, page 549). A human geography, reduced to a context of justification, would not be the product of human thinking.

[4] Theory, in the sense of "*theoria as contemplatio*" (Gould, 1987, page 2) has two meanings: on the one hand it is explanation or contextualization (Gregory, 1985, page 387), depending on the respective epistemology/ontology. As such it is, even when describing transformations, rooted in stability. On the other hand - and only the social sciences are two-handed in this respect - theories are stimuli for change, means to promote control, or new understanding of the self and the other. Rooted in existence, they are effective through nourishing on themselves.

    My argument for the specific dynamics of theories in the human sciences adds a further aspect to Gould's (1987) inquiry into the different meaning of "theory" in the human- and natural sciences. More than Gould ("...both individuals and societies can deny the template [theory] by their self-reflective capacity and assertion that is constitutive of being human. In this world, theoria as contemplatio has no meaning, for if such meaning is carried over unthinkingly from the world of things, it has no capacity to illuminate.") (1987, page 2), I want to emphasize the active role of human beings in making theories "true". (Yes, "true" in quotation marks to save "knowing winks" (Gould, 1987, page 2), and to distinguish it from truth as *a-letheia*!) If seen in this way, *theoria as contemplatio*, although not providing absolute answers, may still have meaning for us.

its basis. Depending on the point of view, paradoxes can be traced either to logical circles, or to existential ones. Both views offer methods of limiting the occurrence of paradoxes to clearly defined and consequently forbidden areas. That is where the circles lie.

The glimpses I catch let me ask for more detailed investigations. I argue that the domain of the human sciences, and of human geography in particular, lies in the area beyond the realm of conventional logic. Research in human geography is based on the circular relationship between subject and object, individual and society, science and everyday practice, theory and facts. If measured by the standards of conventional reasoning, such enterprise is paradoxical.

Research in human geography has an implicit dimension of change. The idea of continuous time lies at its core. If described in the discontinuous time of conventional reasoning, change is lost in discrete, black bars.

One may turn to dialectical reasoning for help and adopt the specific objectives it implies. They demand a different conception of what we mean by a human science, one that is closely related to social processes. Yet, when I am about to consider this as a solution, another, even more fundamental circle turns up. Just as the merits of dialectics take shape in the eyes of those looking from the basis of conventional logic, the dialectic position makes visible the merits of conventional reasoning. In several respects its concept of identity is implied in dialectical logic.

Reaching beyond the area of conventional logic as well as beyond the opposed one of dialectics, the human sciences touch the sharp edge separating the two. There they are: presentiments of the scar of modernity: cut into the cornea of our eyes, the circle refracts our sight. No surprise then: it circumscribes any text written in this context and makes it paradoxical.

... And I demand all the ignorance you can afford, offering you an abstract that pretends it could not be other than it is, that pretends to lie outside the circle, along the smoothness of unbroken razor blades.

Control (4): Adjustment of frame (V-hold): various factors cause interferences in the reception of signals. These may lead to the appearance of "dual pictures": two half images (differing by one phase of time, and appearing simultaneously on the screen) are split by a horizontal black line. To get a single, complete picture, push up control (4). If the picture rolls up or down, pushing knob (4) also will stop continuous change and stabilize the picture. If this does not lead to satisfactory results, please consult a specialist.

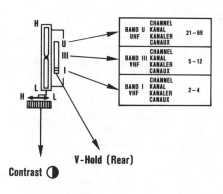

"Dear Colleague,
Thank you very much for the second volume of your "Basic Laws", which I read with great interest. Here we are familiar with the examples you give at the end of your book (page 253). Four or five years ago I found other, more

persuasive contradictions. They convinced me that traditional logic is
insufficient: in particular the theory of concepts requires a tightening and
refinement..."
This was written on a postcard that Frege got from Hilbert in November
1903. Three years later he received a message from Russell, who suggested
the following refinements:
" ... The reflexive fallacies ... necessitate a division of objects. ... Whatever
contains an apparent variable must be of a different type from the possible
values of that variable. We will say that it is from a higher type."[5]

This discussion has important consequences for the contemporary theory of
the human sciences and the concrete approaches to research in human
geography: every investigation we engage in, as well as the whole realm in which
our research problems can be defined, is completely dependent on the formal
possibilities that a logical system offers our thinking.

Russell's suggestion to Frege implies that traditional logical arguments,
conventional reasoning, calculating, and modeling, as we commonly use them in
human geography, only produce meaningful results if a hierarchical distinction
between objects (or between levels of analysis) is made, and only if the
unidirectionality of hierarchical cover-sets is respected. Particularly relating an
object to itself: e.g., using language to refer to this very language, or thinking
about this thought, that is self-reference is excluded. How else could we capture
identity? How could we define the identity of a particular object by relating it
to a more general one, if the general at the same time is defined by the
particular? Reasonable as Russell's proposition may seem, there are many
cases where it cannot be applied. Such cases, as I intend to show, are the
majority of situations we deal with in human geography and in the human
sciences in general. They are cases of *logical circularity*.

In its pure aesthetic harmony, the
circle is a very rich and old metaphor:
earlier, and differing from the inward-
oriented perimeters of our von Thünen,
Burgess, regionalizing, geographical
tradition, it represented a closed path.[6]
In the form of the Ouroboros, the snake
that eats its tail, the circle occurs in all
cultures. It also is a key symbol of
medieval occidental alchemy (referring
to the sun as well as to gold), and
oriental philosophy (appearing in the
artistic drawings of the wheel, the
yin/yang, the mandala symbol).

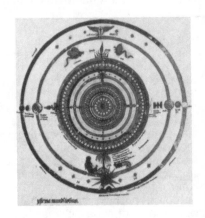

All these traditions share two characteristics which raise the circle to its
privileged position:

---

[5] Cited in Thiel (1972, page 94 and 101). Translator D. R.
[6] Verena Meier drew my attention to the difference between the static view of a circle as a perimeter and its conception
as the path of a movement closed in itself.

Logical circularity: While a straight line expresses a relationship between two distant points, the curved, closed line of the circle depicts the relationship of a point to itself. As a self-referent figure, the circle is the trace of a distance which negates itself.

Existential circularity: In circular movement there is no change. Leaving and returning refer to the same place. At the same time, time is reduced to simultaneity and extended to eternity. This distinguishes the circle from the equally reflexive spiral, which breaks open into a dimension of change.

These peculiarities are also central to the understanding of a variety of terms discussed at the present time, reaching from Hofstadter's (1979) "self-referent structure" (Hofstadter, 1979) to Münchhausen's "moor-rescue-method" (Albert, 1980), from Maturana's and Varela's joint "Autopoiesis" (Maturana and Varela, 1987) to Luhmann's "self-referent systems" (Luhmann, 1984), from Russell's "vicious circle" to Zermelo's harmless one, from the "hermeneutic circle" Schleiermacher inherited from the Reformation to the "ontological circle" Heidegger found when deconstructing human existence. In order to follow this discussion one must not confuse the two dimensions of circularity, the logical one of self-reference, and the existential one of stability.[7] Only their clear conceptual separation permits insight into the intricate connection they form in the paradox.

Surrounded by traditional symbols and innovative thinkers, you may agree to stay at this level of abstraction for a while, and follow the line of their horizon before descending, well oriented as I hope, into the concreteness of the geography it encloses.

He: "I won't say that this does not interest me."
She: "So you are interested in it?!"
He: "No. I did not say that..."

What do you say to such argumentation? It is common, yes, and we know quite well what is meant. But it is logically impossible - illogical according to the forms of conventional reasoning, the rules of traditional logic. In this system $((-A) -A) = A$. This is determined by the specific axiomatic basis of traditional

---

[7] Equivalent to the distinction between logical and existential dimensions is that between reason and cause. Among the variety of causes Aristotle distinguished (*causa materialis, -formalis, -finalis, -efficiens*), the present meaning of *cause* refers to only one of these, namely the *causa efficiens*. The relation between cause and effect is an existential relation. Reason, on the other hand, is defined as the explanation given in order to justify or prove statements or actions. The relation between reason and consequence is a logical relation.

There are many different concepts of causality. This, however, does not limit the possibility of comparing causal dimension and existential dimension. Calling the existential dimension of change a *causal dimension* merely provides it with a direction, and does not further predetermine its nature.

Based on the principle of causality (*nihil fit sine causa*), there exists a variety of propositions about the relationship between cause (*causa efficiens*) and effect. The positivist's emphasis on regular joint occurrence of two consecutive events (whereby the earlier is called the cause of the latter) is challenged by conceptions of causality used in action theory. (Von Wright (1974, pages 76-80) describes the possibility of a simultaneous occurrence of cause and effect and even that of temporally retro-active causation. He suggests that one should distinguish between cause and effect by comparing their different (theoretical) possibilities of being intentionally influenced.) The Realists propose yet another concept of causation. It is linked to inner necessity or essence. "Harrè argues that to view causal relations as consisting only of temporal precedence and regular succession, is to fail to distinguish between the meaning of statements asserting such relations, and the kind of evidence upon which they may be based" (Keat and Urry, 1984, page 29).

logic.[8] The axiom of identity is the origin of its concept of concepts: A = A. Here A denotes itself, here the equality sign denotes identity.[9] It is the transcendent identity of something resting in itself. Simultaneity is implied in this equality sign, as well as eternity. Traditional, formal logic is existentially circular. It does not have a dimension of change. The equations of our statistical calculations and models in human geography also are existentially circular. That is why they qualify for establishing powerful holds.

But this power begins to break where the circle breaks. It occurs when the notion of action demands the recognition of its crucial role in logic. It occurs when thinking demands to be considered as an act.[10] In cases of self-reference this demand becomes imperative. Under the strain of permitting self-reference *and* guaranteeing stability (and therefore excluding change), the power of the circle breaks. Out of the cracks creeps man, the acting subject (were there birds in eggs?), look! ... But the fine cracks may be viciously invisible...

Let's take a closer look therefore: but where from? There are several positions from which to watch and explain the breaking of the existential circle of traditional logic. One of them is its own perspective, that of conventional thinking:

In describing this position I take up a certain position. It is closer to dialectics, and this implies that I have to accept the importance of conventional logic. It is close to dialectics because this position is the one that is consistent in conventional logic' terms. Damned longing for consistency! What else could I do? As long as remain reasoning, my stance is circular itself...

From conventional logic's point of view, the breaking of the existential circl of stability is the origin of the paradox. A *paradox* is defined as a logica contradiction resulting from apparently correct argumentation, based o apparently true premises.[11] Paradoxical arguments thus can neither b considered true, nor false, and appear - from this perspective - as "meaningless"

The definition of classes in set theory is the classical site for findin paradoxes, broken circles. In trying to deduce the arithmetic axioms fror

---

No matter which concept of causality one has in mind; all of them are characterized by an asymmetrical relationsh between cause and effect. This excludes a circular influence of one element upon itself via the other.

[8] The first axiom of conventional, traditional, formal logic is that of identity (for all A: A = A), the second one prohib contradiction (for all A: A ≠ -A), the third axiom is that of the excluded middle (for all A: A = B or A ≠ B). They a supplemented and completed by a fourth axiom, that of sufficient reason (which states that everything has a reason f being as it is, or, more precisely, that the trinity of the former axioms is sufficient for logical reasoning.)

These axioms, reaching back to Aristotle, and partly reformulated by Leibnitz, provide the basis for a theory of concepts (axiom of identity), for a theory of assertion (Schlusstheorie) (axiom of contradiction), for a theory of inferen (axiom of the excluded middle), and for a theory of method (axiom of sufficient reason). See Günther, 1976.

The derived ((-A) -A) = A, the principle *duplex negatio affirmat* is also called 'the stability principle'. Marcha (1979, page 248) discusses it, citing examples from the field of human geography.

[9] For a general analysis of the different meanings of *is*, see Wittgenstein (1962, paragraph 558). For a discussion of t function of the equality sign in logical reasoning in the human sciences, see Olsson (1980, pages 21b-36b and 64b-69b).

[10] In his paper on Hintikka's logic (1986b), Olsson writes about the social conventions inherent in the seeming absolute rules of deductive reasoning. Emphasizing the moment of persuasion and rhetoric in the core of su reasoning, he concludes in a way similar to my argument: "Hintikka's performative readings of Descartes come to mi as well, for there are 'thought-acts' just as there are 'speech acts'.

[11] The notion of the paradox cannot be defined more precisely. The appeal to intuition in the "apparently correct" characteristic. The notion furthermore covers a variety of phenomena ranging from antinomies or paradoxes in a form logical system to pseudo-antinomies or paradoxes in other systems, i.e., the ordinary language. (See also: Kutsche 1964, page 41).

formal logic, it struck Frege, and after Cantor had defined set theory (powerful enough to include and found mathematics), he too had to face it: antinomies arose. Two propositions, well deduced according to the rules of the system, (either Frege's or Cantor's) contradicted each other. Most famous among these antinomies is Russell's paradox of the set of all sets which do/do not include themselves as one element.[12] The result of the occurrence of antinomies was not only a severe crisis of mathematics - it recovered in broken spirits only[13] - but also the designation of a new "danger": the "cercle vicieux" (Poincaré, 1906), or the "vicious circle" (Russell, 1908). Here "circle" refers to a logical relation, not to the figure of existential stability. The vicious circle emerges because classical (Fregean) logic fails to define a directionality which would enable fundamental hierarchical distinctions between the entities it deals with.[14]

In the theory of types[15] briefly referred to above, Russell suggests such a combination of distinction and directionality: the theory imposes a hierarchical structure on objects and sets. (Level one in this hierarchy consists of individual elements, level two of sets of these elements, level three of sets of the sets from level two, ... From one level to the next generality increases.) By imposing these levels, the theory of types distinguishes variables by their power of defining other variables. A high level variable can define the order of a low

---

[12] It is impossible to describe precisely Russell's set-theory paradox in ordinary language notation. Nevertheless, this rough translation is supposed to give a general impression: a set consists of elements that share at least one characteristic. Examples are the set of all geographers, or the set of all words of the English language. While in the latter example, the English word *set* can itself be an element of the class it encloses, this is impossible in the former. The English word *set* cannot be an element of the set of all geographers. As a next step, one can form the set of all the sets that can contain themselves as an element (the set of English words would be an element of this set), and call it "E". Equally, one can form a set "NE" out of all sets that cannot contain themselves as an element. Since the two are exhaustive, every set has to be either an element of "E", or of "NE", and naturally this both holds for "E" and "NE". Now the stage is set for the paradox of sets: if "NE" contains itself as an element of itself, then it is not an element of itself. If, on the other hand, "NE" does not contain itself as an element of itself, then it is an element of itself. ....

[13] Here I refer to the four different schools of mathematics that emerged out of the fundamental crisis brought about by the occurrence of antinomies: the set-theoretical school (represented e.g., by the Bourbaki group), Logicism (Whitehead, Russell), Intuitionism (Brouwer), and Formalism (Hilbert). (See e.g., Heitsch; 1976, Breger, 1982.) According to Thiel (1972, page 128), this fundamental crisis was still unsettled sixty years after its beginning. It was suppressed by the pragmatic output of topologists, number-theorists, probability-theorists, functional-analysts, or algebraic-theorists.

Moreover, it is interesting to note that Brouwer, in his efforts to reconstruct mathematics fundamentally after the collapse caused by the appearance of paradoxes, suggested conceiving of mathematics as an *activity* rather than a stable formal system. He clearly distinguished between the secondary formal expression of mathematics and the primary creative action, the process of doing mathematics.

[14] Hierarchy is a combination of distinction and directionality (V. Meier, personal conversation).

[15] In fact, Russell published two different "theories of types" of which the later one, the so-called "branched theory of types" specified the former more closely (Thiel, 1972, page 99ff)

Poincaré drew an even more radical conclusion from the appearance of antinomies: he challenged the concept of infinity used in mathematics, particularly in set theory. By classifying phenomena into categories permitting vicious circularity, i.e., by forming impredicative definitions, he argues, one is adding one element to the elements of the set. Such classification may lead to the infinite extension of this totality. To him, the concept of "set" only makes sense if it is conceived either as a finite totality, or as an actually existent infinity. Antinomies, then, point to the impossibility of the existence of such actual infinity. Therefore, he thinks that it must have been an ontological misconception that has lead to the formation of antinomies. Poincaré suggested thinking of infinity as of a potentiality instead, as a possibility of infinitely continuing to add one to every number. Thereby he supported the institutionalist's view of mathematics and shared their rejection of the logical principle *tertium non datur* (of two mutually exclusive statements one must be true) for such potentially infinite sets.

level one, but not vice versa.[16] No variable can define its own order.   "No
totality can contain members defined in terms of itself" (Russell).[17]

For the realm of semantic logic, Carnap (1934) and Tarski (1935) suggested a
similar criterion for meaningful assertions. It is based on the logical distinction
between different levels of language: metalanguage and language. The former
is the level used to talk about the latter. The distinction of the object of an
assertion and the assertion itself excludes the possibility of so-called *semantic*
paradoxes. An example of these is the paradox of Epimenides, the Cretan liar
who said "All Cretans are liars.", or, more topically, that of saying that
everything written here is false. That is what it is.

Apart from relations between classes or concepts, and relations between
assertions at different levels of language, there is a third type of relation in
which paradoxes had to be ruled out: relations between actions. Watzlawick
(1985, page 186) calls them *pragmatic paradoxes*, and cites the historic example
of the situation of persecuted Christians who were forced to renounce their
religion by taking an oath referring to their own god. (Appealing to the
authority of their Christian God to guarantee the renouncement from this God
not only put them into the paradox, but also into the inescapable position of
negating the basis of negation through the very act of negating. It also raised
questions as to the obligation arising out of this oath.) Paradox situations like
this are sometimes referred to as "double-bind". The most common answer to
this type of paradox is to become schizophrenic.

In all three types of relations mentioned, relations between classes, between
assertions, and between actions, the methods of eliminating paradoxes are
basically the same. Distinctions are drawn, and hierarchic directionality is
imposed on the whole system. Thus they provide space for defining, talking, or
acting, however limited that space might be, since the directions for these
activities are severely restricted. Familiar structures - secure stability.

The price for this stability is the impossibility of the activity of self-reference.
In a system of existential circularity, the rules for eliminating paradoxes logically
exclude any activity turning back to its origin.   Self-reference leads to
"meaningless" results: language used for reflecting about language, human
beings thinking about human beings, members of a certain society talking about
their society, human sciences investigating human sciences: all this is illegal. All
this remains outside the limits of conventional reasoning. This is the realm of
the unsayable. In the *Tractatus*, Wittgenstein pointed to this realm, the sphere
where things can only show themselves. In response to the *Tractatus*, Russell
once again offered the method of hierarchical ordering as a solution to
Wittgenstein's problem.[18] But this is no definite solution. It merely pushes the
problem into infinite regress. The hierarchy of levels functions as a means of
hiding paradoxes in infinity, well removed from visibility.

The stringent division of objects that the various hierarchy-solutions are
based on directly parallels other familiar divisions: actor and spectator, observer

---

[16] Conventional thinking defines by reference to a higher order level (e.g., by *genus proximum et differentia specifica*,
by a level of operational instruction), i.e., through more general concepts, statements about statements, action
explaining actions. (If we believe that the number of concepts, assertions, or actions is infinite, this becomes more than
just a practical necessity.)

[17] Russell (1908), quoted in Thiel (1972, page 101).

[18] In the last paragraph of his introduction to Wittgenstein's *Tractatus*, Russell wrote: "These difficulties suggest the
possibility that every language, as Mr. Wittgenstein says, has a structure about which one cannot make statements in the
language itself. But there could be another language, dealing with the structure of the former one, having a structure
itself. And it could be that the hierarchy of languages is infinite." (Translator D. R.)

and observed, subject and object... Since their actions are prohibited to influence other than lower order levels, the observed clearly differ from the observers, the untouchables. Yet it must be asked: do we really have to challenge these disctinctions, and up to what point? A paper, a book, a discipline that would do that, and concede a mutual influence between observer and observed, certainly would lie outside the realm of conventional logic.

In this world outside, the possibility of capturing definite identity is lost. Paradoxes viciously undermine such possibility, rendering concepts such as correctness and falsity meaningless. A decision between different statements, all similarly paradoxical, cannot be made on logical grounds. In a system that contains paradoxes, relativity and plurality cannot be excluded.

It is for these reasons that (from the perspective of conventional logic) paradoxes mark a limit to what can be said, a limit to what can be defined or proven, a limit to what can be known. In many different disciplines limitative theorems[19] precisely define the boundary. Any attempt to cross it without falling into paradox must fail and will only push the limit ahead on a way that leads into infinite regress. Do we need a limitative theorem at all for the human sciences, for human geography?

Razor blade in the eye. Cross. Do I have to analyze circularity, dissect the eye that looks at me? Your eye. Looking into your eyes I can't see you. Self-reflection. In your eyes my eyes in which I can see your eyes with my eyes... Forget the razor blade!
... But who are you? "Whatever we see could be other than it is."[20] *Not arbitrarily different, but infinitely other. This I am certain of. - At least until I throw away his ladder. ... Damned scientific steps, up to dissect in the name of security. Who have you been? One more corpse. Deadfined... "Defined what can only be experienced."*[21] *Forget the eyes.*

Self-referent science must stay outside the limits of conventional logic. Its arguments can only provide relative answers to the questions of identity: What is it? What do you mean? Who is the I that is me? Who are you? Relative answers. Still, not arbitrary ones. This kind of thinking takes refuge in the evidence of everyday worlds: at the level of concepts, assertions, and actions infinity is delimited by the Lebensform. Truth is regional, identity is regional[22], the I is open wide...

---

[19] For various types of systems, analyses have pointed out the limits they respectively face in their attempt at describing themselves by means of their own symbolism: Wittgenstein defined the general limit of the sayable. Tarsky that of empirical assertions, Russell the limits for the definition of sets according to Cantor's system, Gödel the limits of decidability in axiomatic systems (used to derive mathematics from logic) like that of Russell and Whitehead and thereby the limits to Hilbert's program of proving the consistency and completeness of this system by means of (a smaller part of) its own methods. Based on Gödel's work, Church limited decidability in classical mathematical logic. Turing revealed the existence of ineluctable limits in even the most powerful computers one can think of. (For a more detailed description, see Hofstadter, 1979.)

[20] Wittgenstein (1982) 5.634.

[21] Olsson (1980, page 27e).

[22] This is how, as I understand it, our thinking can move beyond objectivism and relativism, and transcend the burden of this damned dualism. (For a brief summary of the arguments in favor of its transcendence, see Gregory, 1985).

C.F. Reuterswärd: "THE I" (1984)

Let me, whoever that may be, return to geography to take up and reconside my initial proposition: for most of the research we do within geography and th human sciences in general, the assumption of a clear logical distinction betwee different levels of analysis does not hold. Our investigations tend to be logical circular, they even have to be, if they are to lead to meaningful results.

From their beginning in modernity onwards (Foucault, 1974), this circulari lay in the very core of the human sciences the sciences where human being reflect on themselves: subject and object are not separate, indeed inseparabl They are inseparable because they are profoundly separated. Their unity necessitated by a more profound distinction: the general metaphysical dualisr the crevasse separating thinking and that which is thought, mind and body, the and the "I", does not permit a clear separation of observer and observed. This what "*duality*" means, why it neither means unity, nor difference, but both.

Subject and object of our research in human geography are not separat because they are connected through interpretation. Interpretation presuppos sound knowledge of the world of other men. It presupposes the knowledge its symbolic system, for what is to be interpreted is itself interpretation: doub hermeneutics[23]. Knowledge is the necessary precondition of knowledge.

Recognition of this mutual relationship, of the duality of seemingly distin dualistic opposites, is now generally accepted in human geography. Sayer (198 page 24) considers the dualism between subject and object of analysis a serio misconception. He assigns it to a group of similarly misconceived dualisms, e. that between subjectivity and objectivity, or between the expressive and th referential function of language. The "insider"/"outsider" dualism is anoth example. Buttimer (1984, page 65) argues that "it is the duty of the geograph not to represent solely the insider's or the outsider's perspective, but to acce the challenge that results from the dialectic opposition between these views .. A similar critique of the logical distinction between hierarchical levels in hum geography is raised by Curry and Barnes (1986), Marchand (1979, page 23 Jackson and Smith (1984, page 38), Gregory (1979, page 168ff), Gregson (198 and many others. They plead for a conception that permits an active role f

---

[23] Giddens (1984, pages 95, 179).

agents on both sides of the dual structure and emphasize their mutual influence. Basically, this implies that the various forms of type-theoretical reductions imposed on such mutual relationships cannot be usefully applied in a geography of man. With it collapse - as a logical consequence - conventional logical consequences, and all mathematical and statistical procedures based on this mode of reasoning. Valuable as they are in other realms, when it comes to research of/about self-reflecting human beings, they are inadequate.

The radicality and difficulty of this consequence turns out in practice. Engaged in participant observation, exploratory investigations, or dialogic research, we balance on the thin line between the dualism and duality of observers and observed. In this position it may be less important to listen to people's answers than to listen to their questions:

"What do you want?"
   Who takes the initiative to ask?
"Why are you interested in us?"
   Who defines the research problem?
"Who gives you the right to be interested in us?"
   Who legitimizes this research theme?
"What does this imply for us?"
   What change does it make for those who defined the problem?
   ....
"Who are you?"
   Why are they interested in me?

Questions making me ask. *Are* there general answers? Categorical imperatives? I do not know. Nothing to offer, but a reply from a meta level: accept the struggle with the paradoxy of each situation. Just *because* there is no chance to win. Here too, "every victory in the game of the master is a victory of the master of the game".[24]

The logical circularity of research in human geography accounts for the *relativity* and *plurality* we recognize in this field. It is a relativity and plurality at all levels: from the epistemological and ontological basis of various approaches, the level of different theories of science (e.g., Gregory, 1979, 1984; Johnston, 1983), to different perspectives in the problem definition (Hard, 1973, Bartels and Hard, 1975)[25], and from various hypotheses explaining a defined phenomenon to a multitude of interpretations of the practical and ethical consequences of using these explanations.

The ongoing discussion about relativity and plurality in human geography often is considered to be the result of the specific situation; for example, after the ebbing of the wave of the quantitative revolution, and (in German speaking geography), the late reaction to 1960s self-dissolution of "Länderkunde". In view of the fundamental logical circularity of human geography, and the undecidability resulting from its paradoxical stance, plurality and relativity on

---

[24] Descombes, 1981, page 176. Kafka repeatedly thematized the paradox *exterritoriality* of individual human beings in a (social) world they helped construct. In his notebook he wrote: "Im Kampf zwischen dir und der Welt sekundiere der Welt. Man darf niemanden betrügen, auch nicht die Welt um ihren Sieg." (quoted in Hoffer, 1986, page 148).

[25] Naturally, all these levels are related. Still, it is interesting to see that the pluralism discussion in German speaking and Anglo-American geography focused on different levels when talking about plurality: while Anglo-American geography was interested in the plurality of philosophical approaches, German speaking geographers concentrated on the plurality of perspectives the central concept of "Erdoberfläche" (and later also "sozialräumliche Organisation" was looked at). Hard (1973) describes this difference.

all levels must be considered as its natural condition. Rather than worryin about a "new tribalism" in geography,[26] insight into this logical circularity lea me to question the mechanisms that could - not long ago - produce more uni in the appearance of our discipline. It makes me suspicious abo contemporary calls for a renewed interior homogeneity of geography, uttered c the pretext that disciplinary "foreign policy" would require displaying a cle profile to observers from outside[27].

Much more interest than disciplinary discussions about the reduction plurality and relativity deserve inquiries into their consequences in huma geography. What do they imply for the possibility of dialogue and criticism? What do they mean for (research) ethics? Are there general criteria for these What are the consequences of plurality and relativity for the position of huma geography with respect to covering and legitimizing political decisions?[29] Th logical impossibility of finding a "*common ground*" may oblige us to go beyor the narrow perspective of our own position and to recognize the point in others This, probably, is what is meant by "*common search*".

Let me summarize what I see from the tower of conventional reasonin, unable to accept all the implications of traditional logic, but observing tl standards of logical consistency and completeness, as well as the omnipresei goal of reducing insecurity by defining identity, human geographers caught tl paradox. It is our dependence on the circle of self-reference, and ot simultaneously seeking support in the stability of the existential circle, that pu us in this position. It is very hard to stay there, however, face to face with tl paradox, and to resist the temptation of sneaking away, back into the hallway dualistic distinctions. Its doors are invitingly open. One, for example, is that b which authors shut themselves out from the domain of their texts. Mar philosophical-, social-, and psychological theorists used this escape and gave to the paradox. (Or, should I say, they tucked the paradox under their arms an carried it to another level?) "... If nobody can escape this necessity, and if n one is therefore responsible for giving in to it, however little, this does not mea that all ways of giving in to it are of equal pertinence" (Derrida, 1978, translate in Sturrock, 1979, page 175). Gadamer, for example, certainly knew what h was doing when proposing the absolute, a-historical validity of historic conditionality as a basis of hermeneutic analysis (1975, pages XXI and 324ff Foucault was not the first to question the legitimacy of psychoanalysis as means for the liberation of the self. He himself, provided us with valuab knowledge on the intricate connections between power and knowledge. "Oublier Foucault", Baudrillard suggests, asking if "this era does not have t have ended already, if one is able to express insights ... about it, as definite

---

[26] Berry (1980, page 45) in his presidential address, delivered at the AAG meeting in Louisville, 1980.

[27] These arguments often have very concrete consequences for young geographers. (I feel obliged to write this becau it does not hold for me.)

Apart from this, it is questionable if, from a pragmatical point of view, a multifaceted discipline would not have better stance in a multifaceted society (P. Weichhart, 1987). Also, more fundamentally, it is not evident at all why th need for generalization to increase the "visibility" of geography from the distance should have anything to do with inn homogeneity and discipline.

[28] For a brief discussion of the forms of criticism possible in a pluralistic discipline, see e.g., Reichert, 1987a.

[29] Here we are right in the midst of inquiries about the relationship between power and knowledge, there, where Olsse (1985) asks: "Is the power in the authority of the author or in the auditing of the audience? Or is power at the same tir everywhere and nowhere, always erosive yet in every glance, every touch, every mouthful?"

[30] Foucault (1974), but see also Dreyfus and Rabinow (1983, page 174ff). For an assessment in relation to research geography, see e.g., Driver, 1985.

those Foucault expresses" (1983, page 12). And from where does Baudrillard...[31]

... mere echoes of Hegel's critique of Kant's "Copernican Turn": "Reason, by drawing a limit and distinguishing between the phenomenon and the thing in itself, proves that this distinction actually refers to itself. It does not reach its own limit, but stays inside its boundaries by the act of drawing them. Drawing the limits of reason means that reason already has crossed them" (Hegel)[32]. When the stars no longer turn around the spectator, but the spectator turns around the stars, reflection becomes paradoxical. The limits of conventional reasoning are exposed, when the text is applied to its context. They are exposed, when the content is related to its form.

Seen from the position of conventional logic, the paradox is the essence, the vanishing-point of modern man's epistemological space. How could we human geographers escape the arena of our space?[33] Situated in the circus, cracking the whip, we are chasing more or less trained paradoxes. "Don't be afraid, it's merely self-reference." There it is, then, now that the validity of whatever is said and done is violated by the very act of saying and doing it. There it is that "everything is right in the beginning, but in the end it is all wrong"...[34]

Writing around circularity and self-reference

Dagmar Reichert

---

[31] I use the term "modernity" in the way Foucault (1974) does when describing the epistemological space that began with the Kantian turn.

Insofar as the society or era Baudrillard describes is living Nihilism in its most consequent form, it has not gone beyond modernity. Insofar as Baudrillard, through the very project of his writing, so stimulatingly contradicts its content, neither has he.

[32] It is quoted by Gadamer, 1975, page 325-326. I translated it from the German Original: ... "Dass die Vernunft indem sie eine Grenze ziehe und die Erscheinung vom Ding an sich unterscheide, diesen Unterschied in Wahrheit als ihren eigenen erweise. Sie gelange damit keineswegs an eine Grenze ihrer selbst, sondern sei vielmehr ganz bei sich selbst, indem sie diese Grenze setze. Denn das heisse, dass sie sie auch schon überschritten habe."

[33] Adorno suggests solving the problem of final reason by retreating from the realm of thought to that of the body. The negativity of physical pain would lay behind our intentions. "Die vermeintlichen Grundtatsachen unseres Bewusstseins sind ein anderes als bloss solche. In der Dimension von Lust und Unlust ragt Körperliches in sie hinein. Aller Schmerz und alle Negativität, Motor des dialektischen Gedankens, sind vielfach vermittelt, manchmal unkenntlich gewordene Gestalt von Physischem, so wie alles Glück auf sinnliche Erfüllung abzielt und es ihm seine Objektivität abgewinnt. ... In der Erkenntnis überlebt (das somatische Moment) als deren Unruhe, das sie in Bewegung bringt und in ihrem Fortgang unbesänftigt reproduziert; unglückliches Bewusstsein ist keine verblendete Eitelkeit des Geistes, sondern ihm inhärent, die einzige authentische Würde, die er in der Trennung vom Leib empfing. Sie erinnert ihn, negativ, an seinen leibhaften Aspekt: allein dass er dessen fähig ist, verleiht ihm Hoffnung ..." (1984, pages 202-203).

Recourse to - or primacy of - the body is a central theme in Nietzsche's writings (and not least through him in contemporary French philosophy (Descombes, 1981): "Put briefly: perhaps the entire revolution of the spirit is a question of the body; ... Our lust for knowledge of nature is a means through which the body desires to perfect itself ..." (Orig.: "Kurz gesagt: es handelt sich vielleicht bei der ganzen Entwicklung des Geistes nur um den Leib; ... Unsere Gier nach Erkenntnis der Natur ist ein Mittel, wodurch der Leib sich vervollkommnen will...") (Nietzsche, 1964, page 676). See also; Levin, 1985.

[34] Olsson (1986b, page 5).

Abstract
Cut into the skin of modernity, marking the body of the human sciences, is a
circular scar. One move in the process of dismantling the content and form of
research in human geography is my attempt to get to see it.

When the aim is a circle, the way to describe it cannot be straight. I search
for the limits of conventional reasoning, the paradox. Circular structures form
its basis. Depending on the point of view, paradoxes can be traced either to
logical circles, or to existential ones. Both views offer methods of limiting the
occurrence of paradoxes to clearly defined and consequently forbidden areas.
That is where the circles lie.

The glimpses I catch let me ask for more detailed investigations. I argue that
the domain of the human sciences, and of human geography in particular, lies in
the area beyond the realm of conventional logic. Research in human geography
is based on the circular relationship between subject and object, individual and
society, science and everyday practice, theory and facts. If measured by the
standards of conventional reasoning, such enterprise is paradoxical.

Research in human geography has an implicit dimension of change. The
idea of continuous time lies at its core. If described in the discontinuous time of
conventional reasoning, change is lost in discrete, black bars.

One may turn to dialectical reasoning for help and adopt the specific
objectives it implies. They demand a different conception of what we mean by a
human science, one that is closely related to social processes. Yet, when I am
about to consider this as a solution, another, even more fundamental circle
turns up. Just as the merits of dialectics take shape in the eyes of those looking
from the basis of conventional logic, the dialectic position makes visible the
merits of conventional reasoning. In several respects its concept of identity is
implied in dialectical logic.

Reaching beyond the area of conventional logic as well as beyond the
opposed one of dialectics, the human sciences touch the sharp edge separating
the two. There they are: presentiments of the scar of modernity: cut into the
cornea of our eyes, the circle refracts our sight. No surprise then: it
circumscribes any text written in this context and makes it paradoxical.

... And I demand all the ignorance you can afford, offering you an abstract
that pretends it could not be other than it is, that pretends to lie outside the
circle, along the smoothness of unbroken razor blades.

"Formal logic tells us that two soldiers belonging to the same regiment will
also belong to the same brigade and consequently also to the same division.
This is what the whole theory of inference comes down to. We hear that two
soldiers are in the same regiment and want to infer that they belong to the
same brigade. We can do that, provided that, while we are drawing the
conclusion, none of the soldiers is transferred to another regiment."

(Poincaré, page 100)

Although seeming militaristic and more banal than it is, Poincaré's argument
was not only significant enough to shake the foundations of mathematics (Ch.
Thiel, 1972, page 144ff), it was also the point from which to turn the human
sciences upside down. Maybe this has put them in a better position anyway, but
this is a secondary question.

Primarily, Poincaré shows that the rules of formal logic, those of
conventional reasoning, calculating and modeling in human geography are only

valid if the schema of classification and the assignment of elements to classes remain constant during the time of the inference. With similar arguments one can ask for invariability in the sense and reference of concepts, assertions and actions. Reasonable as these demands may seem (they must not be mixed up with the *ceteris paribus* assumption[35]), there are cases in which they lose their validity. Such cases, as I intend to show, are the majority of cases we deal with in human geography and in the human sciences in general. They are cases where the *existential circle is broken*.

In its pure aesthetic harmony this circle is a vey rich and old metaphor: earlier, and differing from the inward-oriented perimeters of our Thünen, Burg~ regionalization, geographical tradition, it ~resented a closed path~ the Ouroboros, the snake that eats it~ ~circle occurs i~

Self-reflection blows up the metaphysical basis[36] of traditional logic: Günther (1976) shows how it - via its basis axioms - implies the assumption of a transparent relation between human consciousness and things. In a logic of identity, where things are stable and categories are frozen, there is no gap between man and the world. Self-consciousness is the result of a "double reflection",[37] one on the previous taken-for-granted, and one on the reflecting consciousness. Through it, the constitutive activity of human consciousness can first be seen. Man creeps out, the identity and stability of the object vanishes. The logical circle breaks.

The power of traditional logic breaks where the circle breaks. It occurs when the notion of action demands the recognition of its cruciai role in logic. It occurs when thinking demands to be considered as an act. In cases of self-reference, this demand becomes imperative. Under the strain of permitting self-referenc and guaranteeing stability (and therefore excluding change) the power of the circle breaks. Out of the crack creeps man, the acting subject (were there birds in eggs?), look!

... But the fine cracks may be viciously invisible ...

---

[35] A *ceteris paribus* ("other things being equal") assumption usually is made when describing the dependency of (social) phenomena on certain variables (e.g., by means of a regression equation). It implies that the simultaneous effects other variables have on the phenomenon remain the same.

Compared to this, the stability assumption made in the logic of conventional reasoning does not refer to the structure of influences of variables, but to the definition of the variables and phenomena themselves, that is to their conceptualization.

[36] The relationship between logic and metaphysics was already discussed by Russell and Whitehead in the *Principia Mathematica*. In their explanation of the occurrence of antinomies, they returned to the ontological basis of this logic, to the problem of universals. They argued that it is mistaken to make the platonic assumption that abstract constructs such as classes or concepts exist independently of a superior level of human thinking. The platonic world is broader than the area classical logic is able to cover (Kutschera, 1964). Its domain is limited to entities which can be constructed according to certain principles of hierarchical distinction.

Let us look more closely, therefore, but wait: first turn round and see what we have passed: the power of conventional logic comes from the stability in promises. Valuable promise. Dissecting continuity into a series of instant pictures, it makes the world stand still, makes it certain, intersubjectively visible Its existential circularity guarantees stability. The logical circularity of self-reference breaks it. It therefore must be ruled out. This at least is how circularity looks from conventional reasoning's point of view. Forced by paradoxes, conventional reasoning forces us to recognize the incompatibility of existential circularity and logical circularity and provides arguments in favor of the former. [37]

Now we can turn back again to look at circularity from another position, leading us to a different explanation and to different consequences. It is the position of dialectical logic.

He: "I won't say that this does not interest me."
She: "So you are interested in it?"
He: "No. I did not say that..."

What do you say to such argumentation? *"Tertium datur.",* obviously it does, in spite of all (Didn't I understand when he said it?), or, "The middle can't be excluded, it seems."? You may be right, and there are logical systems following these suggestions[38], but I want to proceed in another direction: up into the future!

She may have understood him to suggest that she follow him to a new level of argumentation. The *"tertium non datur"* still held, held so tightly, that the present pressure left no escape but off to a new frame of reference,[39] a frame from which the old distinctions between the mutually exclusive alternatives can be challenged. One, for example, on which spoken words are imbedded in other forms of expressions.

We may understand each other, because we are prepared to give up the initial meaning of the "I", "won't", "say", "that", "this",..., the initial idea of a specific subject, object, predicate order, and perhaps even be prepared to give a

---

[37] Günther, 1976, page 54. Reflection on this double reflection, reflection on the reflection on this double reflection, and its continuation ad infinitum does not increase the extent of our self-consciousness. "Because thinking cannot transcend its self-consciousness, further reflection can only keep repeating this realm of consciousness, and no element of this infinite row of consecutive iterations may extend it" (Günther, 1976, page 54). Furthermore, this infinite regression inhibits any self definition of the subject.

Günther suggests the possibility of bridging this quicksand by a third level of reflection. This level promises a possibility for an extension of human consciousness, and for an absolute self-definition of man, one that cannot be subjected to infinite reflective iteration. Human existence "is the infinite depth of self-consciousness" (1976, page 57). The fundamental basis of this level of reflection is the impossibility of a basis itself. (This third level that Günther describes is not new. It is the level on which the existentialists and many others find refuge. What is new in Günther's work is that he tries to describe this level in terms of axioms.)

Günther argues that this third level of reflection is solid enough to found his "meontic logic", the logic of non-being, of a reflective consciousness that exceeds, and therefore forms, the being which is given to it. It is a logic of change. The axioms Günther defines for this logic are sketches of the skeleton of Hegelian dialectics. This is all very promising. I only wish I could understand how Günther can separate form and content of knowledge to claim that the self-definition of consciousness as an infinite sequence of reflections is not reflection itself.

[38] Stegmüller (1975, pages 147-220) gives a summary of the systems of many valued logic, as well as of other logical systems, e.g., temporal logic, modal logic, or normative logic (deontic logic). For the use of alternative logical systems in human geography, see Gale (1972) or Olsson (1980).

[39] Beautifully mechanistic metaphor! Never. Mind. Suffices.

different answer to the "who is speaking?". We may understand each other because we permit that which we formerly grasped as "identity" to change. It changes as it moves from "then" to "now", it changes by changing contexts of reference. We may understand because we understand the activity of self-reference (Was not his argument logically circular?), we may understand because we understand change (Has not his argument broken the stable existential circle?).

Being logically circular, *hermeneutic interpretation* escapes the paradox through the break in the circle of existential stability. Hermeneutic interpretation is a dialectical movement. On its spiral path, the hermeneutic "circle"[40] leads to new understanding. It is an understanding directed not primarily to the other who speaks, but, via the other, aiming at the shared object of reference[41]. Although such understanding cannot reach an absolute agreement, it is no "meaningless" result, rather results in meaning. From the perspective of conventional logic, this is out of sight. The dialectical perspective makes it visible. Judging from there, Gadamer happily concedes that "it was clear from the beginning, that logically, hermeneutic interpretation is circular" (1975, page 178). It is circular insofar as the whole, with respect to which its parts are to be understood, are not given independently of the parts. Whether in the relationship between the parts and the whole, in the relationship between the present and the past, or that between one human being and the other, all hermeneutic interpretation must presuppose that both sides form a consistent totality, a basic universe of meaning. This may easily be accepted for a text, even for the course of history, but it is very difficult to be identified in the great cultural and individual plurality of mankind. The universal meaning may lie so

---

[40] The hermeneutic circle actually is a spiral. It is the trace of a continuous movement of interpretation between an understanding of the parts determining the consequent understanding of the whole which, in turn, leads to a new understanding of the parts... . For describing the hermeneutic circle in more detail, one has to draw a distinction between the circle as an expression of the method of understanding (Schleiermacher) and hermeneutic circularity and understanding as an existential characteristic of human being. (Heidegger, Gadamer). See: Gadamer (1975, page 164 and 277), Habermas (1973, page 214) or Bernstein (1983, page 131ff).

[41] There are significant differences between the hermeneutic theories of Schleiermacher and Gadamer with respect to the truth-status understanding can demand, and the object understanding can aim for. These differences stem from Gadamer's emphasis on the relative position of an interpreter. Like the texts or actions he/she interprets, the activity of interpretation itself is not independent of its historical (social, political) context. The interpreter does not have a solid ground from which to judge the specificity of a text's or action's relation to its object, i.e., its truth or adequacy. All he/she can do is increase the understanding of the object of the text or action by adding its perspective to the one the interpreter has him-/herself. This, if I understand correctly, is what Gadamer means by extending one's horizon, or by "raising to a higher generality" in the quote given below.

It has two consequences: with respect to the object understanding is aiming at, it means that it cannot address it directly, but only via the way in which it is understood by someone else. Understanding is second-order understanding. "Das Ziel aller Verständigung und alles Verstehens ist ein Einverständnis in der Sache" (1975, page 276). ("The aim of all communication and understanding is an agreement about the object.") With respect to the truth-status understanding can demand, it implies that the interpreter cannot claim to have a final, absolute knowledge of the second-order object. "Die Ausschöpfung des wahren Sinns aber ist ... ein unendlicher Prozess." (1975, page 282). ("But completing the true meaning ... is an infinite process.")

By drawing these conclusions from the "Wirkungsgeschichtlichkeit" of human being, Gadamer transcends the position of the hermeneutics of German Romanticism.

(What I still do not understand is how "historisches Bewusstsein der eigenen Gegenwart" (self-consciousness about our present historical context), which is the precondition for the crucial openness an interpreter has to preserve towards a text or action (to notice possible contradiction), can be reached under conditions of living in the context of "Wirkungsgeschichte". I trust that the answer can be found in the rich source of "Wahrheit und Methode".)

close to us that we cannot see it. We suspect that it lies in the taken-for-granted of our everyday life. ... Did you notice? Low rustle from the edge of dialectical reasoning: what kind of identity is this consistent, universal totality which the dialectical negation of identity has to presuppose? Let's go on, pretending we have not heard anything ...

There is "an unavoidable hermeneutic component in the sciences of man" (Ch. Taylor, 1975, page 178). *Hermeneutic theory*, particularly the enabling role of prejudices and the relativity of the position of the interpreter it emphasizes, bears direct relevance to practical work in human geography: as researchers we may have to learn to listen again.

Still, our work is not reproductive, but productive. It is not done with an accurate description of the problem, even if given by experts such as the people concerned, rather than by those undertaking the research. The productivity of our work unfolds in a dialogic process between the two. "The art ... of understanding is not described correctly and sufficiently by saying that one has to learn to put oneself into a foreign horizon. ... It is ... neither empathy of one individuality with the other, nor subordination of the other to one's own criteria, but always a raising to a higher generality which transcends the own particularity as well as that of the others" (Gadamer, 1975, page 287)[42]. This "raising to a higher generality" is what we aim for in the human sciences. The motor of this dialectical movement is the logical contradiction between a known and an unknown position, the own particularity, and that of the other. Vooom. There it is again: presentiments of the limit of dialectic reasoning: we just stumbled over the identity-relation of logical contradiction in the core of dialectics. Let us clean off the dirt, pretend nothing has happened, and go on a bit further, exploring the position of dialectical logic:

In choosing between existential and logical circularity, dialectical reasoning comes out in favor of the latter, i.e., in favor of self-reference. Nevertheless, i must concede: formal logic determines what self-reference is still looking for: *Identity*.[43]

And what about the identity of self-reference itself? If we use language to refer to language, or refer to science by means of scientific symbolism, we can never completely represent it. We describe the other/prior self they were without/before the act of referring to "itself". It is exactly the attempt at defining its identity by which self-reference undermines the identity i represents and consequently changes in the process. Every act of self-reference either transforms the extension (or intention) of the "self", or even leads to it partial or complete restructuring. This is an opportunity, but at the same time limitation. Logical circularity limits our knowledge, making every assertion dependent on prior conditions (the well known "Wirkungsgeschichte", and historical conditionality are but one expression of this boundary), and it limit the lasting of our knowledge. Naturally, it does not permit a disengage observer. Knowledge, gained through self-reference, cannot be objective,[44] it i moral. It is in these respects that the limitations of our subjectivity form the source of our ability to know.

---

[42] Translated from the German original: "... die Kunst des ... Verstehens ist nicht dadurch richtig und zureichend beschrieben, dass man lerne, sich in fremde Horizonte zu versetzen, ... Es ... ist weder Einfühlung einer Individualität in eine andere, noch auch Unterwerfung des anderen unter die eigenen Massstäbe, sondern immer die Erhebung zu einer höheren Allgemeinheit, die nicht nur die eigenen Polarität, sondern auch die des anderen überwindet." (Gadamer, 1975, page 287).

[43] "Who is man? The one who must create what he would be." (Heidegger, quoted in Levin, 1985, page 7).

[44] For a brief summary of the different meanings of "objective", see e.g., Reichert (1987b).

The notion of self-reference as an activity - one that characterizes all living matter, birds (biological processes) as much as man (biological processes and conscious self-reflection) - radically differs from the lifeless notion of the A = A. When this active component finds a way into definitions or inferences in formal logic, it conflicts with existential circularity and predetermined identity. And when the existential circle is broken, it is time for change: from the dialectical perspective the process of change becomes visible. I remember seeing something resembling it when looking from conventional logic's point of view: existential stability did not imply that conventional logic is blind to the variation of situations over time. But do not be deceived by the resemblance: for formal logic and conventional mathematics change is discrete. Time is the relationship between two moments. Instead of conceiving of it - like Heraclit, James, Turner, or Bergson - as a continuous stream, it captures it as a series of slices, infinitesimally close, perhaps as in the integral, but still discontinuous.[45] Although there are some characteristics they have in common (in both, for example, our knowledge of time is a function of the amount of information available),[46] the *concepts of time* of classical logic and dialectics are fundamentally different.

In dialectical reasoning "everything is seen as in perpetual transition into something else: it is still itself, ... but it becomes, at the same time, another. The thing is realizing itself through ... successive transformation. It accumulates a history, an experience" (Marchand, 1979, page 2). Time as perpetual transition conflicts with "identity", with the stability of our social systems, particularly with the concept structure of our language. Marx called dialectic thinking "a threat for the bourgeoisie, because it understands every historical form in the flow of its movements, i.e., with respect to its transient side".[47] Adorno draws our attention to the static concept of the concept: it "is marked by archaic features which cross the rational ones; relics of static thinking and a static ideal of understanding in the midst of dynamically activated consciousness. Invariant in relation to the changes in what it captures, it creates a stable order. This is its imminent claim. ... In dialectics, thinking raises objections to the archaisms of its conceptuality. Above all, the concept in itself supposes content, its own form versus that which it contains. Thereby, however, it also supposes the principle of identity: that a fact in itself would be a solid, stable entity... . Identifying

---

[45] The terms "continuous" and "discrete" (or "discontinuous") are examples of the numerous spatial metaphors we use when talking about time. Here I want to use two characteristics to distinguish them; characteristics of the process of change, and characteristics of the units of meaning they form. A discrete process, then, is a consecutive series of isolated moments whereby each one can be defined or explained as an independent unit. A continuous process, on the other hand, is an unbroken movement, which cannot be split into isolated elements, because each movement could be defined and explained only by its relations to other moments.

This double criterion may permit a distinction between a discrete process consisting of infinitesimally small steps (a line consisting of points with infinitesimally small extension) and a continuous process.

[46] Writing about discrete time, Couclelis (1982, page 123) describes "urban time as a function of information". "Whatever the metaphysical essence of time may be, in the present context [urban system models] its flow can only be detected through the changes observed from one attribute sheet [here a table of attributes characterizing urban man] in a time series to the next." Since time is equivalent to a relation between attributes, and each attribute added to the table "greatly increases the variety of distinguishable states and, therefore, the probability of observing some change somewhere in the system, ... merely by adding information, we precipitate change." It is important to note the difference Couclelis draws between the *concept* of change and the kind of *evidence* upon which change may be detected.

[47] Marx, *Grundrisse*, quoted in Hubig (1978, page 112) ... translated from the German text: Die Dialektik ist "dem Bürgertum ein Greuel, weil sie ... jede gewordene Form im Flusse der Bewegung, also nach ihrer vergänglichen Seite hin auffasst."

thinking objectifies through the logical identity of the concept. Dialectics, according to their subjective side, aim at a thinking which no longer makes its objects stable and remaining constant in themselves; that they are such, experience refutes" (Adorno, 1984, page 156).[48]

I am not sure if this thinking "which no longer makes its objects stable' implies a concept of time as radical as that of Bergson. Like Adorno, however, Bergson appeals to experience in his remembrance of passed things, trying to comprehend time without grasping it. Like Adorno, he considers the "consecutive snapshots" as a view of time, which "satisfies the requisites of language, but is a poor and artificial reconstruction of change" (1985, page 26). Movement and change, in his experience, are absolutely indivisible. Change is the basic condition of the universe, and there are no objects of change underlying it. "Change does not require a bearer of change" (1985, page 167).[49] Except for the objective dialectic of Engels, dialecticians would not assume such a concept of time to hold for the whole universe.[50] For the development of human consciousness, however, they might, because it is change itself, "the inner laws of motion" (Marchand, 1979, page 251), and not positions which they want to explain. Thus a "spatial concept of time" (Bergson, 1985, page 24), time as the succession of adjacent, isolated moments, will be as inadequate as an ahistorical concept in which the "now" can be characterized independently of what happened before, and in which there is "no need to wait" (Bergson, 1985, page 31).

At that moment *she looked up from the sheet in front of her: how to write to express change as a flow ... the difficulty of following Marx's writing, changing perspectives through additive contextualization, Harvey describes that*[51] *... Santa Barbara discussions about linear descriptions of interwoven structures ... no, this is something else ... well, similar insofar as temporal contexts may be interwoven just like factual contexts ... machetes for thick descriptions ... come on ... metonymies, meaning moving through written environments ... would even characters move, the "in" up there run away from the "adequate" ... no more locations ... it would be interesting to think about the concept of space associated with Bergson's or the dialectician's concept of time ... what is space and materiality without objects, locations, or moments of stability ... what's the time ... I should have called ... it is*

---

[48] From the German original: Der Begriff hat "als solcher archaische Züge, die mit den rationalen sich überkreuzen; Relikte statischen Denkens und eines statischen Erkenntnisideals inmitten von dynamisiertem Bewusstsein. Der immanente Anspruch des Begriffes ist seine Ordnung schaffende Invarianz gegenüber dem Wechsel des unter ihm Befassten. ... In Dialektik erhebt Denken Einspruch gegen die Archaismen seiner Begrifflichkeit. Der Begriff an sich hypostasiert vor allem Inhalt, seine eigene Form gegenüber den Inhalten. Damit aber schon das Identitätsprinzip: dass ein Sachverhalt an sich, als Festes, Beständiges, sei. ... Identifizierendes Denken vergegenständlicht durch die logische Identität des Begriffs. Dialektik läuft, ihrer subjectiven Seite nach, darauf hinaus, so zu denken, dass nicht länger die Form des Denkens seine Gegenstände zu unveränderlichem, in sich selber gleichbleibenden macht; dass sie das seien, widerlegt Erfahrung." Translator D. R.

[49] "Die Veränderung hat keinen Träger nötig". Our contrary, conventional distinction between bearer of change and change itself may be a product of our Indo-European languages. Whorf (1963) describes other languages, e.g., that of the Nootka Indians, which do not distinguish between substantives and verbs and seem to see the world as a continuous interrelation of processes.

[50] The similarities between the Bergsonian and the dialectic concept of continuous time should not lead us to ignore other significant differences: dialecticians, no matter from which branch of dialectics, probably would have difficulties sharing Bergson's emphasis on intuition (e.g., 1975, page 44), or the definition and distinction of metaphysics and science (e.g., 1985, page 55) he makes.

[51] Harvey (1982, page XV).

impossible to discuss meaningfully concepts of space without simultaneously discussing concepts of time ... just violated this ... I don't remember Sack talking about time in his "concepts of space" ... should check again ... time geographers relate space and time ... but not on a conceptual level ... I may need a footnote here, later ... [52] ... Joyce's experiments with stream of consciousness writing ... damned difficult ... how to write to express change as a flow ... water is running out there ... the toilet valve must be stuck again

Compared to dialectic's continuous time, the discrete time of traditional logic rather resembles the pictures on a film: at a projection speed of 15 pictures/second, man begins to progress.[53]

E. Muybridge (1884/85)
Chronophotography - photography of time[54]

---

[52] Buttimer's critique of time geography (e.g., 1984, page 78) may be understood as suggesting that a different conception of time and space may be more adequate when trying to represent the self-reflective capacity of human beings.

    It also would be interesting to analyze the tensions between Giddens' theory of structuration and the time-geographic concepts he seeks to incorporate in this theory (Gregson, 1986) in this respect: could the tensions result from an incompatibility of the space/time concepts of Hägerstrand and the space/time concepts implied in Giddens' definition of the acting subject?

[53] "The locomotive illusion will be regarded as the true way of seeing just as the optical illusion is regarded as true life. 'Movie is 24 x truth per second', the director Jean Luc Godard says. E.J. Maray's chrono-photographic machine only reached 16 x truth per second" (Virilio, 1986, page 57).

[54] These photographs by Edward Muybridge were taken in 1884/1885. His motion studies, as well as those of E.J. Marey, had a strong impact on the work of F. Taylor and G. Gilbreth on the scientific management of factory work and housework (published from 1895 onwards). S. Kern (1983) describes the significant equivalence between Muybridge's and Taylor's work on the dissection of time, the art-works of the Cubists (and subsequently the Vienna school of Kinetism), and the beginning of the cinema shortly after the turn of the century. (At the same time Russell and Poincaré worked on type-theoretical distinctions to prevent the logical paradoxes.) In making time visible and controllable, the techno-logic of mechanization, discrete formal logic underlies all these expressions, even the views of the world that were discussed by the public: Kern (1983, page 115n) quotes a journal article from the Paris of 1912: "'Does everything go by jerks?' ... All processes in the universe might occur by means of a series of infinitesimally small jerks rather than continuously. ... The nature might therefore be 'one vast cinematograph'. In such a world, Charlie Chaplin and Adolf Hitler are equally real.

But the illusion is destroyed if the projectionist does not pay attention to the V-hold: this photograph comes closest to the aim of taking a photograph of the logical structure of paradoxes. It shows the split in the existential circle of traditional logic. Two successive levels appear simultaneously in our view. In the black intervals between them the quality of the phenomenon changes.[55] The contradiction between the two "assertions" becomes visible. In this picture of the paradox, identity cannot be determined anymore. We have chosen the wrong frame, have taken the picture at the wrong moment, have drawn the conclusion at the wrong time, right when Poincaré's soldier ran over to the other regiment. Don't ask *why* he ran!

... writing around circularity and self-reference in geography, my little finger lies on the sheet, preceding the pencil to warn it before it falls down at the end of[56] the

Paradox writing.   Paradoxical writing.   Paradoxes occur when activity stumbles over the ties it has set for time.   Paradoxes occur when writing, based on conventional discrete logic, describes how it goes beyond the limits of an essay.

Are there paradoxes in dialectical logic as well?   The term is not used in this context.   Still, remember what we stumbled across.   Indications for the limits of dialectical reasoning.   Indications for the insufficiency of logical circularity and existential change, even when describing the actions of self-reflecting human beings.   Indications for the need of determined identity and stability.   They can be found on many grounds.   We found them on logical ones.   Dialectical movement is driven by conventional logical contradiction.   It relies on the existence of an ultimate totality, a universal position resting in itself.   It marks the origin as well as the end of this movement.   "Since an origin is that which thinking has yet to think and has always to think anew, it is promised to thinking in an ever closer, immediate imminence, which is never fulfilled" (Foucault, 1975, page 400).[57]   Presupposing the existence of such identity, dialectical thinking nevertheless cannot think it.   "Only on the basis of something which has begun, men can think what they take to be a beginning" (Foucault, 1975, page 398).   So it is that in dialectical thinking, infinite past and infinite future are

---

[55] The movie director, A. Kluge (1985, pages 105-106) comments on the relationship between movie technique and time, particularly on the black intervals between the pictures on a film. "Cinema projection is based on an exposure time of 1/48th of a second, followed by a dark period of transportation. On the average, the cinema is dark for half of the time. The eye looks outside for 1/48th and inside for 1/48th. ... The effect neither lies in the first picture, nor in the next, but is based on an after-effect, ideally an unseen picture. It is the difference, the intermission in a flow of information, ... that leads to this effect. What is the ultimate ideal in the history of movie-making is the production of invisible pictures." (Translator D. R.)

[56] Modified after Beckett, 1976, page 284.

[57] Foucault wrote this when describing the doubles of modernity. Although he does not make it explicit, these doubles are closely related to circularity. The quote is translated from the German text: "... da der Ursprung das wird, was das Denken noch zu denken hat und stets von neuem zu denken hat, würde er dem Denken in einem stets näheren, unmittelbaren, jedoch nie erfüllten Bewusstsein verheissen" (1974, page 400).

united. Time closes to a circle. In order to escape, we may turn to conventional logic for help. It is the old conventional logic which made us turn to dialectics. So it turns out. In their mutual dependency, conventional logic and dialectical reasoning form a circle. Others saw it long ago: "Speakers of dialectics and conventional logic fail to understand each other. ... Both languages are internally consistent. Yet the consistency of the conventional thinker makes him inconsistent, just as the inconsistency of the dialectician makes him consistent. ... The battle will never have a victor, for even though the troops are constantly on the move, they never engage. There can never be reconciliation for compromise leads to everybody's deprivation. The observer can therefore learn little by watching the troops from the distance. Instead he must strive for ... being audience and performer at the same time. ... It is at that stage that we may finally realize that the drama of the human condition is a play of predicaments in which we are damned if we do and damned if we do not" (Olsson, 1980, page 66b, 69b).

Reaching beyond the area of conventional logic as well as beyond the opposed one of dialectics, the human sciences feel the sharp edge separating the two. Is it the scar of modernity?

Well, let me

References
Adorno T, 1984 *Negative Dialektik 3rd Edition* (Suhrkamp, Frankfurt)
Albert H, 1980 *Traktat über Vernunft* (Mohr, Tübingen)
Bartels D, Hard G, 1975 *Lotsenbuch für das Stadium der Geographie* (Verein zur
    Förderung regional-wissenschaftlicher Analysen, Kiel)
Baudrillard J, 1983 *Oublier Foucault* (Raben, München)
Beckett S, 1976 *Malone stirbt Volume 7* (Suhrkamp, Frankfurt)
Bergson H, 1985 *Denken und schöpferisches Werden* (Syndikat, Frankfurt)
Bernstein R, 1983 *Beyond Objectivism and Relativism* (Basil Blackwell, Oxford)
Berry B, 1980 "Creating future geographies" *Annals of the Association of
    American Geographers* **70** (4) 449-458
Buttimer A, 1984 "'Insider', 'Outsider' und die Geographie regionaler
    Lebenswelten" *Münchner Geographische Hefte* **51** 131-147
Breger H, 1982 "Mathematik: Wissenschaft im Wandel der Geschichte"
    Wechselwirkung **15** 31-35
Carnap R, 1934 *Die logische Syntax der Sprache* (Springer, Wien)
Couclelis H, 1982 "Philosophy in the construction of geographic reality" in *A
    Search for Common Ground* Eds P Gould, G Olsson (Pion, London)
Curry M, Barnes T, 1986 "Time and narrative in economic geography" paper
    presented at the Annual Meeting of the Association of American
    Geographers, Minneapolis/St. Paul
Derrida J, 1976 *Die Schrift und die Differenz* (Suhrkamp, Frankfurt)
Descombes V, 1981 *Das Selbe und das Andere* (Suhrkamp, Frankfurt)
Dreyfus H, Rabinow P, 1983 *Beyond Structuralism and Hermeneutics* (University
    of Chicago Press, Chicago)
Driver F, 1985 "Power, space and the body: a critical assessment of Foucault's
    Discipline and Punish *Society and Space* **3** 425-446
Foucault M, 1974 *Die Ordnung der Dinge* (Suhrkamp, Frankfurt)
Gadamer H, 1975 *Wahrheit und Methode* (Mohr, Tübingen)
Gale S, 1972 "Inexactness, fuzzy sets, and the foundations of behavioural
    geography" *Geographical Analysis* **4** 337-349
Gale S, Olsson G, 1979 *Philosophy in Geography* (Reidel, Dordrecht)
Giddens A, 1979 *Central Problems in Social Theory* (Macmillan, London)
Giddens A, 1984 *Interpretative Soziologie* (Campus, Frankfurt)
Gould P, 1987 "Purpose and possibility 3: what does "theory" mean in the human
    sciences? *Environment and Planning A* **19** 1-2
Gregory D, 1979 *Ideology, Science and Human Geography* (Hutchinson,
    London)
Gregory D, 1984 "Review of R.J. Johnston's 'Philosophy and Human
    Geography" *Society and Space* **2** 485-487
Gregory D, 1985 "Thoughts on theory" *Society and Space* **3** 387-388
Gregson N, 1986 "On duality and dualism: the case of structuration and time
    geography" *Progress in Human Geography* **2** 184-205
Günther G, 1976 *Beiträge zur Grundlegung einer operationsfähigen Dialektik*
    (Meiner, Hamburg)
Habermas J, 1973 *Erkenntnis und Interesse 5th Edition* (Suhrkamp, Frankfurt)
Hard G, 1973 *Die Geographie. Eine wissenschaftstheoretische Einführung*
    (DeGruyter, Berlin)
Harvey D, 1982 *The limits to Capital* (Basil Blackwell, Oxford)
Heitsch R, 1976 *Mathematik und Weltanschauung* (Akademie, Berlin)
Hoffer K, 1986 *Methoden der Verwirrung* (Droschl, Wien)
Hofstadter D, 1979 *Gödel, Escher, Bach. An Eternal Golden Braid* (Penguin,
    London)
Hubig C, 1978 *Dialektik und Wissenschaftslogik* (DeGruyter, Berlin)

Jackson P, Smith S, 1984 *Exploring Social Geography* (Allen & unwin, London)

Johnston R, 1983 *Philosophy and Human Geography* (Arnold, London)

Jung C, 1981 *Mandala. Bilder aus dem Unbewussten* (Walter, Freiburg)

Keat R, Urry J, 1984 *Social Theory as Science 2nd Edition* (Routledge & Kegan, London)

Kern S, 1983 *The Culture of Time and Space* (Weidenfeld and Nicolson, London)

Kluge A, 1985 "Die Macht der Bewusstseinsindustrie und das Schicksal unserer Öffentlichkeit" in *Industrialisierung des Bewusstseins* Ed. K Bismark (Piper, München) pp 59-129

Kutschera F, 1964 *Die Antinomien der Logik* (Alber, Freiburg)

Levin D, 1985 *The Body's Recollection of Being* (Routledge & Kegan, London)

Luhmann N, 1984 *Soziale Systeme* (Suhrkamp, Frankfurt)

Marchand B, 1979 "Dialectics and Geography" in *Philosophy and Geography* Eds S Gale, G Olsson (Reidel, Dordrecht) pp 237-268

Maturana H, Varela F, 1987 *Der Baum der Erkenntnis* (Scherz, Bern)

Mittelstrass J, 1980 *Enzyklopädie Philosophie und Wissenschaftstheorie Volume 1,2* (Bibliographisches Institut, Mannheim)

Muybridge E, 1984 *The Male and Female Figure in Motion* (Dover, New York)

Nietzsche F, 1964 *Der Wille zur Macht* (Kröner, Stuttgart)

Olsson G, 1980 *Birds in Eggs/Eggs in Birds* (Pion, London)

Olsson G, 1985 "The social space of silence" *Poetica et Analytica* **3** 6-31

Olsson G, 1986a "Of creativity and socialisation" in *Life Sciences and Society* Eds R Daudel, N Agaggio (Elsevier, Amsterdam)

Olsson G, 1986b "On doughnutting" Paper presented at the Nobel Symposium on "Possible Worlds in Arts and Sciences", Stockholm

Poincaré H, 1913 *Letzte Gedanken* (Akademia, Leibzig)

Reichert D, 1987a "Zu den Menschenbildern in den Sozial- und Wirtschaftswissenschaften" in *Geographie des Menschen* Ed G Bahrenberg, forthcoming

Reichert D, 1987b "Comedia Geographica. An absurd one-act play" *Society and Space* **87** (3) 335-342

Reuterswärd C, 1984 *The Unseen Alphabet Exhibition Catalogue* (Moderna Museet, Stockholm)

Sayer A, 1984 *Method in Social Science* (Hutchinson, London)

Stegmüller W, 1975 *Hauptströmungen der Gegenwartsphilosophie* (Körner, Stuttgart)

Tarski A, 1935 "Der Wahrheitsbegriff in den formalisierten Sprachen" *Studia Philosophica* **1** 1-30

Taylor C, 1985 *Philosophy and the Human Sciences* (Cambridge University Press, Cambridge)

Thiel C, *Grundlagenkrise und Grundlagenstreit. Studie über das normative Fundament der Wissenschaften am Beispiel von Mathematik und Sozialwissenschaften* (Hein, Mesenheim)

Virilio P, 1986 *Ästhetik des Verschwindens* (Merve, Berlin)

von Wright G, 1974 *Erklären und Verstehen* (Athenäum, Frankfurt)

Watzlawick P, Beavin J, Jackson D, 1985 *Menschliche Kommunikation 7th Edition* (Huber, Bern)

Weichhart P, 1987 "Geography as a 'multi-paradigm-game' - a pluralistic discipline in a pluralistic post-industrial society" in *The Role of Geography in a Post-Industrial Society* Ed H Windhorst, forthcoming

Whorf B, 1964 *Sprache, Denken, Wirklichkeit* (Rowohlt, Reinbeck)

Wittgenstein L, 1962 *Philosophische Untersuchungen* (Suhrkamp, Frankfurt)

Wittgenstein L, 1982 *Tractatus Logico philosophicus* (Suhrkamp, Frankfurt)

The eye and the index finger: bodily means to cultural meaning

Gunnar Olsson

"Cum ipsi (majores homines) appellabant rem aliquam, et cum secundum vocem corpus ad aliquid movebant, videbam, et tenebam hoc ab eis vocari rem illam, guod nonabant, cum eam vellent ostendere. Hoc autem eos velle ex motu corporis aperiebatur: tamquam verbis naturalibus omnium gentium, quae fiunt vultu indicante affectionem animi et petendis, habendis, rejiciendis, fugiendisve rebus. Ita verba in variis sententiis locis suis posita, et crebro audita, quarum rerum signa essent, paulatim colligebam, measque jam voluntates, edomito in eis signis ore, per haec enuntiabam."

(Augustine, Confessions, I, page 8)[1]

Thus begins the first paragraph of Wittgenstein's *Philosophical Investigations*. A quote. A launching pad. A germ of reformulation. An instance of inter-textuality. To write is to walk on a pavement of citations.

As a way of showing my desire, I now enter the stage. Silence. A glance catches another. An index finger pins each and everyone down. You. You. You. You. You. You. A mouth opens. Out it comes:

"One".

"Two."

"Three."

"Four."

"Five."

"Six."

And then?

You fill in by silently saying "Seven." Not because 'seven' is a holey number, but because it comes next in the hierarchy of the Order of Numbering. Automatically you extend my writing voice and pointing finger into the rules of counting. Without thinking, you project an individual body into collective meaning.

This is the nature of the word 'seven': to be parasitic on whatever went before. In shared activities like seeing/pointing/speaking/hearing/reading/writing, we become extensions of one another; no body is a self-sufficient entity onto itself, but always a double in need of the other. What I left absent by the question 'and then?', you made present by replying 'seven'. In my words you detected a structure of an already-but-not-yet, of a project to be continued. The taken-for-granted is like Flaubert's God in the Universe: present everywhere, visible nowhere.

---

[1] "When they (my elders) named some object, and accordingly moved towards something, I saw this and grasped that the thing was called out by the sound they uttered when they meant to point it out. Their intention was shown by their bodily movements, as it were the natural language of all peoples: the expression of the face, the play of the eyes, the movement of other parts of the body, and the tone of voice which expresses our state of mind in seeking, having, rejecting, or avoiding something. Thus, as I heard the words repeatedly used in their proper places in various sentences, I gradually learnt to understand what objects they signified; and after I had trained my mouth to form these signs, I used them to express my own desires." Ludwig Wittgenstein: *Philosophical Investigations*, page 1.

It is in such invisible structures that we find both the necessity and the possibility of a social and human science; in the name of reflexivity, the *pre*-sented is *re*-presented, the *re*-presented *pre*-sented. More specifically, our study objects behave predictably because they reflect what is taken to count just as our conclusions become predictable because they reflect the taken-for-granted of counting. In neither case, however, is this predictability intentional. On the contrary. For, as Wittgenstein (1958, page 219) put it: "*This is how it strikes me.* When I obey a rule [like the rule of counting], I do not choose. I obey the rule *blindly.*"

Put differently, I learn the meaning of a word by using it as other people do. To obey a rule is consequently a social practice, impossible to engage in privately; "to think one is obeying a rule is not to obey a rule" (Wittgenstein, 1958, page 202). Obeying a rule is rather a matter of participating in the routinized rituals of day-to-day life, of being socialized into accepting the normal and deploring the different. Unwittingly trained to follow orders, we get rewarded by soft words and punished by hard sticks. Ruler as ruler.

To repeat: "Learning the meaning of a word is to embrace the normal". Even a blind man can see that. Even a mute man can tell that. The question is whether you and I are deaf enough to hear it. Yet it is a well established principle of epistemology that I understand the form and function of a particular rule only when I extend it to its logical and existential limits. Once there, I can remain forever confined or I can try to break loose. From the outside, I am then supposed to review the previously accepted, to transcend the old and create the new. To inquire about society's taken-for-granted is to call its bluff.

Moving from one categorical realm to another is to participate in a revolution. One set of takens-for-granted is replaced by another. Turning one ideology on its head, I put another on its feet. Bottoms up. Underpants. The logical positivist becomes a dialectical materialist, the realist a surrealist, the Christian an atheist. Such Kierkegaardian leaps from one rule(r) to another are incredibly demanding, not the least because they require that one form of life be replaced by another. It is not enough to think differently. I must behave accordingly. Other clothes, other food, other friends. Other gods. All falls together in coherence, for world and life are one.

To me, however, this type of conversion is not challenging enough. The reason is that I take understanding not to be in the crossing of boundaries, but rather in staying right *at* them. Every experience occurs on the border, for at the center everything is so natural that it goes unnoticed. To be at a limit is consequently to have moved from the acceptability of the taken-for-granted to the forbidden of the taboo. To be suspended in that position is to hang in the crevice between categories, to refuse the security of being caught. Rebel instead of revolutionary.

To assume such a position is to cause a serious threat, for the acceptance of a limit is the foundation of social cohesion. As a consequence, various strategies have evolved to repress it, including the normative activities of logic, religion and social psychology. Witness, for instance, the remark by Kristeva (1985, page 220) that "the most profound crises of rationality, which are in this way dramatically organized, are accompanied by a rigid investiture of other archaic and repressive structures, when and if their attempts at becoming semiotic-symbolic fail. These archaic and repressive structures include order, the family, normalcy, normative classical psychological-tending discourse, all of which are just so many characteristics of fascist ideology. Consequently, we may conclude that texts on experiencing limits - this is modern art - constitute the most direct and risky approach to the fascist phenomenon." But why would a certain behavior be taboo, if it were not too dangerous to be practiced? Is the answer in Wittgenstein's (1961, 5. page 632) conclusion that "the subject does not belong to the world: rather it is a *limit* of the world"? (Emphasis added). Thus, "there is no such thing as the subject that thinks or entertains idea. [For] if I wrote a book called *The World as I Found It*, I should have to include a report on my body ... this being a method of isolating the subject - [But] it alone could *not* be mentioned in that book.-" (op. cit., 5. page 631). Yet it eventually turns out that this solipsist viewpoint coincides with pure realism, for "whatever we see could be other than it is. There is no *a priori* order of things" (op. cit., 5. page 634). Perhaps it is such that "language is a labyrinth of paths. You approach from *one* side and know your way about: you approach the same place from another side and no longer know your way about" (Wittgenstein, 1958, page 203).

There is in deed unity, not only between the young and the mature Marx, but also between the early and late Wittgenstein. What ties them together is their common struggle with issues of identity and existence, certainty and ambiguity. The focus is on the relation between I and the other. How could it be otherwise? For the paradox of (post)modernity is the paradox of the liar. Context is pervasive.

Out of these quotations grow a host of therapeutic questions: if the subject is a limit of the world, what then is a limit of the subject? The body, not to be mentioned!? What is a physical and cultural limit of the body? The skin, not to be touched!? Is the skin a bodily metaphor for the culturally taboo of limits? Is the concept of limit too dangerous to know, not because it is constitutive of the subject, but because it is constitutive of truth? Is this why Plato and St. Augustine insisted that poetry and theater present the preeminent threat to truth?

Perhaps. For it is a characteristic of every theory of truth that it obeys some specific principals of law and order. At the same time, it is a major function of art to question these rule(r)s of blind obedience. This usually takes the form of experimenting with the relations between a private or inner act of meaning on the one hand and the collective or outer meaning on the other. Perhaps it is here that solipsism and realism turn into one another, where you and I come together. What is at stake is nothing less than the creation of new cultural meanings out of old bodily forms. Revelation. But in logic there can never be surprises, for "logic is not a field in which *we* express what we wish with the help of signs, but rather one in which the nature of the natural and inevitable sign speaks for itself. If we know the logical syntax of any sign-language, then we have already been given all the propositions of logic" (Wittgenstein, 1961, 6. page 124)

The paradox is that to create new meanings is to break the hitherto taken-for-granted, i.e., to violate the tautologies of connectives. But this means that I simultaneously must follow a rule and stretch the skin of its boundary. Here lies temporary madness. For if I were sometime to see quite new surroundings from my window instead of the long familiar ones, if things, humans and animals were to behave as they never did before, then I should say something like 'I have gone mad'; but that would merely be an expression of giving up the attempt to know my way about" (Wittgenstein, 1970, page 393).

In short: If I am not like you, I am lost. Whenever I encounter the unexpected I have no bearings, no rules to follow, no fixes to keep me steady. Yet, the I is never altogether an I, for the I is always unfinished.

To be lost is not merely a matter of geography. It is also to be morally and socially condemned. Get lost, you bastard, son of a bitch, fruit of unholy intercourse, consequence of category mixing! But a mule is a reliable worker.

In the spirit of mixing categories, I shall now return to my opening scene. What I did there was to rely on my eyes and index finger as bodily means for looking and pointing. At the same time, I asked you to imagine that sounds came out of my mouth, while in fact marks came out of my pen:

"One".

      "Two."

           "Three."

                 "Four."

                       "Five."

                             "Six."

And then I presumed that you behaved normally by saying "Seven". Nothing unusual. In doubt, you ask your anesthetist who will reply that when a patient no longer knows that 'seven' comes after 'six', then he is drugged and ready for operation.

It is, of course, easy to foresee a number of cases when a 'normal' response would strike the informed as mad. For instance, you obviously presumed that I was engaged in the language game of counting, while in fact I could have been performing a naming ceremony. In that case, the proper response would not have been "Seven", but "Gunnar", for what I had used were the abstract labels '1, ..., 6' to denote unknown members of my audience and the name 'Gunnar' to denote myself. What an excellent illustration of Wittgenstein's (1961, 5. page 61) point that "we cannot think what we cannot think; so what we cannot think we cannot *say* either". The conclusion is that what the solipsist "*means* is quite correct; only it cannot be *said*, but makes itself manifest. The world is *my* world: this is manifest in the fact that the limits of *language* (of that language which alone I understand) mean the limits of *my* world" (op. cit., 5. page 62). But what does it mean to point? And what is the function of naming?

It is sometimes held that the proper name provides a key to knowledge; to know is to state what is identical to what. The name identifies. At the same time, however, naming a thing effectively drives a wedge between the namer and the named; naming *is* a queer connection between a word and an object. Notwithstanding, the meaning of a name is sometimes explained by pointing to its bearer. "But that does not make the word ['this'] into a name. On the contrary: for a name is not used with, but only explained by means of, the gesture of pointing" (Wittgenstein, 1958, page 45). The fact remains, however, that the act of pointing is related to the ritual of baptizing. At the same time, it is clearly possible to think not only of what *is* the case, but also of what is *not* the case.

It should now be clear that the possibility of cheating and deceiving is an integral part of language itself. It seems to follow that terms like 'fair game', 'causal prediction' and 'blind obedience' have less to do with detached science and more to do with engaging morality. The reason is that an ostensive definition always can be interpreted in different ways. The lesson is that it is the possibility of various interpretations which at the same time is the threat and the driving force to truth. Such is the normative structure of the already-but-not-yet of the social and human sciences.

The social sciences and their languages are completely intertwined. Not only is human action thoroughly self-referential, but every utterance contains a crucial element of persuasion. There is no description without performance. Telling truths is consequently not enough. Being convincing is equally necessary. Incredible truths are not truths at all, for truth is less an issue of what is the case and more an issue of credibility. The urge to *ex*press is consequently linked with the urge to *im*press, the grasping of meaning with the evocation of meaning. Logic and rhetoric reach out for one another. So do ethics and aesthetics. In the practice of everyday life, the possession of a language is for understanding and acting alike. To be a true scientist is consequently to be a performing artist, for to be an artist is to see a form in the invisible. But even though theory is the death of desire, desire is the birth of theory.

What is desire? Where is a symbol fertile enough to embody it and pregnant enough to bring it forth?

An obvious candidate is the Saussurean concept of a sign, i.e.,

$$\text{sign} = \frac{\text{signifier}}{\text{signified}}$$

Of particular interest here is the limiting penumbra through which signifier and signified are kept together and apart. It is to this Bar of Categorical Meetings that I go to search for fractions of taboo-ridden phenomena and taboo-ridden insights. Intuition tells me that it is in the abyss of this powerfilled void that visible becomes invisible, untouchable touchable. It is here that presence meets absence, absence meets presence. It is in the carnival at the bar that body is transubstantiated into meaning, meaning into body. Here I meet the other, full of dreams, full of realities. Thus, whereas Wittgenstein (1958, page 36) limits himself to the proposal that "where our language suggests a body and there is none: there we should like to say, is a *spirit*", I would add that where we imagine a spirit, there is in reality a *body*. The totality, though, is in the intercourse of the two, one on top of the other, the other on top of the one. There are braids of desire like

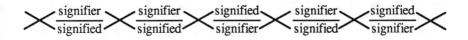

Understanding these intertwined relations is to realize that every sign confounds not only the Cartesian categories of mind and matter, but also the Lacanian categories of real and symbolic. Within itself, the sign contains those processes of ontological transformation which provide the liberating and repressive machinery of power. To use the words of Kristeva (1985, page 217f), it is in the drunkenness of the Saussurean bar that "the speaking subject undergoes a transition to a void, to zero: loss of identity, afflux of drive and a return of symbolic capacities, but this time in order to take control of *drive* itself. This is precisely what expands the limits of the signifiable: a new aspect of the displacement between the referent/signifiable, a new aspect of body, has thus found its signification".

It is authors like Norbert Elias, Michel Foucault, Pierre Bourdieu and Michel de Certeau who have illustrated how cultural conceptions of body and soul determine the boundaries between you and me. Mechanisms of signification indeed reflect and constitute the powerfilled techniques of disciplining, surveilling, ordering and punishing. The insight inherited from Nietzsche is that I simultaneously *have* a body and *am* a body. As I live in and through language, so I live in and through my body; my body is neither thing nor idea, but the measure of things. Like Maurice Merleau-Ponty, I thus conceive of the body as my mode of existence   through my body I express a knowledge which is not objective, but existential.   To form subjects is consequently to form bodies, especially to redraw the boundaries of the body. It is significant that whereas Michel Foucault devoted his life to studies of the constitution of the subject, Anthony Giddens entitled one of his books *The Constitution of Society*.

The physical limit of the body is marked by its own skin. Since boundaries tend to be guarded by the taboo, it is not surprising that the mode of touch is strictly regulated by rules of behavior. Thrusting into another person is clearly to transgress the boundaries of her self and this is regardless of whether the violation is through horrible rape or irresistible love. Here attention should be drawn to the remark of Cixous (1981, page 55) that "bisexuality on an unconscious level is the possibility of extending into the other, of being in such a relation with the other that *I* move into the other without destroying the other: that I will look for the other where s/he is without trying to bring everything back to myself". It follows that to manipulate the body of others is to engage in a kind of political anatomy. It also follows that experimenting with your own body is a sophisticated technique for learning who you are.   My skin is escapeproof, the mode of understanding self-referential. Indeed, "if we were to make completely explicit the architectonics of the human body, its ontological framework, and how it sees itself and hears itself, we would see that the structure of its mute world is such that all the possibilities are already given in it" (Merleau-Ponty, 1968, page 155). Every text is a metaphor of the body, every mark a limiting sign of difference. Painters often claim that what they look at looks at them.

And thus it was that Paul Cézanne could make his revolutionary discoveries in visual art. Since he never took anything for granted, he could suddenly realize that he no longer painted landscapes, but literally pictures, not mountains and houses, but triangles and rectangles, not content, but form. What he was loosing was actually perspective, that single point of vision which hitherto had stabilized what people saw. In his acts of deconstruction, he rediscovered the art of hieroglyphic writing where it is so clear that the cultural bounds of meaning are contained within the bodily limits of form. Nothing is without limits.

Given these relations between physical form and symbolic meaning, it is easy to appreciate why Jacques Derrida's conception of grammatology rests so securely in the two disciplines of geometry and psychoanalysis. While the former teach the techniques of making distinctions by drawing limiting lines, the latter warn that no line is to be trusted; the taken-for-granted is not the content of the distinguished, but rather in the marks of distinguishing. The thinner the boundary between you and me, the greater the risks and the stronger the taboos.[2] The stronger the taboos, the more important to know. Conversely, keeping a distance is considered proper behavior, to be fostered and rewarded. Perhaps it is to Euclid and Freud that I should direct my questions of why it is so difficult to draw the lines differently. Nietzsche, Husserl, Heidegger and Derrida come to mind as well. The conclusion is tempting: if the world is a synthesis of meaning, then the synthesis of meaning is itself the body. As Merleau-Ponty (1968, page 138) put it, "we have to reject the age-old assumptions that put the body in the world and the seer in the body, or conversely, the world and the body in the seer as in a box. Where are we to put the limit between the body and the world, since the world is flesh"?

The categorizing practices of pointing and naming indicate how shared knowledge is obtained through various forms of distanciation. Language is by nature a separation. As if to underscore its own point, this performing essay is itself an instance of the same practices of removal. The only senses I have relied on are those of sight and hearing (assuming, of course, that you have been sensitive enough to read aloud). Your eyes and ears have picked up signals from my voice and hand, especially from my index finger elongated into a real pen and into an imagined pointer. There is no coincidence that the eye and the pointer are the masculine organs of Newtonian physics, that physics which - like geography - deals with action at a distance. All disciplines have their gravity models, don't they? Einsteinian physics, on the other hand, deals with action by contrast; since the mutual action of two electrically charged bodies depends on the character of the intervening medium, the message written by the two bodies depends on the context within which it is written.

---

[2] In Dostoevsky's novel *The Double*, the low ranking clerk Golyadkin hires a magnificent carriage to take him down to Nevsky Prospekt. He wishes to impress. But suddenly another carriage pulls up alongside his. Inside it sits not a woman to be seduced, but his superior Andrei Filipovich to be obeyed. No place to hide. Caught where he should not be. The other had come too close. Eventually Golyadkin was to go mad:

"Should I bow or shouldn't I? Should I acknowledge him? Admit that it is me? Or should I pretend I'm someone else, someone strikingly resembling me, and look completely indifferent?" Golyadkin asked himself in indescribable anguish.

"Yes, that's it: I'm not me and that's all there is to it". So he thought, his eyes fixed on Andrei Filipovich as he took off his hat to him.

"I, I, I ... no, nothing, sir," he stammered in a whisper. "The fact is, it's not me.... Yes, that's all there is to it". (Quoted in Berman, 1982, page 211).

Kissing a Russian on the mouth is not the same as licking the ass of a Swede. Moskivskaya is not Absolut.

What now, if I had produced a text which did not involve my hand and your eyes, but rather my tongue and your nose? Is it even possible to imagine a written document where I did not sit in my study distancing myself not only from you, the reader, but indeed from the very paper onto which I project my marks? Imagine if this text suddenly came really close, sniffing, farting, dripping! You should then say something like 'I have gone mad'. Difficult even in the deceitful theater. Impossible in a truthful publication. Plato again!

Flight of fancy! May be. The unthinkable thought experiment is nevertheless illustrative, for it clearly reveals the role of limits in social discourse. Yet there are, of course, things one can do in the theater which are impossible in the university. Yet it is generally held that creative change always occurs at the boundaries, never at the center. The trick is to mix genres, for it is the non-classifiable that initiates new processes. But only processes smell.

One who successfully approached these limits was Georges Bataille, not the least in his pornographic novel *The Story of the Eye*. On reading this work, it is crucial to realize that its main characters are not the two individuals of Simone and Marcelle. The lead actors are rather a cast of metaphors, especially that of the eye. In its search of meaning, this strange creature wanders from the socket of the face to the suck-it of the cunt. Tsch, tsch! What pushes this imaginary into new symbolic forms is indeed the physical form itself; the spheric eye is metamorphosed first into an egg and then into a testicle. And then suddenly, "there in the sunlight, on Simone's seat, lay a white dish containing two balls, glands the size and shape of eggs, and of a pearly whiteness, faintly bloodshot like the globe of an eye" (Bataille, 1982, page 51).

Immediately after the bullfight, under the sun of Seville, the narrator fuses together the killing of the bull, the loss of the toreador's eye and Simone's orgasm on the plate of testicles: "Thus, two globes of equal size and consistency had suddenly been propelled in opposite directions at once. One, the white ball of the bull, had been thrust into the 'pink and dark' cunt that Simone had bared in the crowd; the other, a human eye, had spurted from Grenaro's head with the same force as a bundle of innards from a belly. This coincidence, tied to death through a sort of urinary liquefaction of the sly, first brought us back to Marcelle in a moment that was so brief and almost substantial, yet so uneasily vivid that I stepped forward like a sleep-walker as though about to touch *her* at eye level" (op. cit., page 54).

It is obvious from these quotes that Bataille's story is less about perverse sexuality and more about the techniques of creativity. A similar, but less revolting example of a metaphor on the loose is Gogol's classical story of the nose. Here the human form is broken into surreal fragments as the barber Ivan Jakovlevich recognizes that the nose he discovers in his morning loaf of bread actually belongs to one of his customers. Will he throw it into the Neva or give it back to its rightful owner? An add in the paper solves the problem. By treating the unreal as real, Gogol here illustrated how humor can serve as a means of insight and change.

As Jacques Derrida (1981, page 81) has remarked, understanding the relation between metaphor and creativity is "to undertake a general reversal of metaphorical directions". We must allow ourselves to be carried away, not only forwards, but backwards as well. Literally. Hence bodily. Yet, whenever a metaphor is let on the loose, the reader easily looses his way. Old lighthouses begin to blink in strange patterns. No longer can I figure out my position. There is nevertheless consolation in Wittgenstein's (1958, page 123) aphorism that "a philosophical problem has the form: I don't know my way about". For an old-time geographer, it is interesting to note that space tends to be associated with corporeality.

And thus is is that the tremulous body is a means of meaning. The eye and the index finger become metaphors for grasping the distanciation inherent in all subject formation. Our only contact with the world is through the holes of our bodies. It is through them that individuals are penetrated by society and its accepted norms of thought-and-action. It is by such bodily means that you and I become obedient and predictable. But it is also through these same organs that we breathe and survive but also suffocate and decay.

Now it seems plausible: the concept of trust has its social origin and destination in the unconscious of the body. But to be trustworthy is nothing less than to be predictable. The screws tighten. "Fucking you" has a double ring. The symbol of marriage is likewise. The double doubles up.

The suspicion is this: our words get their meaningful power less from the things they refer to and more from the taken-for-granted of their physicality. Words, in other words, refer to the presence of other words, not to the absence of concrete things. Signs embrace other signs, intertwining into braids of meaning. Signs copulate. Signs materialize. Words turn to body, body to word. For me, language is like a lover, "not the language of love, but the love of language, not the matter but meaning, not what the tongue touches, but what it forms, not lips and nipples, but nouns and verbs" (Gass, 1976, page 11). Or, as Roland Barthes (1978, page 73) has put it: "Language is a skin ... I rub against the other. It is as if I had words instead of fingers, or fingers at the tip of my words. My language trembles with desire ... Language experiences orgasm upon touching itself".

Whenever I rub my skin against the other, I experiment with the limits of the subject. But the skin of a word delimits its cultural meaning. Whenever I let my words touch the words of another, then, by necessity, I bring forth new meanings and new taken-for-granted. Yet, it should be recalled that even though desire is the birth of theory, theory is the death of desire. The reason is that to create is not to have an idea which searches for its expression, but to have an expression which searches for its meaning.

So: Hold the expressions in the palm of your hand. Mold them there only to let them move on to the tender tips of your fingers. And they will come. Soft and clean. For it is exactly in the crevice between presence and absence that language becomes erotic. The secret is not in the conventional metaphors of desire, but in the devious desires of metaphor. Yet, the *telos* is less in semantics and more in syntax, less in what I am talking about and more in the way I order what I am talking about. It is syntax that leads me by the hand; "I really do think with my pen, because my head often knows nothing about what my hand is writing" (Wittgenstein, 1980, page 17). But the dripping pen is a pet symbol for the new analysts in France. So is the eraser which always leaves a trace. The pen is my spear, the rubber my shield. Double entry. Double protection. Castrated from the outset.

Is this the fate of creative transgression?

In the context of creative transgression, I shall end by returning to Roland Barthes and his marvelous book *A Lover's Discourse*. I do this, not because I feel compelled to repeat what I have written elsewhere (Olsson, 1985), but because Barthes' work is an excellent example of the mixture of genres. Thus it was in his collage of fragments that Barthes performed not an analysis of love, but an act of love. His aim was not to recapture ambiguous human relations in the precise net of descriptive sociology, but instead to set them free into rhythmic waves of subversive action.

At the heart of Barthes' adventure lies the insight that love cannot be rerendered in the taken-for-granted language of society. Indeed, it is the exact opposite of the routinized categories of politics and social science. Rather than being common, love shows itself to be something utterly lonely, something beyond the tragic mean of the common, beyond the law of large numbers, beyond the silent majority of the average. To engage in a lover's discourse is therefore to be profoundly critical, not of others, but of the social system itself. It is an act of extreme revolt when the secretary writes love letters on company time and the geography professor comments on the pornography of writing. What the lover and the rebel have in common is the bricoleur's disregard for the authority of competence. Too much is too important to leave to the experts.

Contrary to public and political action, love does not aim at the realization of well defined wishes. Love is not goal-seeking, its purpose is not to make predictions. All it does is merely to move on, continuously and unpredictably new. Contrary to conventional science, love refuses to be codified, for it knows that every code is totalitarian and that nothing threatens its survival as much as the totalitarian. In everything love is the opposite of the scientific planning document. In everything love is dramatic, poetic and hence non-Platonic. Love is not a fair game, not an instance of the taken-for-granted.

And thus it is that when I say I LOVE YOU, I do not denote, but perform. Whenever I let that verb in present tense be embraced by the pronouns of the first and second person, I do not preach and explanatory sermon, merely join in the chanting of a hymn. What matters is not *what* you are, but *that* you are. I do not analyze, but confess. And you believe me not because I tell truths, but because I make the incredible credible. As a tautological amen at the outer limits of language, those three words 'I LOVE YOU' tell nothing, yet confirm everything. Without the safety net of logic and empirical observations, I throw myself from one trapeze to another, unquestioning, yet driven by an intense curiosity. The crowd does not understand, for the lover's discourse is so exceedingly solitary; in its own actions it is itself a reflection of a loneliness which is not psychological, but systemic. After all, most of us are proud of this little word 'I', that erect letter which denotes identity. But even greater than this little word 'I', spoke Nietzsche in his *Zarathustra*, is your body which does not say 'I', but performs 'I'.

As practicing dialecticians, lovers act first and ask later. Their natural language is not the guarded dialogue whose goal is to reach a common agreement and whose characteristic is to be greedy and cautious. The natural language of love is instead the generous monologue, proud and vulnerable. And thus it is that the lover never resigns, never stays in line, never fights about

the final word. He does not wrinkle his forehead like a concerned sociologist.
All he does is to laugh and cry, unyielding and liberating as the artist he is. So,
once again: hold the expressions in your hand, caress them without intention.
And they will want to come.

And when I beg you to come, I ask not with my mouth, but with my eyes.
You answer not with words, but with glances. Love sees clearly, it is not blind.
Like James Joyce's Molly Bloom, in the cool of the evening, I therefore ask you
with my eyes to ask again. Yes, my mountain flower. And I put my arms
around you, thereby proving that whenever in doubt; the body becomes the
words corrective. The hell with the telephone! Stevie Wonder may well be a
good musician. Philosopher he ain't.

Through this performing essay, I have entered a zone beyond the frontier
lines of a humanistic social science. Once there, I have tried to decode those
sign systems which make you and me so obedient and so predictable. I have
hoped to show what cannot be said and to say what cannot be shown: a juggling
of fragments, and intertextual search for a body beyond the alphabet. To
communicate is to participate in that which is manifest.

What I have illustrated is the obvious: even in phallologocentric writing,
desire streams through some kind of body. In its rhythmic movements, texts are
like kites: at a distance they are like free birds set against the sky; in reality,
though, they are tied down with the strings of social convention.

What is this word 'word'? How do I use my fingers to touch its limits and
thereby those everyday practices that simultaneously keep individual and society
together and apart? How do I sense not the eye, but the seeing of the eye? how
do I discover the alphabet of the body in the body of the alphabet?

More questions than answers. And thus it is appropriate to close with a
quote from Merleau-Ponty (1968, page 155), who quotes Valéry, who quotes
someone else, who quotes God knows who: "Language is everything, since it is
the voice of no one, since it is the voice of the things, the waves, and the forests.
And what we have to understand is that there is no dialectical reversal from one
of these views to the other; we do not have to reassemble them into a synthesis:
they are two aspects of the reversibility which is the ultimate truth".[3]

References
Barker J, 1984 *The Tremulous Private Body: Essays on Subjection* (Methuen,
London)
Barthes R, 1978 *A Lover's Discourse. Fragments* (Hill & Wang, New York)
Batailles G, 1982 *All That Is Solid Melts Into Air. The Experience of Modernity*
(Simon & Schuster, New York)

---

[3] *The Visible and the Invisible*, page 155. "Och i en mening är språket allt, som Valéry säger, eftersom det inte är någons
röst, utan själva tingens, vågornas och skogarnas röst. Och vad det gäller att förstå är att det skogarnas dessa båda
åskådningar inte föreligger någon dialektisk omkastning, vi behöver inte sammanföra dem till en syntes: de är två
aspekter av den omvändbarhet som är slutlig sanning". Translated in *Kris*, page 75.

Bourdieu P, 1977 *Outline of a Theory of Practice* (Cambridge University Press, Cambridge)

de Certeau M, 1984 *The Practice of Everyday Life* (University of California Press, Berkeley)

de Saussure F, 1959 *Course in General Linguistics* (McGraw-Hill, New York)

Cixous H, 1981 "Castration or decapitation?" *Signs* **7**, 41-55

Derrida J, 1976 *Of Grammatology* (Johns Hopkins University Press, Baltimore)

Derrida J, 1981 *Dissemination* (Atlone Press, London)

Derrida J, 1982 *Margins of Philosophy* (University of Chicago Press, Chicago)

Derrida J, 1979 *Spurs: Nietzsche's Styles/Emperons: Les Styles de Nietzsche* (University of Chicago Press, Chicago)

Derrida J, 1984 *Signéponge/Signsponge* (Columbia University Press, New York)

Dryfus H, Rabinow P, 1982 *Michel Foucault: Beyond Structuralism and Hermeneutics* (University of Chicago Press, Chicago)

Elias, N. 1978 *The Civilizing Process: The Development of Manners* (Blackwell, Oxford)

Elias, N. 1982 *The Civilizing Process: State Formation and Civilization* (Blackwell, Oxford)

Foucault M, 1977 *Discipline and Punish: The Birth of the Prison* (Penguin, Harmondsworth)

Foucault M, 1976, 1984) *Histoire de la Sexualité, I, II, III* (Gallimard, Paris)

Gass W, 1976 *On Being Blue: A Philosophical Inquiry* (Godine, Boston)

Giddens A, 1984 *The Constitution of Society: Outline of the Theory of Construction* (Polity Press, Cambridge)

Hartman G H, 1981 *Saving the Text: Literature/Derrida/Philosophy* (Johns Hopkins University Press, Baltimore)

Kripke S A, 1982 *Wittgenstein on Rules and Private Language. An Elementary Exposition* (Blackwell, Oxford)

Kristeva J, 1980 *Desire in Language: A Semiotic Approach to Literature and Art* (Columbia University Press, New York)

Kristeva J, 1982 *Powers of Horror: An Essay on Abjection (Columbia University Press, New York)*

Kristeva J, 1985 "The speaking subject" in *On Signs* Ed M Blonsky (Blackwell, Oxford) pp 210-220

Lancan J, 1977 *Ecrits* (Tavistock, London)

Lemarie A, 1979 *Jacques Lacan* (Routledge & Kegan Paul, London)

McGinn C, 1984 *Wittgenstein on Meaning* (Blackwell, Oxford)

Merleau-Ponty M, 1968 *The Visible and the Invisible (Northwestern University Press, Evanston, Ill).* In Swedish partly as "Sammanflätningen - kiasmen", *Kris* **31-32** 1985 65-75

Olsson G, 1982 "-/-" in *A Search for Common Ground* Eds P Gould and G Olsson (Pion, London) pp 223-231

Olsson G, 1985 "The social space of silence", *Poetica et Analytica* **3** 6-30

Olsson G, 1986 "Creativity and socialization" in *Life Sciences and Society* Eds R Daudel, N L D'Agaggio (Elsevier, Amsterdam)

Staten H, 1985 *Wittgenstein and Derrida* (Blackwell, Oxford)

Stenlund S, 1980 *Det Osägbara* (Norstedt, Stockhom)

Ulmer G L 1985 *Applied Grammatology: Post(e)-Pedagogy from Jacques Derrida to Joseph Beuys* (Johns Hopkins University Press, Baltimore)

Lost words as reflections of lost worlds*

Allan Pred

"I have always been fascinated by the story which a friend found for me in
geography textbook: certain Australian tribes when one of their member
die, eliminate a word from the vocabulary as a sign of mourning. This make
languages equivalent to life, asserts that men are in control of what they sa
and give it orders rather than receive them from it."

(Ronald Barthes, 1985, page 104

To begin the pretexting of this word-weave
I employ Wittgensteinian reverberations of the utter truth.
 The limits of our language mean
 the limits of our world,
 the limits of the region or place we inhabit,
 the limits of the projects we may define and participate in.
 The limits of our world mean
 the limits of our language,
 the words and other linguistic elements
 we are able to encounter and acquire.
To know a form of life,
 a geographically and historically specific form of life,
 a *genre de vie*,
is to know a language.
To actively engage and understand speech acts,
to become embedded in discourse,
to give voice to life, intelligibly,
requires a taken-for-granted common background
of spatially and temporally concrete, nondiscursive practices,
nondiscursive practices themselves influenced by prior speech and discourse.[1]

 The language through which the consciousness of individuals is give
expression and through which certain impressions of the world are differe
tiated, classified, retained and creatively combined cannot be separated fro

---

* This article is a pretext to, and a set of pretexts for, a book that explores the changing nature of daily life in Stockhc
between 1880 and 1900 in terms of the interdependence of locally situated practices, power relations and **
consciousness of individuals and groups (*The Language of Practice and the Practice of Language: Lost Wor[l]ds of La
Nineteenth Century Stockholm* [Polity Press, Cambridge, 1988]). An analysis of words and expressions that have gone c
of use or lost their original meanings since the late nineteenth century reveals that the language of producti
distribution and consumption practices subsumed a language of discipline-avoidance and survival tactics; that the "f
geography", or language used for negotiating the city streets and getting from here to there, subsumed a language
ideological resistance; that the language of social reference and address, the tagging of nicknames on groups a
individuals, subsumed a language of boundary drawing, social orientation and boundary transgression; and that all
these languages were cross-cut and peppered by folk humor, by a vocabulary of comic irony and irreverence, of mock
and ridiculing social inversion, of laughing lewdness and licentiousness.

[1] As Dreyfus and Rabinow (1983, page 62) point out, Foucault and Heidegger, as well as Wittgenstein, "hold tha
whole constellation of practices enables those who share those practices to single out and talk about objects".

the temporally and spatially specific conditions under which people live.[2] As the constraining and yet highly flexible medium in which most organized communication proceeds, language is an absolute precondition for almost all of the social life, or institutional projects, occurring in a given place.

It is largely through language that the local practices are instituted. It is largely through locally situated institutions that language is practiced and given meaning. It is through language that the component tasks of institutional projects are routinely or innovatively defined, made mutually understood and subsequently recounted.

To the extent that language allows memory traces, complex skills, practical knowledge, and rules and norms to be projected from one generation to the next, it helps facilitate the geographically particular perpetuation of institutions, the sedimentation of institutional practices "in deep time-space."[3] The place-bound reproduction or transformation of modes of production, social life and cultural tradition occurs in and through geographically limited forms of language that themselves emerge out of the place-binding reproduction or transformation of modes of production, social life and cultural tradition.

To the extent the internalization of language channels mental associations and facilitates the conveying of thought and experience, as well as the re-presentation of events, physical settings and practice-based memories, it is fundamental to the establishment of common knowledge, a shared sense of place, and other forms of local or wider collective consciousness.

Language does not exist on its own, but comes to life in concrete acts of speaking, writing and reading. It is embodied in people.[4] It is acquired in childhood and beyond through socialization, through entering into an "already constructed network of comprehension,"[5] through participating in location- and time-specified practices, in meaning-filled situations generated by the family and other institutions. Thus,
the assimilation of linguistic rules
    and approved ways of speaking
        that become second nature,
like the assimilation of social rules
    and accepted nondiscursive ways of acting
        that become second nature,
occurs through socialization on particular grounds,
    through the constitution of the subject,
    through inter(con)textuality -
        through learning how to read one here and now situation
        from previously encountered situations, -
    through local patterns of presence and contact.

The words, variable meanings, pronunciation, grammar and other elements of linguistic capital accumulated by a person depend upon the makeup of her daily paths, upon what is successively incorporated into her life path, upon the

---

[2] This position is in some measure consistent with the well-known viewpoints of Sapir (1921) Whorf (1956) and Vygotsky (1962), while also drawing inspiration from *Philosophical Investigations* and other late writings of Ludwig Wittgenstein (cf. Kress and Hodge, 1979). However, as it makes room for creative association on the part of individuals, the position is not to be confused with Whorf's extreme stance on the perception prescribing qualities of language (cf. Wagner, forthcoming).

[3] Giddens (1981).

[4] Cf. Merleau-Ponty (1962, 1973).

[5] Foucault (1973).

formation of her biography through the dialectical interlocking of her dail
practices and long-term commitments.[6] Linguistic repertoire is never uniforml
distributed, but an "inevitable mirror"[7] of one's social roots, one's previous an
ongoing day-to-day history.[8] Individual and collective repertoires are thereb
engendered by the power relations that govern place-bound project admission
project content, and project execution,
by one's place in the world,
the world in one's place.
Situated practical engagement,
the knowing of language,
and power relations,
are never independent threads,
but always part of a three-stranded dialectical helix,
in which one becomes the other
                              the other
                              the other.

At the same time that language acquisition is dependent upon powe
relations, the reproduction of power relations is dependent on language
acquisition.[9] The repeated fine-grained exercise of power on the ground
requires
individual absorption of the language of discipline,
a working knowledge of the language of limit, boundary periphery depiction,
a consistent recognition of the gender-, age-, class-, or group-directed terms and
phrases indicating who may or may not do what, when, and where. If people are
to be kept within project lines or behave acceptably by localized standards, they
must not only come to recognize the content of instructions, commands, role
descriptions or explicit rules. They must also come to recognize the blatant, as
well as subtle terms that either express disregard, disapproval, disgust, ridicule,
and reproach, or some other form of normalizing criticism or censure. And, as
Lacan[10] and others have argued in building upon Freud, the most rigid
categories of language employed in the everyday practices of the family and
other institutions are at the root of the repression that forms the unconscious, at
the root of the "perverse," "decadent," and taboo laden, at the root of subdued
desire, "self-discipline," and that which is absolutely forbidden to take place
locally or become a part of the individual's path.[11]
The linguistic elements encountered and acquired within any place or region
inevitably vary among individuals, groups and classes, as people become

---

[6] The biography formation of individuals may be depicted in terms of a "life path-daily path" dialectic that is central to
the local and wider reproduction of group, class and gender differences. On the one hand, the long-term institutional
roles that dominate any phase of a person's life dictate certain daily path elements. On the other hand, the opening out
or closing off of long-term opportunities, and the actual selection of long-term commitments, depends on the individual's
build up of knowledge, predispositions, and cultural capital at the daily path level. For elaboration and related
observations, see Pred (1984, 1986).

[7] Barthes (1985).

[8] This processual emphasis on biography formation and daily practice is not to be confused with those depictions of
individual speech repertoire and behavior that underline the importance of "age, sex, class, ... cultural cognitive
assumptions" and other synchronic "social variable[s]" (Goffman, 1972).

[9] While of enormous importance, language, of course, is not the only medium involved in the reproduction of power
relations.

[10] Lacan (1968).

[11] Cf. Olsson (1980, 1983)

differently engaged in the social division of labor, become entangled in different sets of power relations and incorporate different practical experiences into their biographies. The common and uncommon discourses of daily life within any bounded area are thereby marked by diversity and stratification, a wide variety of voices, a polyphonic plurality of perspectives, or by what Mikhail Bakhtin has termed "heteroglossia."[12]

As Bakhtin would have it: "At any given moment ... a language is stratified not only into dialects in the strict sense of the word (i.e., dialects that are set off according to formal linguistic [especially phonetic] markers), but is ... stratified as well into languages that are socio-ideological: languages belonging to professions, to genres, languages peculiar to particular generations, etc."[13] Moreover, "all languages of heteroglossia, whatever the principal underlying them and making them unique, are specific points of view of the world, forms for conceptualizing the world in words, specific world views, each characterized by its own objects, meanings, and values."[14] At the same time, "the potential chaos" of an "absolute heteroglotic state" is limited and counteracted, and "a more or less maximal understanding" is achieved, by "the (sophisticated) ideal (or primitive delusion) of a single holistic language," by the "real felt presence" of the linguistic norms of a culturally or sociopolitically centralized "'correct language'".[15]

Within the normalizing confines of a common unitary language, where word flows "cannot fail to be oriented toward
     'the already uttered,'
     'the already known,'
     'the common opinion,'
"discourse in the open spaces of public squares,
        streets, cities and villages,"
"is a social phenomenon ... throughout its entire range ...,
     from the sound image to the farthest reaches of abstract meaning,"[16]
a heteroglotic confrontation
     wherein the singular, biographically and historically rooted resources of

---

[12] Bakhtin (1981). For important comments on this and related ideas, see the burgeoning literature on Bakhtin, especially Clark and Holquist (1984), Todorov (1984), Kristeva (1986), LaCapra (1983) and Morson (1986).

[13] Bakhtin (1981, pages 271-272). Also note pages 262-263. Bakhtin also states: "In any given historical moment ... every age group has as a matter of fact its own language, its own vocabulary, its own particular accentual system that in their turn, vary depending on social level, academic institution (the language of the cadet, the high school student, the trade school student are all different languages) and other stratifying factors. ... [*socially typifying languages exist*] no matter how narrow the social circle in which they are spoken. It is even possible to have a family jargon define the societal limits of a language" (pages 290-291, italic phrase added). Curiously, unlike some of his predecessors in other countries, Bakhtin fails to give any place to gender differences in his conceptualization of heteroglossia. Contrast, for example, the early observations of Gustaf Cederschiöld, *Om kvinnospråk och andra ämnen* [*On Female Language and Other Themes*] (Lund: C.W.K. Gleerup, 1900).

[14] Bakhtin (1981, pages 291-292).

[15] Bakhtin (1981, pages XIX, 270). In elaboration Bakhtin notes: "What we have in mind here is not an abstract linguistic medium of a common language, in the sense of a system of elementary forms (linguistic symbols) guaranteeing a *minimum* level of comprehension in practical communication. We are taking language not as a system of abstract grammatical categories but rather language conceived as ideologically saturated, language as a world view, ..., insuring a *maximum* of mutual understanding in all spheres of ideological life. Thus a unitary language gives expression to forces working toward concrete verbal and ideological unification and centralization, which develop in vital connection with the process of sociopolitical and cultural centralization" (ibid, 271).

[16] Ibid, 279, 259.

each participant are mobilized,[17]
a heteroglotic confrontation
    wherein the fashioning of each spoken word,
        the play of differences within inner worlds,
    is double edged and utterly unique,
    determined as much by whose word it is,
    as by the audience at which it is aimed,
a heteroglotic confrontation
    wherein the utterances of personally different languages
    brush up against, and
    interpenetrate with, one another.

Thus, prevailing power relations need not be merely reproduced in ar
concretely situated discourse where actual meanings are determined by "wh
speaks and under what conditions,"[18] and where rejoinders are contextualized t
one another.   For, in calling upon a virtually inexhaustible wealth «
associations, forms, shadings and nuances, actively engaged human agents ma
wittingly or unwittingly employ discourse as a vehicle for resistance,
    for struggle,
    for rejecting the classifications and categories of the Other,
    for setting up dominance-opposing and identity reinforcing boundaries,
    for ironically confronting the literal and proper with the meaning filled,
    for executing pun-filled sabotage against the Official Wor[l]d,
    for inventing meanings,
    for symbolically reversing hierarchical order,
    for turning the world upside down.[19]

Yes, meaning is an instrument, a conduit of power; but to restate Bakhtin with
foolproof Foucaultian twist: It is through one and the same language tha
people are ruled, or subjected, and exercise opposition to rules, or subjection.
Or, in any geographically and historically specific setting, spoken discourse "
one of the components in the ethical glue that holds individual and socie
together and apart."[21]

In taking on language as "an instrument of action (or power)," rather than a
solely "an object of understanding," Bourdieu similarly reminds us that th
linguistic exchanges making up the everyday discourse of a place or region d
not involve the recognition of invariable meanings, but the grasping of singula
forms in particular social-historical contexts.[22]   Through Bourdieu's window o
reality we see that singular meanings are the consequence of

---

[17] According to Bakhtin, because of the variety of internal heteroglotic resources called upon, "any *living* utterance ir
living language is to one or another extent hybrid" (ibid, 361). Cf. Gumperz (1972, pages 219-231) on "activity sphe:
differences and the variety of "speech styles" commanded by individuals.

[18] Bakhtin (1981, page 401).

[19] Cf. Scott (1985).

[20] Blonsky (1985) and Foucault (1980).

[21] Olsson (1985).   For significant comments parallel both to this observation and the concept of "heteroglossia" s
Roland Barthes' (1986, pages 111-124) arguments regarding the "social division of languages" and the interplay
"sociolects".

[22] Bourdieu (1977a; 1977b, page 645; 1977c)   Also note the discussions of Bourdieu in de Certeau (1984, pages 45-6
and Thompson (1984, pages 42-72).

contexts where different more or less "legitimate" styles or word choice, pronunciation, syntax, intonation, facial expression, and gesture are employed; contexts where the efficacy of performative utterances depend on an institutionally embedded authority to impose reception under certain conditions at certain locations and times, as well as on a deeply inculcated disposition on the part of the receiver to recognize "legitimate" authorized usage as "proper" usage;

contexts where speakers, once having unreflectingly assessed their audience are predisposed to choose a certain level of correctness, to self-censor themselves at what appears to be the appropriate level.

In short, for Bourdieu, the production and reception of speech are one with the reproduction of historically and regionally specific power relations between individuals, groups, or classes.[23]

Different contexts yield different discourses.

Meanings are not fixed,

but multi-layered and shifting with circumstance,

produced in time-space specific settings by particular agents,[24]

particular agents who utter, represent and express

"not only to be understood

but also to be believed, obeyed, respected, [or] distinguished,"[25]

who remark in order to have some effect on others,

to make a mark on the world about them,

particular agents who possess their own set of

previously acquired,

socially derived,

linguistic resources and predispositions,

their own strategies or tactics,[26]

their own capacity "to make a meaning stick"[27] or count.

Not least significantly, the practice of language serves to nourish and reproduce historically and geographically specific power relations to the extent that it aids in the reproduction of ideologies, to the extent the culturally arbitrary classifications of the world it imposes become second nature, taken-for-granted, unexamined and regarded as incapable of being otherwise.

The repres(s)entation of the world contained

in socially given classifications,

the "social construction of reality" impressed by linguistic categories,[28]

the experience-chanelling power of "common sense" word labels,

may often conceal or obscure the relations of domination

---

[23] Bourdieu likewise recognizes that, in certain circumstances, historically and geographically specific power relations also exclude some individuals or groups from discourse participation. Also note comments on power and language in Wagner (forthcoming).

[24] From a rather different perspective, Goffman (1959) also emphasizes the role of time-specific settings in discursive interactions. Also note observations on the impact of situational circumstances on language usage in, among many others, Bernstein (1975), Hymes, (1972) and Labov (1972).

[25] Bourdieu (1977a, page 648).

[26] The use of discursive strategies and tactics is stressed by de Certeau (1984), rather than by Bourdieu, who has a much more passive view of human agents.

[27] Thompson (1984, page 132).

[28] Berger and Luckmann (1967).

with which routine and nonroutine human practices are intertwined.[29]
(Thus, some of those who choose to deal with ideology primarily in terms of th
sustenance of domination have argued that: "The study of ideology i
fundamentally concerned with language, for it is largely within [the] languag
[of everyday life] that meaning is mobilized in the defense of domination, ... i
the interests of particular individuals and groups.")[30] Nevertheless, the languag
of localized practices and social life does not guarantee the reproduction o
ideologically bound power relations. Linguistic classifications, after all, are no
encountered in a vacuum, but biographically superimposed on one another an
thereby open to mental associations and internal incompatibility and no
automatically persuasive or accepted as legitimate.[31] "Classification is a livin
process, and language offers not only an existing set of classifications, but also :
set of operations to enable the individual to further classify or reclassify hi
reality."[32] People are not merely the bearers of taken-for-granted, traditiona
linguistic categories; but also "culture builders,"[33] the constructors of nev
meanings. Through the exercise of creativity, human agents frequently becom
"involved in extending the meaning of words, in providing new meaning
through metaphor, word-play and interpretation; and ... thereby, knowingly o
not, in altering, undermining or reinforcing [their] relations with others and witl
the world,"[34]

The spoken language of any settled area does not stand still, a frozen cultura
form. It is, instead, ineluctably historical, always in a state of becoming. Socia
"stratification [of usage] and heteroglossia widen and deepen as long as [a
language is alive and developing."[35]
As practices and power relations emerge out of one another,
                                         and into one another,
as new practices appear and former practices are discarded or modified,
as power relations are transformed through consensus or struggle,
as new powers of technology are developed
          and new technologies of power are implemented,
as migrants arrive with their cultural and biographical baggage,
the language of particular groups, institutions, occupations and
          generations inevitably undergoes shifts and transformations.[36]

---

[29] Such concealment or obscuration does not require that specific interests intentionally employ systematic distortion o
employ language and other signs for trickery.

[30] Thompson (1984, pages 35, 37).

[31] Cf. Bakhtin (1981, pages 342-346) on the struggle among internally persuasive discourses.

[32] Kress and Hodge (1979, pages 64-65).

[33] The concept of "culture building" is imaginatively employed in the writings of Löfgren and Frykman. See, fo
example, Frykman and Löfgren (1985, 1987).

[34] Thompson (1984, page 6) in commenting upon the "social imaginary" as developed in the writings of Corneliu
Castoriadis and Claude Lefort.

[35] Bakhtin (1981, page 272). With considerable fervor Bakhtin also notes: "... language is something that is historically
real, a process of heteroglot development, a process teeming with future and former languages, with prim but moribund
aristocrat-languages, with parvenu-languages, and with countless pretenders to the status of language--which are all more
or less successful, depending on their degree of social scope and on the ideological area in which they are employed"
(ibid, 356-357)

[36] Cf. the concise summary of the different traditional schools of language-shift interpretation in Gumperz (1972).
Under modern circumstances, localized lexicological changes often result from the internationalization and
interregionalization of capital, from the invasion of practices and power relations associated with both investments of
nonlocal origin and new trade linkages.

Words, expressions and forms of discourse sometimes die quickly as institutional projects are abandoned or radically reconstituted, sometimes slowly weather away, gradually or unintentionally altered in the course of prolonged daily use in relatively stable projects.[37] Old meanings are likewise disrupted or altered. New words and usages are adopted as significantly different institutionally embedded projects are introduced. New discourses are born at the same time that new pronunciations and deeper changes of syntax and generative grammar may also occur.[38]

Because words, expressions and other discursive elements that have fallen into disuse, or become lost, are bound up with lost place-specific practices and power relations, they are one with lost worlds, lost *genres de vie*, lost forms of consciousness.

Thus,
to uncover lost worlds, no longer durable meanings and expressions,
to retrieve elements from no longer spoken dialects,[39]
jargons and
slangs,
is to lift the lid from a treasure chest of past social realities,
to reveal fragments shimmering with the reflections of lost worlds of
everyday life.
To recapture lost worlds,
to resurrect dead (hetero-)glossaries,
is "not only [to] capture the attributes ... of particular practice[s] but also [to] begin to conjure up the ghost of the whole language of practice and practice of language associated with living a set of social relations in a specific physical setting."[40]

The history of lost wor(l)ds
as the story of transformations
in institutionally embedded
practices and power relations,
as the story of changes in consciousness --
refract(ur)ed reverberations of Vico's voice
invoked as closing pretext.[41]

---

[37] Cf. Foucault (1973).

[38] The interpretation of changes in syntax and generative grammar is beyond the scope of my subsequent treatment of late-nineteenth century Stockholm materials. This is so partly because such changes are rather difficult to document, partly because I lack the competence to conduct any such analysis in Chomskian or other terms.

[39] This term is here employed in a broad sense of relation-reflecting vocabulary and usage differences, rather than being largely confined to subtle phonetic distinctions. Wagner's geographically oriented definition is appropriate: "A dialect is a more or less widespread local system of speech usage, regionally discrete and historically continuous" (Wagner, forthcoming). Cf. Trudgill (1984).

[40] Thrift (1985). The intimate connections between the practice of language and the conduct of other social practices in specific local or regional contexts are also suggested in, among others, Kirk, Sanderson and Widdowson (1985).

[41] Vico, of course, was the first to consider at length the history of words in terms of changing modes of thought as well as the connections between institutional changes (and thereby altered practices) and changes in consciousness. See Vico (1948); as well as Burke (1985) and the literature cited therein.

References

Bakhtin M, 1981 "Discourse in the novel" in *The Dialogic Imagination: Four Essays* (University of Texas Press, Austin) pp 259-422

Barthes R, 1985a "Barthes to the third power" in *On Signs* Ed M Blonsky, (Basil Blackwell, Oxford) p 189-191

Barthes R, 1985b "Day by day with Roland Barthes" in *On Signs* Ed M Blonsky, (Basil Blackwell, Oxford) pp 98-117

Barthes R, 1986 *The Rustle of Language* (Hill & Wang, New York)

Berger P, Luckmann T, 1967 *The Social Construction of Reality: A Treatise in the Sociology of Knowledge* (Anchor Books, Garden City)

Bernstein B, 1975 *Class, Codes and Control: Theoretical Studies Towards a Sociology of Language* (Schocken Books, New York)

Blonsky M, "Introduction--the agony of semantics: reassessing the discipline" in *On Signs* Ed M Blonsky (Basil Blackwell, Oxford) pp xiii-li

Bourdieu P, 1977a *Outline of a Theory of Practice* (Cambridge University Press, Cambridge)

Bourdieu P, 1977b "The economics of linguistic exchange" *Social Science Information* **6** 645-668

Bourdieu P, 1977c *Ce que parler veut dire: l'économies des échanges linguistiques* (Librarie Arthème Fayard, Paris)

Burke P, 1985 *Vico* (Oxford University Press, Oxford)

Cederschiöld G, 1900 *Om kvinnospråk och andra ämnen [On Female Language and Other Themes]* (C.W.K. Gleerup, Lund)

Clark M, Holquist M, 1984 *Mikhail Bakhtin* (Harvard University Press, Cambridge, Mass)

de Certeau M, 1984 *The Practice of Everyday Life ((University of California Press, Berkeley)*

Dreyfus H, Rabinow P, 1983 *Michael Foucault: Beyond Structuralism and Hermeneutics* (Chicago University Press, Chicago)

Foucault M, 1973 *The Order of Things: An Archaeology of the Human Sciences* (Vintage/Random House, New York)

Foucault M, 1980 *The History of Sexuality Volume 1: An Introduction* (Vintage/Random House, New York)

Foucault M, 1983 *Beyond Structuralism and Hermeneutics* (University of Chicago Press, Chicago)

Frykman J, Löfgren O, Eds 1985 *Modärna tider - Vision och vardag i folkhemmet* (Liber Förlag, Malmö)

Frykman J, Löfgren O, Eds 1987 *The Culture Builders* (Rutgers University Press, New Brunswick)

Giddens A, 1981 *A Contemporary Critique of Historical Materialism Volume 1 Power, Property and the State* (University of California Press, Berkeley).

Goffman E, 1959 *The Presentation of Self in Everyday Life* (Penguin Books, Harmondsworth)

Goffman E, 1972 "The neglected situation" in *Language and Social Context* Ed P Giglioli (Penguin Books, Harmondsworth) pp 61-66

Gumperz J, 1972 "The speech community" in *Language and Social Context* Ed P Giglioli (Penguin Books, Harmondsworth) pp 219-231

Hymes D, 1972 "Toward ethnographies of communication: the analysis of communicative events" in *Language and Social Context* Ed P Giglioli (Penguin Books, Harmondsworth) pp 21-44

Kirk J, Sanderson S, Widdowson J, 1985 *Studies in Linguistic Geography: The Dialects of English in Britain and Ireland* (Croom Helm, London)

Kress G, Hodge R, 1979 *Language as Ideology* (Routledge & Kegan Paul, London)

Kristeva J, 1986 "Word, dialogue and novel" in *The Kristeva Reader*
Ed T Moi (Columbia University Press, New York) pp 34-61
Labov W, 1972 *Sociolinguistic Patterns* (University of Pennsylvania Press,
Philadelphia)
Lacan J, 1968 *The Language of the Self: The Function of Language in
Psychoanalysis* (John Hopkins University Press, Baltimore)
LaCapra D, 1983 *Rethinking Intellectual History: Texts, Contexts, Language*
(Cornell University Press, Ithaca) pp 291-324
Merleau-Ponty M, 1962 *Phenomenology of Perception* (The Humanities Press,
New York)
Merleau-Ponty M, 1973 *Consciousness and the Acquisition of Language*
(Northwestern University Press, Evanston, Ill)
Morson G, 1986 *Bakhtin: Essays and Dialogues on His Work*
(University of Chicago Press, Chicago)
Olsson G, 1980 "Ord om tankar/tankar om ord" *Svensk Geografish Årsbok* **56**
89-94
Olsson G, 1983 "Of creativity and socialization" *Archivio di studi urbani e
regionali* **18** 143-154
Olsson G, 1985 "Inledning" (unpublished manuscript)
Pred A, 1984 "Structuration, biography formation, and knowledge: Observa-
tions on port growth during the late mercantile period" *Society and Space* **2**
251-275.
Pred A, 1986 *Place, Practice and Structure: Social and Spatial Transformation in
Southern Sweden, 1750-1850* (Polity Press, Cambridge)
Sapir E, 1921 *Language: An Introduction to the Study of Speech* (Harcourt,
Brace & World, New York)
Scott J, 1985 *Weapons of the Weak: Everyday Forms of Peasant Resistance* (Yale
University Press, New Haven)
Thompson J, 1984 *Studies in the Theory of Ideology* (Polity Press, Cambridge)
Thrift N, 1985 "Flies and germs: a geography of knowledge" in *Social Relations
and Spatial Structures* Eds D Gregory, J Urry (Macmillan, London) pp 366-
403
Todorov T, 1984 *Mikhail Bakhtin: The Dialogical Principal* (University of
Minnesota Press, Minneapolis)
Trudgill P, 1984 *On Dialect: Social and Geographical Perspectives* (New York
University Press, New York)
Vico G, 1948 *The New Science of Giambattista Vico: Unabridged Translation of
the Third Edition (1744) with the Addition of "Practice of the New Science"*
(Cornell University Press, Ithaca)
Vygotsky L, 1962 *Thought and Language* (The MIT Press, Cambridge Mass)
Wagner P, "The geographical significance of language" forthcoming
Whorf B, 1956 *Language, Thought and Reality* (The MIT Press, Cambridge
Mass)
Wittgenstein L, 1953 *Philosophical Investigations* (Basil Blackwell, Oxford)

The truth seekers: geographers in search of the human world

Helen Couclelis

Love among the robots

In a delightful essay entitled "Love Among the Robots", Melvin Konner recollects the moral outrage he experienced as a teenage boy when, in a "Twilight Zone" episode, he watched a stunningly life-like android being summarily destroyed for reasons of practical convenience. The laser gun that ripped open "her" beautiful synthetic skin revealed the underlying wiring (glaring proof of faked humanity, if there ever was one), but did not detract from the moral conviction that the artifact, capable of every human appearance, including that of love, had earned the right to a human soul just like the beings it so closely resembled[1].

What does this have to do with science and humanism in geography? In itself not much, but please read on: you will soon discern a pattern. This essay is about truth in human science, as I assume that something or other resembling truth is what we all seek in our work. Because the issues are difficult and abstract, I can best hope to lead you there through concrete examples. Here then is the next one:

The Mark III Beast was nothing but a roughly assembled, vaguely beetle-like contraption put together by an engineering student (who also happened to be a subtle psychologist, as it turned out). But when "Mark's" creator asked a friend to watch "him" "explore" his surroundings, "hurt" himself by banging against a table leg, "drink" at the electrical outlet to "restore his energy", "bleed" as a result of a deliberate blow that caused some lubricating fluid to leak, "scream in pain" when the disrupted mechanism started making grinding noises, "feel terrified" as some red lights came on, the friend found himself incapable of carrying out his part of the bet and "crush Mark dead" with a heavy hammer.[2] The shrewdly used anthropomorphic language had transformed a rough electrical toy into something animate, to which the taboo against killing suddenly applied. Anyone who ever hugged a stuffed bear called Monica or Teddy, or refused to eat a lamb who had a name, will appreciate the hefty rearrangement of categories that is the theme of this story. Widely documented outside the realm of science fiction and fable, this phenomenon has become particularly topical in these days of computers that pretend to be minds. The creator of "Eliza", the computer program that responded like a nondirective psychiatrist, abandoned the field of artificial intelligence in horror when he realized that intelligent, grown-up people were becoming emotionally involved with the appearance of human understanding generated by a few hundred lines of computer code.[3] The effect had been anticipated by Turing who, in the early fifties, invented the test named after him for deciding whether thought and intelligence may be attributed to a computer. The test is a variation of an old

---

[1] Konner M, 1987 "Love among the robots" *The Sciences* 27 (2) 12-14.

[2] Miedaner T, 1981 "The soul of Mark III Beast" in *The Mind's I* Eds D Hofstadter, D Dennett (Bantam Books, Toronto) pp 100-113.

[3] Weizenbaum J, 1976 *Computer Power and Human Reason: from Judgement to Calculation* (Freeman and Co., San Francisco).

parlor game whereby a person has to guess, on the basis of interaction through written messages with two people in another room, which of the two is a man and which a woman. This time communication is through a remote terminal, and the two invisible entities to be distinguished are a person and a computer. If, after being given plenty of time to experiment, the subject still cannot tell the two apart from their typed responses, then the computer can think, in every relevant sense of the word.[4] Thought, so the argument goes, is whatever is indistinguishable from thought. Turing died over thirty years ago but the debate is still raging.

Why do we find these games with appearance and reality so deeply unsettling? This is, after all, the age of proliferating substitutes, clones, imitations, copies, stand-ins and look-alikes. From the life-like artificial flowers on your dining table and the nice Monet reproduction (where the frame, incidentally, happens to be worth ten times more than the print itself), to the faked scientific data supporting "findings" found to be void only years later, it would seem that such switches between "is" and "as if" would have long lost any power to shock. "If you can't tell the difference, why pay the difference", is the logo of a local discount store. Whether the lower price signals inferior merchandise, or just the absence of big brand names that do nothing but give the buyer's vanity a condescending pat in the back, the fact is that reality and appearance are so casually mixed-and-matched in our society that, at least at the level of gut reaction, this should no longer be an issue at all.

Something else is going on with Love Among the Robots, the Mark III Beast, the Turing test and Eliza. The disturbing quality of these examples, both fables and facts, does not lie in any attempt to fool us by passing something for something else, which it isn't. In every case, the artificial nature of the offending entity is *a priori* well known. Rather, their power lies in their irreverent blurring of the boundaries between animate and inanimate, human and non-human, animal and machine, same and other, suggesting that lines between such fundamental categories may be much thinner than we may care to think. Like a well-researched and rationally explained optical illusion, their effect coexists with the knowledge of what they are not.

The means by which the effect is achieved differ somewhat from one case to the other. In Love among the Robots, it is external appearance and behavior that endow with personhood a mere machine. The Turing test attributes thought on the basis of a sufficiently convincing appearance of thinking, and Eliza's power to seduce lies in the enabling of a particular mode of emotionally charged interaction characteristic of the relation that sometimes develops between patient and psychiatrist. The case of Mark III is even more remarkable because here it is the strongly animistic language used by a third party, rather than anything inherent in the artifact itself, that is responsible for the dramatic Gestalt shift from gadget to living being. This very same device - creation of a new reality through astute use of language - was used very effectively a couple of years ago in a short anti-abortion film shown on television, which produced tremendous emotional response in some and raging cries of "foul" from other viewers. The sequence showed a sonogram of a human embryo being aborted, while a narrator's voice was describing in most vivid terms the drama of "her" escalating agony, from initial thumb-sucking contentment in the comfort of her mother's womb to the "primal scream" uttered at the onset of the savage death through gradual dismemberment. (Note the use of the female pronoun, rather

---

[4] Turing A, 1950 "Computing machinery and intelligence" *Mind LIX* 236. Reprinted in *Minds and Machines* Ed A Anderson (Prentice-Hall, Englewood Cliffs, 1964) pp 4-30.

than the more impersonal "he"). Speak of "her" as you would of a six-month-old baby, and the vaguely discernible gray blur on the screen becomes one. Talk about "it" as a growing mass of invading tissue, and it is more akin to a cancer requiring to be promptly removed. Here is a case where a word is worth a thousand pictures, but this is by no means the only case where words create what is. Thinkers such as Foucault have made their name by showing how the essence of some of our most celebrated concepts (sanity, sexuality, freedom, even life) seems to have changed over time according to how people thought, wrote and talked about them.[5] John the Evangelist was probably right: in the Beginning *was* the Word.

Cognitive Science and the New Search for Meaning

My purpose in bringing in these various instances of major semantic confusion is to explore what they may reveal about the world we think and write about, to help me show why traditional notions of truth from both philosophy and science may be unable to account for these and many other anomalies, and to suggest that human geographers may have a lot to learn about notorious intangibles such as truth and meaning from cognitive science, a rapidly growing interdisciplinary field.[6]

So let us begin to unravel the common thread running through these examples. What they all have in common is that they describe situations in which observers are forced into an ambiguous mode of cognitive interaction with particular things. The ambiguity lies in the fact that the responses, the dispositions, the expectations, the general mental imagery elicited by the appearance, the behavior, or the description of these objects are known to be appropriate for objects belonging to some fundamentally different class. In terms of the theory of knowledge adumbrated by Arbib and Hesse, these objects elicit *schemas* not compatible with our prior experience of the categories to which these objects are known to belong.[7] That cognitive dissonance between *presentation* and *expectation* - between present experiencing and past experience - rather than any clash between Error and Truth, is what accounts for the disturbing quality of these and other similar puzzles.

If this is the case, it should be clear why science as traditionally understood cannot be of much help in resolving this type of dilemma. Guardians of the Truth in a world so often seduced by appearance, scientists often see the unmasking of falsehood as being a major part of their role. So much in the commonsense world appears to be what it isn't: the sun *looks like* it is moving around the earth, but the physicist has established that it is not; Nutrasweet *tastes like* sugar, but the chemist and the nutritionist will tell you exactly why it is not; religion *makes you feel* that a benevolent deity cares, but this is only false consciousness, as the Marxist scientist knows. It is X-ray and chemical analysis

[5] Any of Michel Foucault's works could be cited in this context. Most relevant perhaps to our discussion here is his analysis of the various mutations of the concept of man since the seventeenth century, in *The Order of Things* (Random House, 1970). For a perceptive discussion of Foucault's thinking, see *Michel Foucault: the Will to Truth* by Alan Sheridan (Tavistock, London, 1980).

[6] A comprehensive and highly readable introduction to cognitive science is Howard Gardner's *The Mind's New Science: a History of the Cognitive Revolution* (Basic Books, New York, 1985).

[7] Arbib, M and Hesse, M, 1986 *The Construction of Reality*, (Cambridge University Press, Cambridge). Michael Arbib is Professor of Computer Science, Neurobiology and Physiology at the University of Southern California. He is best known for his work in artificial intelligence linking motor responses in organisms to aspects of perception and cognition. Mary Hesse is Reader in the Philosophy of Science at the University of Cambridge. Together they delivered the Gifford Lectures in Natural Theology at the University of Edinburgh in 1983. The book developed out of that lecture series.

that revealed the un-Rembrandtness of the "Man with the Golden Helmet", thus invalidating the worshiping admiration of several generations of people who grew up with a false belief. But what kind of truth does science have to reveal concerning the likes of Konner's android, Turing's thinking computer or the Mark III Beast? We have *known* all along that they are but machines: and yet we ask the questions, regardless.

Mainstream philosophy will not be of much help either. Not that philosophers have not contributed greatly to debates on the humanity of embryos or the possibility of minds in machines. But their romantic vision of Truth as something out-there to be discovered by a privileged few through clear, hard thinking and study of the Masters, parallels that of the scientists in its neglect of more immediate realities governed by different forms of truth. The fact is that much of the world has always been run outside scientific laboratories and philosophy classes, and it has been run by and large successfully, or we would not be here to make these remarks. Yet the practical wisdom guiding the everyday world has only recently begun to be taken seriously in academia. Long dismissed as vulgar, degraded reflections of essences that only a select few could ever hope to glimpse, the forms of truth to which ordinary men and women respond are now beginning to be studied systematically, sometimes with very surprising results.

Cognitive science is a discipline still very much in the making, which, according to the broader definitions, encompasses every field of study that is concerned with aspects of the human mind. This includes psychology, linguistics, neurophysiology, computer science, anthropology and philosophy, thus bringing together perspectives from the natural and social sciences, the humanities, and even engineering. Cognitive science has sometimes been described as "experimental epistemology" because, in the process of studying how the ordinary human mind understands and deals with the everyday world, it has stumbled upon, and in some cases even begun to answer experimentally, many of the classical questions of traditional theories of knowledge. Next to philosophy, the explicit, a priori authority on truth and meaning, and science, which defines truth implicitly and a posteriori, as it goes along building up *its* version of the world, cognitive science is already becoming a third major source of insights on truth and knowledge, from which human geographers may have a lot to learn.

Take, for example, the largely empirical work done in psychology on categorization, and its implications for cognition, as drawn out by Lakoff.[8] In contrast to the accepted wisdom on classification, according to which a class is defined by a set of characteristics shared by all the objects in that class, people seem to categorize things on the basis of the principle of "family resemblance", which Wittgenstein made famous in his later work.[9] That is, commonsense categories usually include some "prototypes" that are the most representative examples, and many other items that are less representative but are perceived as full members of the category nevertheless. Thus a robin is a "better" bird than a duck, which is a better bird than either a penguin or an ostrich. As in the case of human families, there are features that characterize the category as a whole, but no single member needs to possess all or most of them, and any two members of the category need not share many (or even any) characteristics.

---

[8] Lakoff G, 1987 *Women, Fire, and Dangerous Things: What Categories Reveal About the Mind* (University of Chicago Press, Chicago).

[9] Wittgenstein L, 1958 *Philosophical Investigations* Macmillan, New York. Wittgenstein's best-known discussion of a category to which membership is not determined by the classical set-theoretic criteria is that of game.

(What do the games of Ring-a-Ring-a-Roses and the Prisoner's Dilemma have in common?..) Prototype effects exist even in the case of categories that are explicitly defined on the basis of certain attributes. For example, nine is a "better" integer in most people's minds than two thousand and ninety-one, although both numbers share to an equal extent all possibly relevant integer characteristics.

Now, basic though categorization may be for our thought, perception, speech and action, it is itself but a manifestation of deeper cognitive principles and mechanisms. That is, the recent experimental findings on categorization do not determine a theory of cognition, but on the contrary beg one. In "Women, Fire and Dangerous Things" (all included in an actual category of the Australian aboriginal language Dyirbal),[10] Lakoff adumbrates a theory capable of accommodating the shift from classical categories to prototype-based categories suggested by the psychological evidence. But Lakoff's theory does more than that: it entails, in the author's words, "changes in the concepts of truth, knowledge, rationality - even grammar".[11] In particular, it implies that reason is embodied rather than disembodied, thought is imaginative rather than representational, language is metaphorical rather than literal, and truth is contextual rather than transcendental. In this view, the tenets of mainstream "objectivist" theories - that reasoning is abstract symbol manipulation, that words correspond to discrete meanings, that knowledge represents the structure of what really is - are not necessarily false but simply too limited, resulting from special applications of the general cognitive principles that govern both practical and abstract thought.

Seen in the light of Lakoff's arguments, the conundrums presented by Konner's robots, Weizenbaum's Eliza or the Mark III Beast begin to dissipate. The category of machine, like most other categories, is prototype-based. Determinism, predictability, artificiality, materiality, clockwork regularity, reliance on laws, repetition, closure (not to speak of the properties of being noisy, metallic, large, and made of cogs and wheels), are all attributes associated with the category of machine, but no machine need have all or even many of these characteristics. That is, the category contains good examples and not-so-good ones. Car mechanics is "better" mechanics than celestial mechanics, which in turn is better than quantum mechanics; typewriters and steam engines are "better" machines than robots - unless we are talking of the "Little Engine that Could",[12] in which case the schema elicited is closer to Mark's borderline animality. Because engrained habits of thought (the result of decades of acculturation in the classical views of category) lead one to believe that either something is a machine (in which case it has no business behaving differently than a typical machine) or it isn't, atypical and borderline cases and cases that appear to "bleed" into some other category cause great intellectual and emotional distress. The effect is of course strongest when the categories involved are fundamental for our own self-understanding, as is the case with the concepts of life, intelligence, humanity, and soul.

There are striking similarities between Lakoff's ideas and the theory of schemas developed by Arbib and Hesse, to which passing mention was earlier

---

[10] See footnote 8. The Dyirbal category *balan* alluded to in the title of the book also includes the sun, birds that are not dangerous, and some unusual animals such as platypus and echidna.

[11] Ibid. page 9.

[12] The allusion is to a children's story about a (somewhat underpowered) little train engine that makes it up a slope by repeating to itself "I think I can, I think I can..."

made.[13] The authors of these two books, published at about the same time, do not seem to be aware of each other's efforts. It is thus all the more remarkable, though not really surprising, that a psychologist, a computer scientist and neurologist, and a philosopher should have come up with such similar insights.

The notion of schema as cognitive representation has a long history in psychology and philosophy. What is novel and particularly powerful in the theory of schemas proposed by Arbib and Hesse is the attempted synthesis of every level of the mental, from the substratum of neural machinery and bodily sense and motion, to the rarified heights where some of the most intangible aspects of individual and social experience - culture, freedom or religion - can be addressed. And unlike any other speculative theory relating body, mind, society and culture, this one can be tested, in principle at least. Not only does it predict cognitive and linguistic phenomena such as the ones Lakoff is describing, but the implied mechanisms of individual and social schema generation, interaction and change can be translated into artificial intelligence programs that allow empirical experimentation.

What follows from the Arbib and Hesse framework many will find deeply disturbing: the dependence of even the most advanced forms of thinking on the embodied self; the pervasiveness of analogy and metaphor, in science as well as in everyday life; the definition of knowledge as a network of shifting metaphors connecting the most abstract of concepts with the realities of ordinary experience. Other insights follow from these basic principles: boundaries between categories are forever shifting; language is governed not by precise meanings but by the use of schemas resulting from the interaction with a physical and social world; scientific knowledge is only in degree different from commonsense knowledge or even myth and religion; and truth is defined not in *essence* but in *use*.[14]

What this implies is that in the case of scientific theories, truth is the same as old-fashioned predictive success. In the case of schemas "representing reality" in some less rigorous manner, it means the generation of attitudes, expectations and actions that adequately anticipate eventual outcomes.

This pragmatic criterion of truth is what distinguishes sharply the Arbib and Hesse theory from both idealist and realist positions. There must exist a real world out there to provide the proof of the pudding at the time when expectation meets outcome; and yet, our conceptions and theories about that world need not be themselves reflections of how reality is *really* constituted. The world is only knowable through its manifestations: all else may be nothing but metaphor and myth.

These arguments, which challenge so much of conventional philosophical wisdom, but also so much of our understanding of what scientific theory is all about, interestingly enough converge towards a notion of truth very close to that propounded by the rather neglected pragmatist philosophers: Namely, that the place of things in the world is determined by their effects and not by their essence, and in particular by the elements of experiential deja-vu, situational recognition, dispositions, and expectations they generate. This assimilation of

---

[13] See footnote 7.

[14] A good example of a classical position on truth and meaning diametrically opposed to the arguments of Arbib, Hesse and Lakoff, is Peter Gould's discussion of the concept of theory (this volume). Gould seeks to define the true meaning of "theory" by going back to the original, literal senses of the term - indeed as far back as the ancient Greek meaning, according to Heidegger's highly controversial etymologocal analysis. The meaning of "theory" which, according to Gould, is the only correct one, would in fact be, in the terms of our discussion here, the prototypical one.

"reality" with what coheres with and gives meaning to experience is the idea expressed in the following passage by William James:

"'Truth' in our ideas and beliefs means the same thing that it means in science. It means ...nothing but this, *that ideas (which themselves are by parts of experience) become true just in so far as they help us to get into satisfactory relations with other parts of our experience.*"[15]

The implications of such an "interactionist" view of truth are far-reaching because it makes so many of our taken-for-granted assumptions difficult to maintain. Among the consequences most pertinent to the present discussion is the blurring of the line between truth and falsehood, reality and appearance, literal meaning and metaphor, description and narrative, science and myth. All these distinctions indeed presuppose the validity of the set-theoretic notion of category, the literalist theory of meaning, and the correspondence theory of truth. Searching for the Truth in the sense of hoping to discover "what really is" presupposes the existence of fixed essences, and of a language of words with fixed meanings to correspond with these essences. It might be more appropriate to ask of the world "what is it really *like*?" - but note how this expression has strongly metaphorical overtones.

In this view, then, the search for truth is the search for the development of *appropriate schemas*. These are the schemas which "make sense" because they cohere with our accumulated experience of the world, which are meaningful because they elicit dispositions and actions leading to pragmatically successful outcomes, and which are intellectually fruitful because they help connect together disparate pieces of the broader network of meaning, thus leading to ever more appropriate, though ever shifting, truths.

Scientific approaches to the human world seek to develop schemas appropriate to the understanding of ourselves as embodied agents in a world of space, time and events. Schemas based on the analytic perspective describe not what we "really" are, but where we stand relative to our understanding of the rest of the world, of which the most appropriate descriptions are also analytic. Humanist approaches, on the other hand, help highlight and focus schemas pertaining to our view of ourselves primarily in relation to ourselves (or our ever-shifting schemas of ourselves), in relation to our historical memories, our artistic creations, our cultural and linguistic categories, the abstractions (class, society, power) that our collective schemas generate.

On with the search for truth, then, and let us leave Truth for the logicians to play with in their Truth-tables. Is the human world sufficiently like a natural system to be captured by formalisms and approaches adapted from those used to study the physical world? Or is the human world so irreducibly human that in order to illuminate anything of substance, radically different ways of seeing and explaining must be devised? The question is moot, of course, because the world *is* neither this nor that, but what we make it; and we need both this *and* that perspective before we can even begin to understand.

Τά πάντα ρεῖ[16]

In the flow of intellectual history, our most cherished geographical ideas share the fate of all time- and place- contingent concepts. Bubbles in the stream of geographical invention, they come together and are carried in the current for a

---

[15] James, William, 1907/1974 *Pragmatism* (Meridian, New York) page 49.

[16] For the benefit of those whose Greek may be a bit rusty, this is the famous dictum by Heraclitus, "All is flow".

while before they burst, reflecting different lights and different landscapes as they swirl by and we watch, captivated. Then they merge back into oblivion, their scattered molecules soon claimed by other sparkling bubbles further downstream. Heard any good ones on environmental determinism lately? Where do things stand with general equilibrium on the plane? Did you watch the structure of the spatial relations of production collapse under the burden of impossible theoretical premises? And you, the underprivileged of the sixties, why are you hiding under ever new names?

Emergent phenomena of the collective professional unconscious, or loans from elsewhere somewhat too hastily guaranteed to fit, ideas populate our lecture rooms and journal pages for a brief decade or generation, before other ideas become your, her or my new obvious truths. So why the debates and the discussions, why the symposia, why the bad blood, why the "us" (right) and "them" (wrong) in human geography, if most of what we singly or collectively believe now we shall collectively or singly tomorrow discard?

Pleas for mutual respect and tolerance are well taken but insufficient. Mutual understanding would be more desirable but is hampered by the inability of the human mind to be at two places at once. Common ground, if it exists, may be too narrow for anyone to stand on. But an appreciation of the deeply complementary role of science and humanism in illuminating the human world is not out of the question. All we need to do is to agree that each perspective can be a rich source of *metaphors* (literally: transports) of conceptual schemas from intellectual worlds that necessarily have some structure, to a real world which, for all we know, may have none.

If the role of human geography is to illuminate human experience, take a moment to reflect on what *this* last metaphor may mean. Illumination depends on the position and character of the light source, the distance, orientation, shape, size, and texture of the object being illuminated, the place, shape, size, and other properties of surrounding things, the nature of the intervening medium, the rules of propagation, reflection, and diffraction of light of that particular frequency, and so much else that is relative, contingent, contextual, and even accidental. And, in any event, only the side turned towards the light source is ever illuminated: whether that source be Science, Marx or Heidegger, all else remains in the dark.

We can only illuminate one cognitive creation at a time, but all of these together can help us build up what we really must have - an adequate repertoire of *appropriate schemas*. This applies to the findings of individual pieces of research as well as to the broader pictures adumbrated by science and humanism, the two apparently conflicting perspectives. Schemas generated through a humanist approach place us in opposition, dialogue, or dialectical relation with nature: whether the emphasis be on the tension or the harmony, we are an anomaly in the picture of the natural world. Schemas generated through analytic methods, on the other hand, stress the logical continuity between person and natural world, but are not very good at distinguishing continuity from identity. Leave out the humanism and we are nothing but sublime machines; leave out the analytic and as part of the world, we are incomprehensible. Is it necessary to choose?[17] Good human geography is not a matter of choosing the "right" perspective. Good human geography is never having to say "so what?".

---

[17] Gould, Peter, 1982 "Is it necessary to choose? Some technical, hermeneutic, and emancipatory thoughts on inquiry" in *A Search for Common Ground* Eds P Gould and G Olsson (Pion, London) pp 71-104.

Index